Noncommercial Foodservice

Noncommercial Foodservice

An Administrator's Handbook

John Cornyn
Joyce Coons-Fasano
with Mitchell Schechter

JOHN WILEY & SONS, INC.
New York Chichester Brisbane Toronto Singapore

This text is printed on acid-free paper.

REQUIREMENTS:
An IBM PC family computer or compatible computer
with 256K minimum memory, a 3.5″ high-density floppy drive,
PC DOS, MS DOS, or DR DOS Version 2.0 or later, and a printer.

Published by John Wiley & Sons, Inc.

Library of Congress Cataloging in Publication Data:

Cornyn, John, 1945-
Noncommercial foodservice management : an administrator's handbook/
John Cornyn, Joyce Coons-Fasano.
p. cm.
Includes bibliographical references.
ISBN 0-471-00880-X (book/disc : acid-free paper)
1. Food service management. I. Coons-Fasano, Joyce, 1945- .
II. Title.
TX911.3.M27C66 1995
647.95′068—dc20 94-17566

Printed in the United States of America

10 9 8 7 6 5 4 3 2 1

Contents

Throughout this book, documents that are also available on the enclosed computer disk are identified by a small diskette:

For readers' convenience, passages within the text that are of particular interest to foodservice administrators in the following settings are identified by the appropriate icons in the margin:

Medical

Educational

Correctional

Cultural

List of Exhibits

The documents listed below are also provided on the enclosed formatted disk in Microsoft Word for Windows 2.0, WordPerfect 5.1, and ASCII.

Preface

We set out to produce this book (as well as the disk that accompanies it) for a single clear reason: to offer institutional and corporate administrators the information they need to oversee and improve their organizations' foodservice programs.

This book is designed to inform and assist administrators of service departments, as well as organizations' foodservice liaisons, financial officers, human resource managers, facility commanders, business managers, government representatives, law enforcement officials, and legal counsels. The information presented here should be of value to these and other professionals, whether their organizations' foodservices are self-operated or contractor-managed, single or multi-unit, or nonprofit or for-profit. To ensure that this book-disk set serves as both a complete introduction to foodservice administration for those new to the field, and as an informative reference work for more experienced administrators, we have included chapters (and exhibits) on all aspects of program oversight and evaluation. Our effort has been to present pertinent instruction and advice on such common administrative concerns as foodservice quality assurance, selection of appropriate management, facility construction and remodeling, legal and social obligations, and financial accountability.

We acknowledge that this book does not include guidance on how to operate a foodservice program on a day-to-day basis. The focus is on providing administrators with key information that will enable them to ask questions and have a framework for the answer or where to find it.

In order to help readers better understand the actual duties and myriad details involved in foodservice administration, we have also provided a "model" character—Dana Jones—as a guide. Jones is a Support

Services administrator at Acme United, a fictional organization located somewhere in middle America. From the book's opening to its conclusion, readers can follow Jones up the knowledge curve, as this administrator first becomes familiar with basic resources and service systems of AU's foodservice, then sets out on a thorough program of inspections, assessments, renovations, changes, and improvement. Along the way, Jones encounters the challenges and setbacks that administrators will recognize from "real-life" work situations. We hope Jones' learning experiences will further enrich readers' understanding of the research and control-systems necessary to achieve successful foodservice management.

Another tool offered to readers is the computer disk. Accessible on this disk, in Microsoft Word for Windows 2.0, WordPerfect 5.1 and ASCII formats, are sample worksheets, requests for proposals and contracts (all of which are also included as exhibits in the appropriate chapters of the book). Readers will not only be able to review these alterable documents to see how Jones has built a database of foodservice information and resolved AU's foodservice challenges, but will also be able to use them as models to produce customized documents suitable to their own administrative responsibilities. We sincerely hope that readers will be well rewarded by their perusals and use of its contents.

This book is a culmination of 40 years' consulting in the foodservice industry. Its inspiration comes and a great deal of thanks go to a long list of great clients. The authors have been privileged to work with representatives of organizations such as Alameda County Sheriff's Department, CA; Amdahl Corporation, Sunnyvale, CA; Baltimore City Jail, MD; Bexar County Commissioners' Court, TX; Booz Allen & Hamilton, San Francisco, CA; Bridges Restaurants, Aberdeen, WA; California State University, Chico; California Youth Authority; California State Board of Corrections; California Department of Corrections; California State University, Sacramento; Caltrans, Sacramento, CA; Cerritos College, CA; Chicago Symphony Orchestra, IL; Chico Unified School District, CA; Children's Hospital of Pittsburgh, PA; Coldwell Banker, Portland, OR; Colorado Department of Correction; Comstock Casino & Hotel, NV; Cornerstone Development, Seattle, WA; Country Cousin, Chehalis, WA; Cushman Wakefield of Oregon; Dan & Louis Oyster Bar, Portland, OR; Deere & Company, Moline, IL; Disney Development Corp., Burbank, CA; Donald E. Long Juvenile Home, Portland, OR; Duke University, Durham, NC; Elk Grove Unified School District, CA; Elliott Bay Design Group, Seattle, WA; Emanuel Hospital, Portland, OR; ERA Care, Inc., Seattle, WA; Gaston County Schools, Lowell, NC; Good Samaritan Hospital, Portland, OR;

Gray's Harbor Community Hospital, WA; Hale Koa Hotel, Honolulu, HI; Harvard University, Boston, MA; Hewlett Packard Corporation, CA, MD; Holiday World Theme Park, IN; Honeywell Inc., Minneapolis MN; Iowa State University, Ames, IA; Illinois State University, IL; Intel, Hillsboro, OR; Jones & Jones Architects, Seattle, WA; King County Corrections, WA; Kitchell CEM, Phoenix, AZ; Laschober & Sovich Inc., Pasadena, CA; Legacy Health Services, Portland, OR; Loehmann's (Cascade) Plaza, Beaverton, OR; Marion County Sheriff's Department, OR; McCormick & Schmick Management, Portland, OR; Mehlville School District, St. Louis, MO; Melvin Simon/Lloyd Center Corp., Portland, OR; Mentor Graphics, Beaverton, OR; Middlesex County Corrections, NJ; Mills College, Oakland, CA; Modesto Junior College, CA; Monterey County Sheriff's Department, CA; Morgan-Stanley/PacWest, Portland, OR; Mt. Hood Meadows Ski Resort, OR; Mt. Zion Hospital, San Francisco, CA; Multnomah County Sheriff's Department, OR; Multnomah County Aging Services, Portland, OR; Multnomah Athletic Club, Portland, OR; Museum of Flight, Seattle, WA; Nature's, Portland, OR; New York City Department of Correction; North Clackamas Parks and Recreation District, Milwaukie, OR; Norwest Bank–Denver; Old County Kitchen Restaurants, Portland, OR; Olson Sundberg Architects, Seattle, WA; Omaha Royals Stadium, Omaha, NE; Orange Julius Franchisee, Aberdeen, WA; Oregon Museum of Science & Industry, Portland, OR; Oregon Department of Correction, OR; Oregon State Hospital, Salem, OR; Oswego Lake Country Club, OR; Pacific Gas and Electric, San Francisco, CA; Pacific Power & Light, Portland, OR; Pierce College, Tacoma, WA; Placer County Sheriff's Dept., CA; Point Defiance Zoo, Tacoma, WA; Port of Portland, Airport, OR; Port of Seattle, WA; Portland General Electric Portland, OR; Portland State University, OR; Portside Properties, Oakland, CA; Providence Medical Center, Portland, OR; Reed College, Portland, OR; Sacramento County Jail, CA; Salem/Keizer School District, OR; San Francisco County Sheriff's Department, CA; San Diego Bar Association, CA; San Diego County Sheriff's Department, CA; San Joaquin County Sheriff's Department, CA; Sandpiper Restaurant, Roseburg, OR; Santa Clara County Corrections/Juvenile, CA; Seattle Art Museum, WA; Seattle Times Newspaper, WA; Select Enterprises, Olympia, WA; Sequent Computers, Beaverton, OR; Sonoma County Sheriff's Department, CA; South Dakota Human Services Center, Yankton, SD; Space Needle Corp./Windows, Portland, OR; St. Anthony's Hospital, Pendleton, OR; St. Mary's Hospital, San Francisco, CA; Stanford University Residential Food and Housing Services, CA; State of Oregon, Department of Justice; Sverdrup Purcell, St. Louis, MO; Tahoe/Donnor, CA; Tektronix, Beaverton, OR; The Marshall Associates, San Mateo, CA; The Minnesota State Universities, MN; The Evergreen State College, Olympia, WA; Timberline Lodge, Mt. Hood, OR; Tressider Memorial Union, Stanford, CA; UCSD Faculty Club, San Diego, CA; University of California, Irvine, CA; University of California, San Diego, CA; University of Minnesota, Minneapolis, MN; Washington State Ferries, Seattle; Washington State University, Pullman, WA; Washington University, St. Louis, MO; Washington State Historical Society Museum, Tacoma; Washington Park Zoo, Portland, OR; Washoe County School District, Reno, NV; Wenatchee Valley College, WA; Westates Development, Bellevue, WA; Westchester County, NY; Westin/O'Hare, IL; Willamette Valley Senior Citizens, Salem, OR; Wood County Adult Detention, OH; Woodland Park Zoo, Seattle; Yale University, New Haven, CT; Zimmer, Gunsel, Frasca, Portland, OR.

Special thanks and appreciation go to our agent Bobbi Feldman; the long time friendship and writing skills of Mitch Schechter; Judith McGee, who opened a number of doors and provided the encouragement to take the leap into a full-scale book effort; and Marjorie Redbird, our office manager, for the ability to keep client work and book drafts in some degree of order. Also, we wish to thank Kelly Zusman for reading the manuscript. There are two people who have bestowed the authors with remarkable patience while the preparation of this book was in progress. Actually, they have shown remarkable patience with the ups and downs, horrendous travel schedules, frantic deadlines, and unforseen client emergencies for many years. A very sincere and heartfelt thanks to John's wife, Patricia Benner, and Joyce's daughter, Jessica Fasano.

CHAPTER ONE

A Global Approach

IT WAS not quite 8:00 A.M. on a cold, clear morning in early January when Dana Jones pulled into the still-dark parking lot of Acme United (AU) Corporation. After turning off the engine of his sedan, Jones paused for a moment, reluctant to leave the car's warm interior.

"Sure is bitter outside today," Jones thought to himself. "True, but that's nothing compared to how *hot* it is going to be in the office these next few weeks. What a way to start the New Year. Never expected the company to transfer Alex Cotter, our Employee Services administrator, just before Christmas. They sent him all the way to Portland. Wish I knew who will be picking up foodservice here. Us maybe? My people in Support Services already have full plates, and I hardly know anything about it. Just know good food when I taste it, like anyone else. Still, how hard could foodservice be to administrate? Write a few menus, keep the facilities clean, make sure everyone pays for their meals—what else could the bosses want? Guess that's one of the things we'll find out at the big 8:30 meeting. Time enough to stop in the cafeteria first, pick up a cup of coffee to go; be great if they had the right size cup lids for once."

Scarf pulled snug and overcoat collar turned up, Jones locked the car and hurried through the chill of the rapidly filling parking lot, stomach aflutter with butterflies at the prospect of the unknown responsibilities about to be assigned at that morning's meeting.

Two hours later, Jones slowly walked into his large, windowed office, closed the door that bore the neatly printed legend, "D. Jones, Support Services Administrator," and sat down behind a broad, bare desk. The butterflies that had earlier filled his stomach had now turned to lead weights.

"Wow," he murmured, unclipping a fountain pen and staring blindly at the handout notes that had been distributed at the meeting. "I knew a reorganization was in the cards, but this is corporate-wide, bigger than I ever expected," he mused silently. "Look at this first item: a new boss. Patricia Bell, Vice President, Human Resources and Support Services. She must be from outside the company—never even met her before the meeting. But everyone says she's a real no-nonsense professional. Hope she knows her way around foodservice, because we don't, and now it is *ours*. Some job the catering people did at the meeting; everyone got the sweet rolls the president ordered, but they never delivered any coffee." Jones looked balefully at the thin pile of file folders, several of them empty, which he had also received at the meeting. "Thanks a lot, Mr. Cotter," he muttered wryly. "You apparently either kept foodservice records in your head, took them all to Portland, or never bothered to keep them at all.

"How can I be expected to take over this department, in addition to managing all my other duties, without knowing what we've been paying for supplies, what our labor costs were, even how much money we lost last year?" Jones wailed to himself, one hand cupping his forehead, the other picking fruitlessly through the meager information with which he'd been provided.

In fact, the entire reorganization plan, announced at the meeting by the company's president and CEO, had been somewhat short of specifics. The message behind the announced reorganization, the executives had emphasized, was simple but urgent: To stay competitive, AU had to become more efficient and cut its operating costs. From now on, consistent and effective management controls would have to be implemented in all company departments—*especially* those areas that had not previously been directed with all due diligence.

"Sounds like they certainly could have had foodservice first in mind when they planned this reorganization," Jones thought, pushing the near empty record files aside. "Who knows how we are ever going to meet cost and revenue targets for this department—assuming we ever get any. Well, have to worry about foodservice later."

Spreading open his schedule planner, Jones reviewed the day's upcoming meetings with his Support Services staff. First up was Facility Management's monthly reports, until lunch; then a two-hour session with Grounds Maintenance, probably to determine snow-fence allocations. Finish the day with the employees' Quality of Work Life team to discuss more lighting in the parking lot and shuttle bus service to the three nearest commuter rail stations.

Jones grinned, tapping his pen against the edge of his desk, recalling that many of the Support Services' functions, such as these, which he had been overseeing for nearly a decade had also first arrived on his desk without extensive records or support. "Turned departments around before for this company. We can do it again with foodservice," he assured himself. "Spent 10 years building a great career here. There's no way I'm letting the 'lunch program' put a boulder in *my* path," Jones vowed to himself.

Suddenly there was a rapid knocking on Jones' closed office door. Marjorie Lowry, his assistant, came in with the morning mail. "Good morning. I think you better take a look at this first, Dana," Marjorie said quietly, handing Jones a large interoffice envelope and placing a clutch of holiday cards and letters on a far desk corner. "It's from Ms. Bell's office."

"Good morning, Marge. Looks like our new vice president doesn't waste any time, does she?" Jones asked, smiling up at his dutiful aide.

"No, sir," the woman gravely replied. "And from what I hear, she expects the same from you. Good luck."

"Thanks," he replied dryly to the closing door.

Within the interoffice envelope, which was tightly taped shut and stamped "Personal and Confidential," Jones found a handwritten note and several neatly typed computer printout pages. The note, on Patricia Bell's new executive stationery, read:

> Dana,
>
> It was a pleasure to make your acquaintance at this morning's meeting, and I look forward to working with you. I was also glad to hear that you share my opinion about our corporate foodservice program—it needs a thorough reorganization and a new, problem-solving operational plan. ["All I said was, 'Boy, it really looks like this foodservice program has been running itself.' Dana, you have a big mouth," Jones reminded himself.]
>
> What I am asking you and your staff to do, on a first-priority basis, is to undertake a careful, cost-conscious review of every aspect of our foodservice. Our goal is to answer three key questions: How can we do the best possible job of controlling costs? How can we improve production and service efficiency? How can we raise our participation and average check?

Jones dropped the papers onto his desk, sat back in his chair, a light film of sweat beading up on his brow and the lead weights churning uneasily in his stomach. "Oh boy, here come the late weeknights and overtime weekends," he thought. "I don't have a clue how to get this new VP the information she wants. What to do? Wait a minute, there's more. Read on."

> To help Support Services attain these critical answers, and to assist our company in confronting the inherent challenges of operating an employee foodservice program, I have prepared a 'hot file.' This is a short list of urgent concerns and projects that will help identify the strengths and weaknesses of our current program, the answers to our key questions, and your appropriate role and responsibilities as foodservice administrator. Please let me know by this time next week how you and your people will be addressing these challenges. Good luck with your new duties.
>
> Patricia Bell

Jones squared his shoulders, preparing to read over the "hot file." Then he picked up the crisp printout pages and began to scan the new assignments awaiting Support Services.

1. Harry Daulton, AU's veteran foodservice manager, has tendered his intention to accept the company's early retirement package and retire at the end of this business quarter after 26 years of loyal service. Your recommendations are needed on the following points: How do we replace Harry? Should our foodservice program remain self-operated after Harry retires? Is this the time to outsource foodservice, the way our company has already contracted janitorial and landscaping services? If we were to explore contract foodservice management, how can we find, evaluate, and select the best, most competitively priced management company?
2. Construction of our new corporate campus across the highway will begin this spring. Our employees have indicated their desire for a foodservice program to be operated there when construction is complete. Can we afford to put a program on West campus? What sort of facilities should it include? What level of foodservice should be provided? Should this campus have its own foodservice management?
3. Shortly after new campus construction is completed across Highway 61, extensive renovations on our 30-year-old headquarters building will commence. During this four-month (projected) period, it will be necessary to shut down one of our two main cafeterias. Funds for remodeling this facility have also been requested. How will you provide interim foodservice while our headquarters' cafeteria is closed? How much will the temporary program cost? Should we revise our menus during this time, and how? What sort of renovation program should the main cafeteria undergo? Who should be hired to conduct this project?
4. The headquarters' renovation planning has brought forth the fact that this organization has been providing foodservice since its founding 30 years ago—to a large extent with original or retrofitted equipment. How

soon can Support Services complete a thorough assessment of all our foodservice production and serving equipment? Can you include a comparative analysis of the value of continued maintenance versus new equipment purchases? Can you determine if all equipment is functioning according to codes? Finally, which pieces of new equipment does foodservice need to purchase, why, and how long will it take to recapture purchase costs via improved sales and productivity?

5. As is now apparent to us all, foodservice's operational records are sketchy at best. We need to develop an accountability system to identify which costs foodservice alone is generating. How long will it take to devise and apply this accountability system? Which costs will be isolated and tracked over time? How can the company determine if foodservice's component services, such as catering, are competitively priced and effectively cost-controlled? Since it appears that our foodservice subsidy cost this company a minimum of several hundred thousand dollars last year, how much can we realistically expect to cut our losses this year? Or do we just have to live with the current subsidy? Ultimately, will this system allow you to estimate accurately future annual budgets for foodservice?

6. According to all available records, our foodservice customers have not been formally surveyed for the past two years. Are you and your staff able to gather statistically valid information on foodservice customers' dining preferences? Can you use this information to designate which improvements need to be made to foodservice to give our customers what they want? How much will these new resources cost? What is our current participation rate? What was the average check last year? What were our sales per labor hour? How do our figures benchmark against those of comparable organizations? Can you determine why a large number of our employees do not patronize foodservice, and what would be required to convert them into customers? Finally, by which means will you be able to track customer reactions to foodservice in the future?

Dana Jones let the papers he had been studying settle soundlessly back on his desk. For a moment, he merely stared off into space. "Funny how warm it's gotten in here," he heard the voice in his head say. "Can't lie to myself. Right now, I have *no* idea how to help my new boss measure foodservice's productivity. All right, don't panic; remember, we've handled situations this tough before. What to do first? Get in touch with some colleagues at other organizations who can recommend competent foodservice consultants? We need both management and design advice. Need to think. Let's see, I have another meeting in 20 minutes—time for a cup of coffee. Maybe I can find a vending machine that can change a dollar. If not, Benefits Office has their own coffee service; I can get a cup from them for a quarter.

"You know something, Dana, old boy?" Jones asked himself as he slid his responsibilities' packet back into its envelope and rose to leave his office. "Running a foodservice department just might turn out to be a little more challenging than we thought. Now, let's see how smart we can become before tomorrow."

CHAPTER TWO

Orientation to Foodservice—A Walk Through Your Facilities

Shortly after receiving his new responsibilities, Jones, like any administrator put in this position, realized that the next step was to identify the components of his organization's foodservice program. He especially needed to determine which components were contributing to and which components were detracting from foodservice's operational and financial success.

"But how can I get a fair and complete appreciation for foodservice's attributes and drawbacks?" Jones asked himself. By reading several foodservice trade publications and Harry's few, dust-caked management manuals, Jones determined that an informal walk-through of his organization's dining and food production facilities would be the most effective means of gathering data.

This course of action would be equally appropriate for any Support Services administrator, whether the foodservice to be scrutinized consists of just a small cafeteria or comprises a large complex including multiple cafeterias, restaurants, convenience stores, and a central production facility with an array of satellite serving areas. In some organizations, the identification process is made more difficult by the particular makeup of the customer base. Some examples:

- Hospitals—Their foodservice must prepare and serve food to critically ill patients (who usually require a large number of medical/ therapeutic diets), operate one or more staff and public cafeterias, and/or restaurants or doctors' dining rooms, and meet a wide range of catering requirements.
- Colleges/Universities—Besides a constantly changing student population that lives either on or near campus, foodservice must provide retail-style programs for faculty, staff, and visitors. Students include those who live on campus and participate in a defined board plan and those who live either on- or off-campus and do not participate in a board plan. On some campuses, foodservice must provide services at major events, such as commencements, football and basketball games, and numerous meetings and conferences throughout the year.
- Schools—The basic foodservice challenge in this market is to provide varying menus and service levels to children from kindergarten to high school age within the guidelines of the National School Lunch Program.
- Government Institutions—Government entities either operate or administer foodservice contracts for groups such as Head Start, children's summer play programs, homeless shelters, senior citizen centers/meals-on-wheels programs, and adult and juvenile detention centers. Each group has unique nutritional needs and varying amounts of money to pay for them on a per meal basis. In addition, many government buildings require that full-service cafeterias and/or snack bars be available for the convenience of employees and visitors.
- Amusement/Recreation Venues—Whether private or government-operated /administered, these organizations are characterized by a wide variety of places/events that require foodservice. Zoos, museums, performing arts centers, stadiums, arenas, and county/state fairs represent just a few of the possible locales where food and beverages may be served to members of different market segments, each of whom has specific menu and price/value expectations.

We will now follow Jones as he attempts to discover and evaluate the strengths and weaknesses of AU's foodservice during his informal walk-through. Along the way, we will offer commentary about different sorts of foodservice facilities and pose several series of questions that any Support Services administrator charged with overseeing foodservice will want to consider.

To begin, Jones prepared to walk through his organization's cafeterias, executive dining facility, and catering and vending areas. His primary intention is to identify the foodservice department's obvious and common components. His first stop will be AU's main employee cafeteria.

Sometimes known as central dining rooms, self-service cafés, canteens, mess halls, or lunchrooms, the number of these facilities should reflect the daily number of persons working on or visiting an organization's campus or site, as well as the size of the campus itself. Some cafeterias are referred to as "stand-alone," which means that they are more or less self-sufficient in regard to food production and storage. Other cafeterias may be "dependent on" or "satellites of" a stand-alone facility. It is important to distinguish between these two types because their operating costs are usually substantially different. If an organization operates more than one foodservice facility, reasons for doing so may include the following:

- The organization has insufficient space to accommodate comfortably and/or practically the number of persons who wish to eat during peak service times.
- The organization's campus is so big that it takes potential foodservice patrons too long (i.e., more than eight to ten minutes) to walk to a single foodservice facility without sacrificing a major portion of their available mealtime. (Some organizations give staff only a half-hour lunch, which places extreme limits on meal choices. While longer meal breaks are more advantageous for in-house foodservice programs, they can also offer the detrimental opportunity for personnel to dine off-site.)
- There are distinct customer groups that need (or prefer) to have their own dining facility. An example would be white- and blue-collar workers or graduate and undergraduate students who wish to dine separately.
- Although a site population has declined from its previous level, no one has yet thought about the operational and/or financial implications of shutting down one or more foodservice facilities.
- No one has considered the operational and financial implications of reducing food production and/or service levels at one or more facilities.

From the moment he decided to tour his organization's foodservice facilities, Jones had begun making a list of key questions whose answers he would have to acquire in subsequent meetings with foodservice's management and his boss, Vice President Bell. His first series of questions includes the following:

- Are financial and operational records available that accurately detail the sales and expenses at each foodservice facility?
- Given current physical appearance and condition, what is the remaining useful life of each facility and its equipment?
- How do each facility's managers and customers assess their units? What do persons who don't patronize foodservice think of each facility and the overall foodservice program?
- In general, how well have the organization's foodservice facilities been operated over the past few years?

Dining Rooms

With his preliminary questions entered into a notebook, Jones set out on a midmorning tour of AU's ground-floor main cafeteria. In the 600-seat, glass-walled dining room, he watched foodservice staff mopping the linoleum-covered floor and spray-wiping Formica tabletops to the blare of a radio. "Looks clean in here," Jones thought to himself, "but without customers it feels so plain and open. I wonder how we could make this space more inviting?"

While decor and atmosphere are highly subjective topics, inspiring individual decisions as to what is appropriate or might work in a given space, administrators should consider the following:

- Do dining room(s) contain one big contiguous space, or are they divided into sections that offer different types of atmospheres or views? Room dividers or planters, raised seating sections, or private booths can help break up a large space into more interesting subdivisions.
- On "normal" days, are seats equally occupied? Unless there is a good balance of table sizes (for two, four, six, or more persons), seating utilization can be as low as 50 percent. Depending on individual foodservices' customer profiles, many patrons may feel uncomfortable sharing tables with strangers, so be sure cafeteria seating contains a majority of two- and four-person options.
- What are traffic patterns like as patrons transverse the servery

(serving and merchandising area)? If patrons have to cross one another's path as they go to condiment stands or return their trays with dirty dishes, their comfort level declines and the potential for accidents increases proportionately. In other cases, patrons coming into a foodservice facility must pass by a tray return area or cross paths with persons carrying dirty trays, neither of which is a particularly appetizing situation.
- How comfortable or uncomfortable are furnishings? Hard seats, uncomfortable back-supports, improper spacing (either too high or low) between chairs and tables, insufficient table space, and too many tables and chairs crammed into a room are just some of the possible mistakes foodservice should avoid.
- What is the noise level? Rooms with high ceilings or no carpeting or other sound-absorbing materials can make a dining environment very uncomfortable. In some cases, however, a high noise level will be desirable, such as when foodservice's intent is to have customers eat and leave as quickly as possible.

Servery

Moving past the deserted cashiers' stations, Jones entered the cafeteria's servery. The brightly lit, narrow, rectangular area contained five separate points of sale (or stations), including a hot food/main entrée counter, a deli/sandwich area, a salad bar with end-mounted soup/chili wells, a grill, a dessert area, and two beverage islands. Also there was a "grab 'n go" refrigerated case stocked with premade items, a self-service novelty ice cream freezer, a self-service frozen yogurt dispenser, a popcorn cart, and, closest to the cash registers, merchandising racks for candy and snacks. Looking over the empty, stainless-steel stations, Jones thought, "It seems to me that if we turned the salad bar 90 degrees, we could reduce crowding by the deli during lunch. And why are those menu boards so hard to read? Come to think of it, do we have to offer only two entrée choices a day? Could we add stations?"

Jones' questions are all valid, but require a certain amount of research before the answers can be framed. Today most organizations want their foodservice to achieve a break-even or defined profit/not-to-exceed-subsidy financial objective. Therefore, administrators must study their current menus (content and variety) and service levels relative to the number of potential patrons and the staffing required to serve them before initiating any program additions. While not an absolute rule, the more potential customers, the more extensive a foodservice's menu and service levels can be. Within a servery there are usually three to four high-traffic (or potential congestion) service points. They include the following:

- Salad Bars—Depending on the number of selections, traffic movement in this self-service area can be very slow. A two-sided, mirror-image (i.e., both sides exactly the same) setup of products and serving ware can double customer throughput.
- Made-to-Order Sandwiches—As the name implies, each sandwich is made to order at this station. Depending on the number of staff making sandwiches, items' relative preparation difficulty (i.e., a club versus a submarine versus a regular roast beef, lettuce, and tomato sandwich) as well as the number of orders and the manner in which orders are taken (verbal versus preprinted forms), waiting times can become extensive.
- Grills—This station is where patrons come for mostly made-to-order hamburgers, cheeseburgers, grilled chicken breasts, fried fish, french fries, and similar items. Grills are almost always crowded and can subject customers to service waits of up to 10 minutes.

The final pressure point is the cashier station(s). It is vital to have the most efficient service possible at various food stations, but if customers have to wait four or five minutes to pay, they are not going to be happy. Not only will their food grow cold, but a good part of their meal period will have been taken up waiting in line. Therefore, the best design for a cashier stand is double-sided. With this design, cashiers can swing back and forth from one customer to another. This allows patrons to get money out or put it away and move on before the cashier is finished with the opposite person. Where food is sold by the ounce, automatic scales linked into cash registers work best. Automatic change dispensers work well if they can be positioned so patrons on both sides can easily access them.

Kitchen

Walking behind the hot entrée station, Jones pushed through a swinging door and entered the main cafeteria's production kitchen. In this busy workspace, lunch production was in full swing. The huge kitchen was filled with workers stirring steaming kettles, garnishing chicken breasts in roasting pans, and pushing racks of plated desserts and carts of clean dishes. Equipment included twin ranks of ovens and grill-tops, several banks of deep fat fryers, three large kettles and two steamers, and walk-in storage areas all along the farthest wall. Not wishing to disturb the intently occupied staff, Jones carefully picked his way back toward the kitchen's receiving area and loading dock. Here, too, staff members were hard at work, checking produce; dairy and baked goods deliveries were being off-loaded from a large truck and stored in nearby freezers, refrigerators, and dry storage areas. "Sure is hectic in here; look at all the labor just making lunch requires. What if we upgraded our equipment? Or tried to prepare more items out in the servery, in front of customers? Just how efficient is our kitchen, anyway?" Jones asked himself.

Chapter 7 addresses the importance of good kitchen design. At this point, it is essential simply to understand that a good working kitchen needs to be laid out in a logical fashion. The best work flow pattern is one in which everything moves forward from the back of the kitchen (where all dry, refrigerated, and frozen foods are received and stored) through the ingredient preparation areas (where functions such as chopping onions, washing and cutting fresh fruit, and filleting fresh fish are done) to the food preparation area (where dishes like meatloaf, fresh fruit salad, and halibut Florentine are prepared) to points of service (such as cafeteria lines, dining rooms, or catering sites). What administrators should look for in a kitchen is how easy or difficult it is to accomplish the principal processes of preparing, cooking/baking (if necessary), holding until service (under optimum temperature and environmental conditions), and service of foods. Some factors that could negatively impact this process include the following:

- The kitchen consists of a series of partially or fully enclosed (i.e., hidden from view) work areas.
- Cooks constantly have to run to the storeroom or refrigeration unit to get ingredients as there is no convenient place to keep such items near prep areas.
- Insufficient smallwares such as pots, pans, and cooking utensils, are available to support staff throughout a meal period. This causes cooks to stop and wash equipment or wait until equipment is washed before they can finish their tasks.
- Hallways and aisles are not wide enough for carts and people to move efficiently.
- There is insufficient storage or assembly/holding space for the

various utility and food transport carts used to support foodservice operations throughout the building or campus. As a result, carts are put anywhere there is an open spot.

- Prepared hot food holding capacity is insufficient. As a result, hot food is left in kettles, in ovens, on top of grills/hot tops (sometimes in containers stacked four or five high) or, worse yet, is left on tables under the assumption that the aluminum foil covering will hold the contents at optimum temperature until service. Oftentimes this practice results in food being placed out on a service line steamtable up to two hours in advance of service.
- There is insufficient prepared cold food holding refrigeration. As a result, cold food can be found inside overstuffed walk-in refrigerators (sometimes balanced on top of four cases of lettuce), sitting on top of ice-filled pans, left on top of a work table, or placed out on the service line two or more hours in advance of service.

There are literally hundreds of examples of inefficient kitchen design. In some cases, poor designs occur when a kitchen planner fails to anticipate food production and service requirements. In many cases, food production demand will grow to the point where it far outstrips the practical capacity of a kitchen. Besides the resulting inefficiencies, the even more compelling need to ensure efficient kitchen operations is to make sure that no food safety or sanitation rules are violated.

Executive Dining Room

Jones continued his tour by riding an elevator to the top floor of AU's headquarters building to check out the firm's executive dining program. (These elaborate facilities are not just a corporate phenomenon, but exist as faculty clubs at many universities and doctors' dining rooms in hospitals.) The organization's executive dining facility, with its panoramic views of the landscaped campus and surrounding wooded hills, consists of a 70-seat, wait-service dining room; six private dining/meeting rooms, each with its own service pantry; a cocktail/reception space capable of accommodating 150 guests; and a small production kitchen adjoining the dining room and outfitted with expensive restaurant-style equipment. Jones admired the elegant furnishings, the china, silver, and crystal place-settings at the still-empty tables, the movable walls available to subdivide the reception area, all the while sniffing the aroma of fresh foods being prepared by chefs in the small kitchen. "This is a beautiful facility; it really shows the class and quality of our organization," he mused. "On the other hand, I'm sure we're running a loss because hardly anyone eats in here. I wonder what we're *really* getting for our subsidy(ies).

Though not as ubiquitous as in years past, many organizations still operate (and expect their Support Services administrators to oversee) executive dining rooms. These facilities typically consist of one or more wait-served or buffet-style eating spaces. Customers most often include senior organizational personnel such as executive-level officers, doctors, or faculty and board members, as well as visiting dignitaries and potential or current customers.

At some organizations, employees of all ranks are eligible to eat in any dining facility, but, most often, executive dining patrons are generally senior-level personnel who expect and appreciate a quiet and/or private dining environment and an extremely high level of service, and who can afford to pay premium prices on a regular basis. It is therefore essential that any executive dining does honor to the image and reputation of the parent organization. As one executive at a high-tech electronics firm put it, "We are an organization dedicated to providing quality products and services, and we expect our foodservice to be a glowing example of that."

Although certain exceptions exist, the vast majority of executive dining programs are designed to operate at a loss, and must be supported via direct subsidies or from profits generated by employee cafeterias, vending or catering services, or other revenue centers. However, executive dining program expenses are in part determined by whether facilities are supported by a dedicated kitchen or if production is being provided (in part or entirely) from a kitchen shared with another dining operation. Note that due to the low volume of its production a separate kitchen for executive dining usually incurs higher labor costs and, thus, loss of economies/efficiencies of scale.

After conducting an initial tour, administrators may wish to list any questions that have arisen about the operational aspects of their executive dining programs. These questions could include the following:

- Are separate sales and expense records maintained for this foodservice program?
- Based on the number of persons eligible to use an executive dining facility, how many people actually eat there on an average daily basis? If available, do records show when the dining facility was used to entertain important clients or guests, rather than just an internal group that decided to lunch together?

- Do records show how often local off-site commercial restaurants are patronized by the eligible customer group instead of the executive dining room(s)?

Before leaving the executive dining floor, Jones got a steaming cup of fresh-brewed coffee from a facility staff member and retired to an unbooked dining/meeting room to spend some more time evaluating and thinking about the two kitchens he had seen.

It is important to realize that, depending on circumstances such as those already described, a foodservice kitchen may have either a single function (such as supplying meal items to an employee dining facility) or may serve as a resource for multiple services, such as executive dining, in-house or social catering, and the operation of satellite dining facilities located on-site or nearby.

It is also important to understand how efficiently and productively foodservice kitchens are functioning, since these facilities are generally the most expensive (in capital dollars) to build and maintain. In addition, kitchens are where most better-paid foodservice staff members (other than management) perform their work. What's more, it is incumbent upon administrators to ensure that neither the physical plant nor equipment is responsible for diminishing the all-important quality of foods served to customers.

With that in mind, at this early stage of administrators' evaluation of their foodservice, a single primary concern should be kept in mind: Production facilities and their equipment must be maintained in a clean and sanitary condition. Support Services administrators, in attaining a complete understanding of how well their foodservice production facilities and systems are performing, should ask the following questions of the foodservice unit manager(s) or director:

- Who is responsible for repairing and maintaining kitchen equipment? Who is expected to pay for regular preventive maintenance and repairs? What is the annual cost of maintenance?
- What is the best way to determine when new or replacement capital equipment should be purchased?
- Is a process in place that allows cost justification of new equipment purchases?
- What are the kitchen's annual utilities costs? Is there a way to monitor utility usage in foodservice areas efficiently?
- Who is responsible for the cleaning and day-to-day upkeep of the kitchen(s)?

- Are the kitchen(s) and other foodservice facilities subject to the local Health Department's jurisdiction? If yes, are copies of the last few inspections available for review?
- Are security measures in place that restrict unauthorized personnel from entering kitchen(s) and that prevent theft of expensive foods and supply items?

Catering Facilities

Having finished his initial appraisal of the foodservice kitchens (and his delicious cup of coffee), Jones returned to the headquarters building's ground floor to inspect the catering storage and product assembly area.

The catering pantry at AU was a high-ceilinged, windowless room adjacent to the main cafeteria's kitchen and storage spaces. It was filled with long, stainless-steel makeup tables, two wet sinks, and row upon row of shelving packed with chafing dishes and serving platters, bowls, pitchers and tureens, china plates and silver hors d'oeuvres trays, and cases of flatware—all behind locked chicken-wire fencing. In the room's closets hung dozens of clean uniforms worn by staff at different catered events. "My gosh!" Jones exclaimed silently. "We must have $250,000 worth of inventory in here. Who parcels out what's needed each time we call for catering? I guess they cook the meals and brew coffee in the main kitchen and put together the trays and such in here, but who's in charge of that? I wonder if we could transfer catering records into Support Services' computer database?"

Jones' questions reflect the complexity of administering an in-house catering program in a workplace or health care, educational, government, or nonprofit organization. In most institutions and corporations, catering is rarely confined to rooms proximately located to (or easily accessible from) production kitchens. Instead, catered foods and beverages must be presented in distant offices, conference rooms, lobbies, or patios. In some cases, catering takes place in organization members' homes or at local attractions such as museums or public parks. What's more, as employee demand for quiet places to meet or work is usually intense, catering must often fit its presence in these spaces around others' schedules. Thus, the key to successful administration is to prioritize various departments' needs and use-schedules so that catering does not have to be turned over to a local restaurant, hotel, or commercial (outside) caterer. On the other hand, there may be times when an off-site caterer can provide the expertise, foods, and service levels in a more cost-efficient and effective way than an in-house foodservice. The responsibility for ascertaining the best approach to catering for both the organization and the foodservice provider remains with individual administrators.

The upside to catering administration is that this service can become a cash cow for an organization's foodservice department. In fact, the positive revenue stream generated by catering is oftentimes used to offset losses from cafeterias and/or executive dining programs. This positive cash flow, however, usually only occurs when a parent organization is operating profitably. When a financial crunch hits an institution or corporation, catering is usually one of the first services to be cut back, often in dramatic fashion. Therefore, administrators who decide to oversee profitable, customer-pleasing catering programs need to meet with foodservice management to answer the following questions:

- Which rooms and spaces are normally used as sites for catering events? How far are these areas from production facilities?
- Do spaces exist in or near catering preparation rooms that can be used to stage and/or support catering events more efficiently?
- Is properly working equipment available to transport and hold hot and cold foods safely at or close to where catering events are held?
- Is a process in place to assure that all catering events are accurately booked and billed?

Vending

With his first impressions of catering now in mind and duly recorded, Jones made his way to his final inspection site: AU's main vending area. Although individual snack-food and hot/cold beverage machines were located in all five buildings on the organization's campus, the main vending area was situated in a large employee "break" room at the rear of the main factory floor and adjoining enclosed patio with seating for 50. The vending area contained three candy and snack machines, two coffee/tea/hot chocolate machines, two soft-drink machines (one a post-mix, the other offering canned drinks), one machine stocked with premade sandwiches, salads, and microwavable items (made in and delivered from the foodservice main kitchen), and one machine vending ice cream novelties. There were also three microwave ovens and assorted, single-serve condiments set out on separate tables.

"Let's see, it's just 11:15 A.M. and all the seats are filled; there are lines at two machines and all three ovens," Jones observed silently. "Even though the lighting glares and the seats are uncomfortable, our people really flock here. What if we improved the decor and started bringing in some hot entrées at lunch to augment machine selections? How would that affect our sales and costs?"

Jones' thoughts reflect the attractive sales opportunities inherent in the operation of vending machines (also known as "automatic merchandisers" or "silent sales agents"). Given the right circumstances (such as when there are not enough personnel to support manual (i.e., staffed) foodservices at small buildings/remote locations; cafeterias are too distant for staff to reach during 10- to 15-minute work breaks; and when an organization is on a "flex" hours schedule, which means that personnel will be working at times when the cafeteria is not normally open), vending machines can offer an economical alternative to a manual foodservice operation. In most cases, vending success depends on the number of potential customers, the amount of on-site "off-hours" activity, and the ease of accessibility to the machines. Vending customers are highly prone to making impulse purchases, so situating vending machines near rest rooms or major traffic-flow areas is critical to attracting the maximum number of available customers. When vending is the only alternative (such as for personnel who work on weekends or second/third shifts or in buildings without cafeterias), there is an implied need to make vending programs as attractive as possible. In some cases, the food provided in the cold food display units is prepared and packaged by cafeteria staff rather than coming from a vending contractor's commissary. When this option is practicable, potential vending customers will usually feel better about purchasing foods that are the same (in terms of quality, quantity, and price) as those found in the cafeteria.

Dana Jones closed his rapidly filling notebook and breathed a sigh of relief. His initial tour of foodservice's physical resources was finally complete. But even as he left the vending area, Jones realized that his evaluative tasks were far from over. (In Chapter 8, Jones will continue his research by looking into some of the less obvious, competing, "unofficial" food and beverage services that can threaten any organization's "official" foodservice revenue and, equally, Support Services administrators' ability to ensure their department's success.)

CHAPTER THREE

Contract or Self-Operated Foodservice—An Objective Analysis

On that fateful morning—was it only last week?—the new vice president had asked Dana to look into the issue of whether or not to contract with a foodservice management company. Given Harry's imminent retirement, now seemed to be as good a time as any to make such a change. But then Dana's mind started whirling with second thoughts. "Would a decision to contract foodservice affect current employees' jobs and earning potential? Especially Mabel, who has been the cashier *forever*. People just love Mabel. They come just to visit with her and hear her latest joke. It would not do my career any good to be responsible for Mabel losing her job or, worse yet, her benefits," Dana told himself. "Her family relies on her benefits. Besides, what are the usual terms of the foodservice contract? Would subsidy go up or down? Would a contractor be willing to participate in some of our popular traditions like the Halloween Lunchtime Costume Judging Contest? More important, how much control would the organization lose?"

CONTRACT FOODSERVICE

Reasons to Consider Contract Foodservice Management

The purpose of this chapter is to discuss the common advantages and disadvantages of contracting, as well present a process for assessing these advantages and disadvantages. Perhaps one of the best ways to analyze whether to contract foodservice is to look at the reasons why some organizations choose to go this route. Based on his study of foodservice trade magazines and Support Service management guides, Dana assembled the following list of reasons why certain organizations consider contract foodservice as an option.

- The current program is mismanaged. Generally speaking, if the existing program is efficiently managed with few staffing problems and the facility is in good working order, organization administrators do not consider contracting out foodservice.
- An organization-wide effort to downsize the workforce has resulted in a move to outsource support services and shrink expenses.
- The new "state-of-the-art" kitchen that was built takes more sophisticated management skills than are available in-house. As new kitchens are constructed with ever more advanced and sophisticated preparation and delivery systems, administrators are finding that managers familiar only with traditional cook-serve systems do not have the skills to manage the new systems. It is precisely for this reason that administrators need to keep abreast of emerging foodservice technology.
- The foodservice concept desired by the organization lies outside the experience or vision of the existing management. Sometimes, a foodservice is still serving meat, potatoes, and gravy when its customers have started going out for espresso, taco salads, or croissant sandwiches and ordering pizza or submarine sandwiches from a nearby delivery operation. Change is not easy for some foodservice directors, and these individuals often remain convinced that the way they have run their programs for 15 years will suffice for another 15.
- The cost of foodservice has become more than the organization is willing/able to subsidize. In light of many organizations' efforts to decrease operating budgets, some of the built-in costs of self-

operation have made contract feeders' fees look comparatively attractive. With their purchasing power, well-developed training programs, and existing accounting and control systems, contract management companies contend that they can provide employee meals for less money than self-operators, even if a self-operator is doing a quality job of management.

- The organization's foodservice needs new equipment but cannot afford the capital expense. A contract feeder may be both willing and able to purchase the necessary equipment for a client and amortize the cost over a given period of years. At the end of this time the equipment belongs to the client-organization.
- The organization is unable to build and sustain a viable foodservice management team. Because there is no real career path for managers in a self-operated foodservice, it is sometimes difficult to retain a competent staff. Talented individuals will move on to improve their careers, leaving the company with less motivated or trained staff. There is also a tendency for those who remain, no matter how good they were initially, to become isolated in their organization and therefore lose touch with the marketplace. The best advice to a self-operated manager is to get out and stay current with the foodservice industry. Attending professional meetings and trade shows and networking not only with other managers of self-operated foodservices but also with persons from all aspects of the foodservice industry are ways to keep pace with an ever-changing profession.

  Perhaps the manager of the foodservice is retiring and there is no one who appears qualified to take that individual's place. Sometimes, a very efficient and effective program will simply fall to pieces when the "indispensable manager" retires. Even though that manager may leave everything in writing, sometimes there simply isn't anyone in the organization capable of carrying on the former manager's quality of work. Occasionally, especially in isolated or rural workplaces, this situation is simply unavoidable, since really good managers usually choose to take positions in larger metropolitan or scenic areas.

  The loss of one or two key individuals could, in effect, leave the administration with a major management challenge (i.e., headache). Without question, this can be the most difficult issue to analyze. An assessment has to be made as to whether the foodservice department operates via a well-defined system or by the strength and knowledge of a few key people. During this assessment, personal reputations and egos could possibly be on the line, so caution is recommended. If everything is in the head of the current management, it goes away with them. ["Hmmmmm. I need to follow up with Harry and get those operations policies and Quality Assurance manuals he was talking to me about the other day," thought Jones.]

- Differentials between the organization's wages and those paid in the private sector for comparable foodservice jobs make the cost of the program prohibitive. This is especially true when there is a desire or demand for retail concepts with the same or comparable pricing. If the wages and benefits are higher than those paid locally, it is unlikely that financial objectives will be met.
- Management perceives there would be an increase in purchasing power with contractors. Sometimes this perception is valid; other times other purchasing options are open to an organization. For example, many hospitals join purchasing groups that achieve the goal of increased purchasing power without a contractor.

One institution's foodservice had the greatest purchasing volume in its locale and its prices were on a par with many contractors. However, because the institution had a central purchasing process that added a 15 percent handling charge on all purchased goods, the food cost was higher than in similar institutions. This institution benefited not from the increased purchasing power so much as from the fact that the contractor passed its purchasing prices on to the institution without the handling charges. Even with the management fee/administrative charges billed by the contractor, the department was able to achieve a net savings through contracted foodservice.

Perceived Negative Aspects of Contracting

Dana mused to himself, "What about the potential downside of hiring a contractor to manage our foodservice?" By consulting his growing reference library and networking with other Support Services administrators in friendly organizations, Dana was able to complete this list of commonly perceived drawbacks to "going contract."

- "Since profit is the only motive for contract feeders, they won't be willing to provide decent food and service. All they care about is their bottom line."

- "Nutrition will be thrown out the window because they all try to promote fast food."
- "Contractors cannot provide service as cheaply as self-operators since they cannot use student or inmate labor or commodities." (This last constraint applies to schools, colleges, and correctional institutions.)

The truth of the matter is, contract foodservice companies *are* interested in the bottom line. So is government these days. There is nothing wrong with making a reasonable profit; it is business taxes that help pay for government services. How good the food is under a contract feeder is quite simply a function of how good a contract an organization writes.

Most contract feeders have registered dietitians on staff who help write and evaluate the menus, which ensures appropriate nutritional standards. Again, well-defined specifications, monitored on a regular basis, will assure the contractor's adherence and performance level.

Note: Those organizations qualified to receive USDA commodity foods may allow contractors to use those foods on their behalf. In 1978 the USDA rewrote the restrictions on the use of commodities to allow contract feeders to use such products as long as they follow the rules and regulations set for institutional use. Commodity programs are closely monitored by appropriate state agencies. Administrators of foodservice in correctional facilities should be aware that there is no reason that closely supervised inmate labor cannot be used in a kitchen run by a contract management company. For programs at colleges and universities, work–study students can be employed by contractors.

Potential Negative Aspects of Contract Foodservice

So what are the real downsides to contract foodservice management?

- A perceived loss of control of the day-to-day operations. For some organizations, it is difficult to lose direct control. They have a tendency to want to "give direct orders" to the foodservice staff rather than working through the contract process, which usually involves addressing all changes and complaints to a designated manager. This process takes more time and is frustrating to some.

  Experience has shown that it is as easy for an administrator to lose control of a self-operated foodservice as it is to lose control of a contractor operation. In all cases, it is imperative that someone knows enough about foodservice to administer it properly regardless of who is operating it. ["Boy," Dana said to himself. "Am I learning *that* one the hard way!"]

- A certain amount of trauma accompanies the transition from self-operated to contract management. While an organization may think that it is ready for the transition, there are always unforseen shocks to the organization's culture. For example, people used to walking into the kitchen to grab a cup of coffee or a cookie (whether or not it was against the policies) may no longer be able to do so. There is also the trauma that surrounds changing from a subsidized self-operation to a profit and loss account. Under that scenario, the organization cannot withhold pricing increases. If prices were substantially lower than market because of the subsidy, there will undoubtedly be a price increase required to eliminate or reduce the subsidy.
- A share of the income goes to the contractor. Sometimes an organization's foodservice has been losing money and a contractor is able to increase sales and effect efficiencies that result in a lower subsidy or increase in profit. At that point some memories are short, and people begin to point to the amount of money that is flowing out of the organization to the contractor. For some organizations, the contractor fee is well worth not having the day-to-day headaches. For others, the money is more important. In most cases, the amount of profit a contractor makes can be negotiated.
- The organization now has to deal with an outside entity that has different goals and objectives. While not an insurmountable challenge, these different goals and objectives need to be identified and resolved if the relationship is to succeed. The process of meeting the challenge is more stressful to some organizations than others. Most contractors want to establish and maintain a long term relationship, so it is in their best interest to integrate the two.
- There is the human resources issue of what will happen to an organization's employees if a decision is made to use contract foodservice. That is always a concern not just of foodservice personnel, but also the rest of the organization's community. Foodservice personnel are often highly visible, long-term members of the community and no one wants to see them harmed. Again, there are means of dealing with the issue, such as requiring that all existing employees receive a trial period with the contractor. Another solution is to offer them jobs elsewhere in the organization. The key to success is carefully thinking through the issue and its solutions early in the process.
- Through the low-bid process or for other reasons, an organization

may be locked into a contract with an incompatible contractor. This becomes more of a problem with government contracts than for private industry. With the Request for Proposal (RFP) process, there is more latitude to determine the quality of the proposal and the ability of an organization to implement its proposal. An RFP is a formal written process for soliciting qualified companies to submit proposals based on parameters established by the requesting organization. If price is the sole or primary determinate, then it might be called a Request for Bid (RFB). Sometimes a government agency is required to use the low-bid process and will find itself in a contract with a company that is not meeting its needs.

The challenge is the imperfect mediums of people and food, which vary too much to quantify. Foodservice is not a clearly defined "item" that can be bid. No matter how detailed the specifications, there is still the issue of whether a company can really meet the challenges of a given foodservice operation. In the low-bid process, if even one variable surfaces it is sometimes impossible to solve the challenge.

For example, a foodservice management company was awarded a contract at a psychiatric hospital based on the low-bid process. The company that won the award had other hospital foodservice accounts, and the purchasing office contended that that alone qualified them to operate foodservices at its institution. The reality was that the contractor had no experience with the special needs of a psychiatric hospital. The contractor offered the low bid based on its knowledge of staffing levels at general care hospitals, and that price did not permit adequate staffing to compensate for some of the security delays that affect a psychiatric hospital. The contractor's learning curve related to psychiatric hospital needs frustrated the institution's management. At the same, time the contractor was frustrated because its "profit" was spent on adding the necessary staffing. There was general dissatisfaction with the account on the part of both parties. However, because it was a three-year contract and there had been an investment made in the facilities by the contractor, it was nearly impossible to break the contract.

It is important to think through all these issues in advance. In some instances an organization has elected not to contract because it would be required to seek a low-bid price rather than use the RFP process formatted to select the best, most qualified company without money being the primary determinate.

In yet another instance, an organization's administrators were able to build a strong case for developing a request for proposal, rather than a request for bids. They presented their case to the state's attorney general and subsequently to the legislature to obtain an exemption from the bid process for its foodservice facilities.

ANALYZING AN INDIVIDUAL SITUATION

The most important question to answer is, Who can operate foodservice at a given facility most efficiently and cost-effectively? If self-operation is working for an organization and the manager is keeping on top of industry food and marketing trends, that organization will probably not want to consider contract foodservice. If, however, there are problems and foodservice management is lagging behind the times, it is essential for responsible administrators to look at contract foodservice as an option. One thing is certain: turning over foodservice to contract management does not mean that a client-organization never needs to be concerned with its program again. The contract between an organization and a foodservice company will only be as good as the way in which it is administered (see Chapter 5).

Even with a foodservice contractor in place, most organizations will assign an administrator who will need to become knowledgeable enough about foodservice to monitor the contractor's performance. This administrator will be required to do operational audits, review and process contractor billings, handle customer and staff complaints, and perform similar duties. With this in mind, Dana Jones sat down and wrote a list of the major issues he would present to Patricia Bell to consider when deciding whether to go to a contracted foodservice. Here's what Jones' list included:

- The aptitude and attitude of staff relative to the foodservice program. Please note that the same administrative/oversight requirements apply whether foodservice remains self-operational or is turned over to an outside contractor. The question Support Services administrators must answer is, Do they want to be involved in the day-to-day operations or just the policy decisions? "Hey, if we were contracted and our manager was retiring I wouldn't have to worry about it so much. I'd just tell the contractor to have someone new in here six weeks before Harry leaves!"

- The skills and talents of the existing staff. Professional attributes are especially critical if a foodservice has or will soon be expanded or has otherwise become more complex. "It seems to me that there are also some problems with our current operation that staff just never seems to address," Jones thought. "Like the fact that caterings are usually late, if they arrive at all. Or what about the long lines in the cafeteria each lunch hour? Couldn't the manager/staff do something to alleviate the problems? It seems to me that they are not proactive in solving the challenges."
- Labor cost. "Has our corporate effort to treat all employees equally resulted in foodservice workers receiving higher wage and benefit packages whereas their counterparts in retail foodservice do not?" Jones wondered. "If we stay self-operated, can we pay more for labor and charge less for food without incurring substantial losses? Even my understanding of economics tells me that won't work for long." Thanks to his research, Jones had learned that comparable wage scale rates can be secured from local culinary workers' unions, state employment offices, restaurant associations, or [by surveying other] similar foodservice programs. (If you choose to conduct a survey, it is important to make sure that the job titles and responsibilities of those contacted are comparable.)
- Purchasing power. With the aid of local purveyors, businesses, and private and government institutions, the relative dollar volume purchasing power can be determined. It is important to verify that like-quality products are being compared. "I am sure we could serve more or better quality food for less if our purchasing power was greater," mused Jones.
- Financial record keeping and performance. Sometimes the lack of past financial/operational data prevents an administration from validating improved performance levels. Organizations can rarely tailor their financial reporting system to accommodate the particular needs of an individual department such as foodservice. This sometimes results in a compilation of data that are difficult, if not impossible, to track, never mind analyze effectively. This situation is especially common in institutions where more than one foodservice function exists (e.g., a hospital that has patient feeding, cafeteria, doctors' dining room, catering, and other foodservice responsibilities). The ability to reconstruct financial statements and to assign costs and/or develop productivity data that

have any meaning may be difficult under these circumstances. The ultimate goal is to have the kind of data available that permit the benchmarking of an organization's foodservice against comparable operations in similar organizations.

- The mission of foodservice within the organization. "What is it that our organization expects foodservice to accomplish?" Dana asked himself. "To keep employees on campus? Provide meals subsidized only to the de minimis level set by the Internal Revenue Service? Provide a glamorous image to assist in raising funds, selling product, or influencing high-powered visitors?" In Dana's case, the expectations are for all of the above in varying degrees. He would be interested in how Vice President Bell would perceive AU's goals for its foodservice.
- Capital investment. While an organization may lack funds to make the necessary capital investment, if sales potential and customer base are stable and sufficient to support current facilities, a contractor may make the capital investment and amortize it over a period of years. This issue confronts primarily local, state, and federal government more than private organizations. This type of arrangement is much more attractive to contractors if they can operate in a retail environment, such as arena concessions, public cafeterias, and similar operations. Dana knew that AU would not be interested in a direct capital investment by the contractor. He might, however, indicate to Bell that if they decided to contract they might want to have the contractor provide the smallwares or some other facet of the program as a "token" investment. Personally, he always thought people and organizations performed better if they had a financial commitment to any program.

Sitting back, Dana said to himself, "I guess the key to our situation is how I want to replace Harry. Yet even if we can replace Harry with another qualified manager, this analysis makes me see that there may be some merit to hiring a contract foodservice provider. As a result of my own self-education process, I have most of the other elements required to make this decision. I better put this data together and then call a meeting of some of the key players to go over the primary points. Whatever we do, it is becoming crystal clear that I'll still have to supervise the program."

Jones completed a discussion paper considering each of the positive and negative aspects of contracting AU's foodservice. He was ready for an audience with Bell to discuss the issue. Perhaps they would consider contracting the new operations across the freeway and continuing to operate the existing facility as a means of comparison. In that way, there would be an in-house staff in place to pick up the operations if contracting did not work for AU. And, if contracting proved to be the better option, it would be relatively easy to bring the existing cafeteria under the contract at the appropriate time.

It is acknowledged that there are many more reasons and unique situations that justify the contracting out of foodservice. The key is an analytical process for making such a decision. As many administrators will agree, it is far more difficult to return to self-operation after an outside contractor has been used. The answers are not easy and the issue must be considered carefully by each and every organization.

CHAPTER FOUR

Selecting and Managing an Outside Foodservice Contractor

Returning from Harry Daulton's retirement party on a Friday afternoon, Jones gratefully settled back behind his desk. "Well," he thought, "all the signs now point to our selecting an outside contractor to take over our foodservice responsibilities at the new facilities." However, Jones had decided that for the time being, the existing facilities would be self-operated. Daulton's assistant could help with planning the new facility. As Jones saw it, he would then have a mirror operation to compare the merits and negatives of contract food service.

"Now, all I have to figure out is how in the world we go about the contracting process. What if we make this change and foodservice fails to meet everyone's expectations? This could be another critical cross-roads in my career! I can't afford the risk of just calling up a few contractors and asking them to give us their proposals. What do I do?"

By calling a friend at another organization who also had responsibility for foodservice, Jones learned that a national foodservice professional association was offering a one-day seminar on the topic of "Selecting

Foodservice Contractors" in Seattle in just two weeks. He decided to sign up for this seminar in order to learn as much as possible about the process.

While at the seminar, Jones learned a great deal about selecting the appropriate foodservice contractor and administering contracted foodservice. To make sense of the copious information distributed at the seminar, Jones spent his long return flight home reviewing the handout materials he had collected and his own notes. During the uninterrupted hours of travel, Jones began to put his own contractor-selection strategy together, as well as some thoughts on how a contract foodservice company could best serve his organization.

One of the most important facts Jones learned at the Seattle seminar was that in order to keep the number of unpleasant "surprises" to a minimum, both the selected contractor and the client organization must share the same expectations for the management of the organization's foodservice. If the contractor thinks that the client wants gourmet food, but the real goal is to minimize subsidy even though employees have limited discretionary income, there *will* be an unpleasant "surprise." Therefore, the best way for a client organization to communicate its goals and objectives to potential foodservice contractors is through the preparation of a Request for Proposals (RFP) document. Prior to creating an RFP, however, some very important research must be conducted, as the best contractual arrangements result from a carefully thought-out planning process. Paying attention to detail before selecting the contractor will make all the difference in the success of that contractual operation.

To begin, someone must sit down and list all current positive and negative aspects of the organization's foodservice program. It is essential that this appraisal be honest and realistic. It will do absolutely no good to hide any "skeletons in the closet," such as policies or union work rules that have created avoidable costs or inefficient/nonproductive practices, in the hope that the selected contractor can deal with them after winning the account. If some of these policies or work rules are to be eliminated, it is far better for the organization's administration to deal with the situation now, rather than expecting the foodservice contractor to do so later.

Since contractors are generally under no obligation to employ the foodservice staff of a formerly self-operated department, administrators considering outsourcing foodservice should consult their personnel and legal departments regarding the issue of job displacement. One important question to ask is, If jobs are to be eliminated, will the contractor be required to interview or hire any of our existing employees? The key point here is that nothing positive will be accomplished by making a new contractor take the negative hits on the first day of business to fire the organization's employees. That's why it is important that any policy decisions/changes regarding current employees be made in advance and clearly expressed in the RFP.

Some organizations require a foodservice contractor to interview its existing employees and, if they are qualified, to give them first preference for jobs with the newly contracted operation. In other situations, an RFP may go so far as to require a contractor to hire current foodservice employees for a trial period of three to six months. Others hire employees and replace them by attrition or simply retain the contractor to manage that organization's employees while taking advantage of expertise, purchasing power, and accounting support. The conditions an organization may wish to cite in an RFP should be based on current foodservice staff performance, popularity, and tenure.

On a less controversial front, if the contracting-out process is expected to produce any improvements and cost savings in foodservice operations, these, too, should be identified in the RFP. An example might be repairs and maintenance of kitchen equipment. In many organizations, foodservice fails to get adequate in-house maintenance support due to overworked maintenance staff and/or an unwillingness to contract the work to outside suppliers. Some maintenance department heads will, in fact, welcome the opportunity to turn over this function (especially maintaining and repairing refrigeration and other specialty foodservice equipment) to a foodservice contractor and/or its outside subcontractors.

On completion of the needs assessment and with initial policy and operational decisions resolved, Jones began the process of preparing his organization's RFP. While at the Seattle seminar, Jones had been taught how to prepare an outline for this document. His outline for the step-by-step process was as follows:

A. Put together an in-house committee to prepare the RFP and evaluate the responses.
B. Perform a needs assessment.
C. Establish a contractor selection time schedule.
D. Prescreen the potential foodservice contractors through a Request for Qualifications (RFQ). An RFQ is essentially a prescreening process. This document tells potential contractors the scope of services required and requests that they submit certain key background information concerning their ability to successfully meet that scope.
E. Prepare the RFP.

F. Distribute the RFP.
G. Proposers' meeting.
H. Defined question-and-answer period with deadline.
I. Evaluation Process.
J. Reference checks.
K. Contractor site visitations.
L. Contractor interviews.
M. Contractor selection.
N. Final contract negotiations.
O. Transition Planning

IN-HOUSE COMMITTEE

Upon review of his detailed seminar notes Jones knew he needed to get started by forming a committee to help him develop the RFP's various segments, so he decided to wait until he returned to work to write up his outline. The seminar leader had explained that this in-house committee would both provide information and serve as an evaluation board for the RFP and the contractor responses/selection process.

Following the seminar leader's advice, Jones decided to include representatives of the following departments on his committee:

- Personnel (to provide guidance on how foodservice employees who would be displaced or have to work for the contractor should be treated, as well as to develop a demographic profile of employee-customers)
- Finance (to provide input on corporate financial goals, accounting and audit requirements)
- Facilities (to provide information on the facilities and equipment assigned to foodservice, as well as safety and sanitation issues)
- Executive Staff (to gain insight from those who arrange the majority of AU's catering and are best able to assist in defining catering needs)
- Purchasing (to provide input on the organization's general purchasing policies)
- Legal counsel (either in house or retained legal counsel should be used to review the "boiler-plate" language in the contract, as well as the RFP. The best arrangement is for the RFP and the proposal response to be incorporated into the final contract. That requires detailed attention to both documents from a legal perspective.)

PERFORM A NEEDS ASSESSMENT

Assessing the current foodservice program and determining future needs are a critical step in the process of developing an RFP. The process for conducting a needs assessment is thoroughly discussed in Chapter 7.

ESTABLISH A TIME SCHEDULE

Jones established a contractor selection time schedule that he would present to his committee for review. He followed the seminar leader's advice and allowed plenty of time for each step of the process. In particular, he knew he needed to allow from five to six weeks for the contractors to respond to the RFP. A sample time schedule is presented in Exhibit 4-1 and on the disk.

Exhibit 4-1
TENTATIVE RFP TIME SCHEDULE

TASK	*DATE*
1. RFQ release	August 10
2. RFQ responses due	August 24
3. RFP released to contractors	September 10
4. Rejection notices sent to other contractors	September 10
5. Notification of intent to participate due	September 18
6. Mandatory proposing contractors meeting	September 20
7. Questions/clarification requests cutoff date	October 15
8. Questions/answers released to contractors	October 17
9. Proposal responses due	October 25
10. Contractor client site visits	October 28–29
11. Contractor interviews	November 1
12. Contractor selection	November 2
13. Contract execution	November 15
14. Contractor to assume control	December 31

[Note: It is generally wise to allow a new contractor at least six weeks to prepare for a new account. The above schedule has sufficient flexibility to permit a more rapid selection process without sacrificing the ability to achieve high-quality results.]

REQUEST FOR QUALIFICATIONS

Ideally an organization will send out a separate Request for Qualifications (RFQ) before the RFP. The purpose of an RFQ is to ascertain which potential contractors are most qualified to operate an organization's foodservice in order to solicit proposals only from those qualified companies. Note: This process is sometimes, but not always, precluded by the purchasing laws of federal, state and local governmental agencies. (A sample RFQ is included at the end of the chapter as Exhibit 4-2, and on the accompanying disk.) The critical points Jones included in his document were the proposal schedule and the identification of submittal times and places.

Keep in mind that even though a contractor provides foodservice at 200 colleges and universities it may not be the best company to operate corporate foodservice for an electronics firm. By the same token, experience operating foodservice at a hospital may not cross over to a program at a correctional facility or performing arts center.

Finally, organizations seeking to hire a foodservice contractor should ask for proof of the financial stability of the company. Adequate proof may be a copy of an audited annual statement or a letter of credit from a bank. Sometimes it is appropriate to accept federal tax returns and references from vendors, banks, and other financial institutions. In the case of private companies, administrators will need to be sensitive to the fact that such financial documents are not public information and should be treated as confidential. Any form of recent legal protection from creditors should be investigated and considered in the selection process.

Over the past few weeks Jones had been developing a list of contractors who might be suitable for AU. His first source had been the file of business cards and literature sent by various contractors. In addition, he had contacted some of the professional associations (see Chapter 14) and a few of his associates at other contracted operations. He was surprised to have a list of 22 companies. After debating whether to send the RFQ to all of them, he decided it was best to do so at this early stage of the game. After all, that was the purpose of this separate process, to determine who was interested in AU and which contractors had the qualifications to meet AU's needs. Jones scheduled the submission of contractors' pre-qualification materials to coincide with the committee's review of the draft RFP, so that both parts of the selection process could proceed simultaneously.

PREPARING THE REQUEST FOR PROPOSALS

Preparing to begin the proposal drafting process, Jones recalled that the seminar leader stressed that proposals should be clearly defined and in accord with organizations' existing purchasing practices. To guide his draft, Jones consulted AU's purchasing department to see which criteria AU applied when requesting proposals. After meeting with the department's head, Jones decided to follow a process that met AU's requirements but also incorporated some of the elements discussed at the seminar. (His basic points are listed as RFP Exhibit 4-3 and on the disk).

Background and Scope of Assignment

To begin, Jones recalled that the "Background and Scope of Assignment" introductory section of each RFP will be unique to the needs of different organizations. The critical point is that this RFP section must provide potential contractors both the history of the organization's foodservice department and a description of what the organization hopes foodservice will accomplish in the future. Referring to his seminar notes, Jones considered which factors should be presented in this section of the RFP. His first list looked like this:

- State the goals/purpose of the foodservice department.
- List all facilities, including square footage and number of seats.
- Provide floor plans and equipment lists, preferably as attachments.
- Identify all facility improvements that need to be made and indicate whether the contractor is expected to participate in the funding, planning, and/or design of those facilities.
- State the organization's specific financial goals and the type of contract being sought.

Smaller organizations (those with base populations of 750 or less) may need to subsidize their dining programs, with the amount dependent upon the type of foodservice requested, intensity of local restaurant competition, length of lunch periods, and other issues. It will also be necessary to subsidize extended hours of service, particularly if the population is smaller during those time periods. For example, keeping a cafeteria open to serve 125 people working on a night shift will usually not be profitable for a contractor. As a result, many organizations which, in the past, insisted on keeping their cafeterias open all hours have gone to vending machine service on the second and third shifts to reduce or eliminate subsidy. Rising costs of doing business, lower profit margins, and de minimis tax laws (see Chapter 6) have all influenced organizations to limit foodservice hours. Finally, those administering foodservice may wish to consider offering prospective contractors profit and loss contracts, if the employee population and hours of operation generate sufficient revenue to allow the contractor to make a profit.

General Contract Language

The most efficient way to ensure that responding contractors understand the basic contractual conditions an organization seeks is to provide a sample contract as an attachment to an RFP. (See Exhibit 4-4 at the end of this chapter and on the accompanying disk). Such concerns as indemnity, insurance, exclusive rights, and other clauses should be included, but only *after* the proposal has been reviewed by the organization's legal department.

This document serves two purposes. It clearly identifies the responsibilities of contractor and client, and also allows contractors to challenge and/or accept basic contract terms before (not after) the selection process is complete. The contractors should be required within the proposal to state any objections/revisions to that contract language.

Dana recalled a story told by a fellow seminar attender who had recounted how her organization had proceeded all the way to the contract negotiation stage before it found that neither its attorney nor the contractor's would compromise on an insurance liability issue. After several weeks of intense negotiations, the would-be client had been forced to go to its second choice contractor to complete a contract. Dana shuddered. "I don't *need that* kind of hassle or embarrassment with our new VP," he reminded himself.

Responsibilities of the Organization

At this point, it is important to list the areas for which your organization will be responsible. These areas should include which, if any, facilities, equipment, utilities, or janitorial services will be provided to the contractor. This section also usually specifies that the client-organization will provide access to designated foodservice facilities and to what extent designated foodservice areas will be secured from unauthorized access by the organization's employees.

Responsibilities of the Contractor

This section of the RFP should outline all of the selected contractor's responsibilities regarding facilities management, janitorial services, maintenance, menus, pricing and portion control, security, safety, expected transition plan, and other requirements. (The RFP on the disk provides a generic sample of issues to be addressed in this section.)

Mandatory Proposal Requirements

This is the section in which client-organizations must tell would-be contractors what they should propose. The best way to do this, of course, is to ask for specific program features, such as a set cycle menu designed for your employee population, a proposed staffing chart, wage rates and salaries, proposed revenue projections, and a pro forma statement of income and expenses. You should also include specific requests about any other operational areas in which you want contractors to tell you what they would do for your organization. Dana very clearly recalled the seminar leader saying, "If you want product or service delivered a certain defined way, then write it up in the sample contract under contractor responsibilities. However, if you want a contractor to be creative and *tell* you how it would provide a given product or service, then put your request in the Mandatory Proposal Requirements section." Responses to the mandatory requirements will enable you to evaluate the "quality of thinking" that the proposers put into assessing your situation and how to meet your needs.

Evaluation Criteria

The most effective way to select the "right" contractor for your organization's foodservice is to provide the criteria for evaluation of proposals within your RFP. Looking up from his notes, Jones recalled asking the seminar leader, "Why would you tell potential contractors your criteria? Wouldn't that be comparable to giving students the answers to study before the exam?" The leader's response had made a lot of sense to Dana. The leader had said that the reason for telling contractors the evaluation criteria was to reinforce for them what is important to the client-organization. "You will not get the best proposal if contractors are trying to guess what is most important to you," the seminar leader had advised.

The evaluation process must also include a thorough review of each proposal. To do so, it is useful to make a comparative chart to highlight the most important variables. Jones set about developing a list of the most important variables to AU.

Whatever the bidding contractors propose must be reviewed in light of how their vision of foodservice fits in with your organization and its goals. For example, at a manufacturing plant, most of the employees do physical labor throughout the day and, thus, are usually very hungry when they come to their cafeteria. What these employees are looking for is a hearty meal priced within their budget. In an administrative setting, by contrast, employees work at desks and are more interested in light fare. Hot turkey sandwiches with mashed potatoes and green beans, therefore, will appeal to the first customer group but likely not to the second. Avocado and sprouts in pita bread, on the other hand, would probably be of limited appeal to the first group, but might be highly desired at the second location. Jones realized he was beginning to understand how important the initial research stage was to support the development of an RFP *and* the evaluation of contractors' proposals. He made a note to himself to spend time discussing the findings of the research phase with his evaluation committee, to remind them what would be and what would not be important when it came time to evaluate contractors' proposals.

Having completed his draft RFP and a collection of attachments, Jones set up the next meeting of the evaluation committee to review his document and make sure that nothing had been left out.

Evaluate the Qualifications and Distribute the Request For Proposals

Two days before the planned evaluation committee meeting, Jones received a letter from one of the contacted contractors that at first he found disturbing. This contractor's president had written to say that he did not think that his company's goals were compatible with those of AU. This was especially disturbing to Jones since he had visited a cafeteria operated by that contractor while in Seattle and had loved the food. However, after reading the letter a second time, Jones recalled another piece of advice the seminar leader had offered: "Do not let personal tastes drive the decisions you make on behalf of your organization." At this point, he realized that the contractor had actually done him a favor, because if the supplier did not have an interest in AU's vision of foodservice, it was unlikely that it would have done as good a job as would other established companies.

At the evaluation meeting, committee members offered some constructive reactions to the draft RFP. Peters from Personnel pointed out that AU should ask to see contractors' benefit packages so the committee could evaluate how different suppliers treated employees. Martin from the Marketing Department reminded Jones to add to the RFP the fact that AU held six fly-ins a year, bringing in top distributors to view demonstrations of new products. Martin added that each of these demonstrations had to be supported by a variety of catered events over a week-long period, which required both increased staffing and opportunities for foodservice to earn significant revenue.

"Over the past few years, however," Martin noted, "we in Marketing have been taking our guests to nearby hotels because, well, frankly, our catering could have been better. I sure hope these contractors can propose the sort of catering program that would encourage departments to spend dollars in-house." Jones shook his head, careful to keep a smile on his face while he thought, "Here's our organization subsidizing foodservice, while the departments are spending money on outside catering. What a waste."

At the same meeting, the committee reviewed the 10 responses to the RFQ. Based on several criteria, they selected four. The criteria used were the following:

- The existence of accounts of a similar size and type in the geographic area surrounding AU. They arbitrarily selected a 250-mile radius.
- The number of accounts that the district manager had to supervise. In one case they eliminated a company because the district manager was expected to supervise 17 accounts in a five-state area. No way could that poor individual provide quality supervision to those accounts and travel the hundreds of miles necessary to visit them all with any regularity.
- Financial stability. They rejected one company which was in the middle of a Chapter 11 reorganization and, while all might turn out well in the end, no one wanted to be responsible if the company failed and AU was left "holding the bag".
- Specialization. Two companies were rejected because it seemed that they specialized in hospital foodservice. While there were some similarities, AU wanted a company with real business and industry experience for its first venture into contract foodservice.

After the committee meeting, Jones' amended RFP was mailed to the four qualified vendors and the Support Services administrator began planning for the mandatory proposers' conference he had scheduled for the next week.

PROPOSERS' CONFERENCE

According to what he learned at the Seattle seminar, Jones knew that the conference should include a tour of his organization's foodservice facilities; a brief discussion of the organization's goals, emphasizing the reasons for considering contract foodservice operations; and, at the end, an opportunity for the contractors to ask questions.

This reminded Jones that all questions should be asked and answered in front of the whole group. He had been warned by colleagues that a contractor might try to get representatives of potential clients aside to ask questions and get answers in private. He wanted to preclude that kind of behavior and ensure that all contractors were working from the same information base. Still, Jones chuckled to himself, recalling the fellow at the seminar who had said that any contractor who did something like that should be disqualified. Jones' own reaction had been, "Well, you can't blame a person for trying!"

The following week, a successful proposers' conference was held at AU. The next day, Jones' secretary typed up all notes taken during that conference, along with relevant questions and answers. Jones' secretary also compiled copies of additional data (such as a list of the foodservice equipment repair records) requested by several of the contractors during the meeting.

Defined question and answer period with deadline.

There should be a deadline for contractors to submit questions in writing. That deadline should allow time to develop the answers and return the written response to all of the potential contractors. Generally that means that the deadline for questions is from one to two weeks before the date the proposals are due.

Proposal Evaluation Process

The day finally came when the contractors' proposals arrived on Jones' desk. Along with four blank sets of the evaluation form, Dana sent copies

Exhibit 4-5
OPERATING PROPOSAL EVALUATION

REVIEWER ____________________ DATE ______________

OPERATING PROPOSAL EVALUATION	*PTS.*	*CONTRACTOR A*	*CONTRACTOR B*	*CONTRACTOR C*	*CONTRACTOR D*
CYCLE MENU	10				
CATERING MENU, PORTIONS & PRICES	5				
CONCEPTS/CREATIVITY	10				
MENU PORTIONS & PRICES	5				
STAFFING FTE'S	10				
QUALIFICATIONS OF SITE MANAGER	5				
TRAINING PROGRAMS	5				
MARKETING PLANS	5				
QUALITY ASSURANCE PROGRAM	5				
COST CONTROL PLAN	5				
PROMOTIONS/PACE CHANGERS	5				
UNIFORMS	2.5				
SERVING HOURS	5				
VENDING PLAN	10				
RECYCLING PLAN	2.5				
NUTRITION PLAN	5				
FACILITIES PLANNING ASSISTANCE	5				
TOTAL	100				

Exhibit 4-5 continued

FINANCIAL PROPOSAL EVALUATION

REVIEWER ____________________ DATE ______________

FINANCIAL PROPOSAL		*CONTRACTOR A*	*CONTRACTOR B*	*CONTRACTOR C*	*CONTRACTOR D*
RETURN ON VENDING	10				
MANAGEMENT FEE/ADMINISTRATIVE AND GENERAL	25				
PROPOSED PROFIT SPLIT	10				
EQUIPMENT INVESTMENT VALUE	10				
PRO FORMA SALES PROJECTIONS	10				
PRO FORMA EXPENSE PROJECTIONS	10				
TOTAL	75				

NOTE: The following are typical questions for some of the evaluation points. It will be important to develop the specific evaluation criteria, assign the points and develop the questions based upon your organization's goals and scope of work.

MENU EVALUATIONS

- Are the menus complete? Do they meet the minimum standards set in the RFP?
- Is there variety each day and from day to day?
- In general, does the menu appear to be nutritionally balanced?
- Are the menus interesting?
- What have they proposed to break the monotony of dining in one facility all the time? i.e, specials, theme days, etc.
- Are the menu proposals realistic or are they more than might be feasible at your facilities? i.e., do they propose stir-fry to order but you do not have woks nor do they propose install them.

Exhibit 4-5 continued

PRICES AND PORTIONS

- What is the price of retail items compared to local retail market?
- What is the price:portion relationship for items prepared on-site? i.e., Is a quarter-pound cheeseburger comparable to a quarter-pound cheeseburger at a fast food restaurant?
- How reasonable are the catering prices?

CONCEPTS

- Is there any creativity in the concept/decor plan?
- Is what is proposed compatible with the general nature of the organization?
- Are there special programs proposed during the year such as outdoor BBQs in the retail areas?
- Is there any proposal to maximize foodservice availability through the use of carts?
- Is there any creative proposal to maximize use of branded products?

PERSONNEL AND SUPERVISION

- How does the contractor propose to train new staff?
- How many full time equivalencies (FTEs) does the contractor propose to schedule? Is there a chef, or if not, what is the quality of the training for the main production person?
- What does the contractor propose to pay for salaried and hourly workers?
- Is there a benefit plan available? Who pays for it? Who qualifies?
- What is the caliber of the proposed district and site management candidate(s)?
- Do they appear to have adequate experience?
- What are the uniforms? Are they in keeping with the decor and concept?

FINANCIAL PROPOSAL

- Does the contractor agree to the financial terms set forth in the request for proposals?
- Are the sales revenue projections realistic? If a contractor tells you that they will double the sales, but they also say they are keeping the current menu and prices, limiting branded concepts and cutting the hours, something is not right.
- Are the expenses realistic? Again, if a contractor says that they can lower food cost to 30% and they are not proposing to raise the pricing, then the only way is to cut food quality. If they propose to pay higher wages but cut labor cost . . . will there be more than one cashier at lunch? The key to remember is that the financial proposal must ''jive'' with the operational proposal.
- Is there an investment in additional equipment to develop the proposed concepts, what will that equipment cost, how will it be depreciated and does it pay itself back in a reasonable amount of time? Is their sufficient new equipment to do what they propose, i.e., if they propose hot pretzels, how will they heat/display those items? If they propose 8 kinds of soft yogurt and current capacity is 4, have they shown how they will accomplish the other 4? You do not want them coming to you in September saying, ''Sure **you** can have the other 4, after **you** buy a new yogurt dispenser!''

to all committee members for their evaluation and scheduled a meeting for the following Monday. He then prepared himself for the meeting over the weekend by doing his own preliminary evaluation of contractors' proposals and filling in his scores on the evaluation forms.

The committee members came to the meeting prepared to compare and discuss their preliminary scores. Sometimes the reader had not interpreted the proposal accurately. In other cases, there were holes in the proposal. From this meeting, the committee drafted a list of questions to ask each of the companies in the interview process. Jones recommended to the committee that they send most of the technical questions in advance to each of the companies so that they could come prepared to answer those questions at the interviews. He also suggested that they reserve one or two more generic problem solving questions to ask directly at the interview. He was interested in the interaction between the various people who came to the interview. Would the District Manager respond or would that person have to look to the "higher ups" to answer the question. It would reveal something about how autonomous the District Manager would be in dealing with AU and how fast AU would get a response to its needs in the future.

One of the committee members objected to sending the questions in advance, believing that the surprise element was best. Jones reminded them (kindly but firmly) that their objective was to get good proposals and select the best contractor, not play a game of "gotcha" with the contractors. That would serve no one's interest, least of all AU.

Telephone Reference Checks

Telephone reference checks should be made to the current and previous clients submitted by contractors. Whether one person conducts the interviews or the committee members divide up the list, it is important to work from a common base of questions. Organizations are becoming increasingly reluctant to speak up in a reference check for fear of being sued. The best responses come when you ask specific questions and, where possible, provide a numerical rating system. A sample telephone reference check form is presented in Exhibit 4-6 and on the disk.

Contractor Site Visitations

Between the initial review of the proposals and before the interviews, it may be appropriate to schedule site visits to key accounts for each of the contractors. Jones knew to make the site arrangements through the contract administrator and/or the contractors. Whenever possible, he asked

Exhibit 4-6
TELEPHONE REFERENCE CHECK FORM

Contractor: ______________________________

Reference Source: ____________________ Date: ____________

Person Contacted: ____________________ Phone: ____________

1. How long have you had a foodservice contract with "this management company"[1]
2. What type of foodservice does "the contractor" provide at your organization?
3. Have you had other foodservice contractors? (If yes):
   A. What was the reason that you changed contractors?
   B. How would you compare this contractor with your previous contractor(s)?
4. On a scale of 1 to 10, with 1 being low, 5 average, and 10 high, how would you rate "the contractor" on the following:

A. Food quality	1 2 3 4 5 6 7 8 9 10
B. Menu variety	1 2 3 4 5 6 7 8 9 10
C. Response to complaints/ problems	1 2 3 4 5 6 7 8 9 10
D. Equipment maintenance	1 2 3 4 5 6 7 8 9 10
E. Sanitation	1 2 3 4 5 6 7 8 9 10
F. Employee training/service attitude	1 2 3 4 5 6 7 8 9 10
G. Employee turnover	1 2 3 4 5 6 7 8 9 10
H. Ability to "fit in" as a part of your organization	1 2 3 4 5 6 7 8 9 10
I. Quality of catering	1 2 3 4 5 6 7 8 9 10
J. Merchandising/display/appearance of food	1 2 3 4 5 6 7 8 9 10
K. Availability/support/responsiveness of corporate or regional staff	1 2 3 4 5 6 7 8 9 10

5. How would you rate "the contractor's" overall performance:
   Poor Fair Average Good Excellent
6. If you did not *have* to go out for *[public]* bids *[or rebid the contract every x years]*, would you retain this contractor or solicit other proposals?
7. From your perspective, has "the contractor" met the commitments it made to your organization in its proposal/contract?
8. Are there any other comments you would like to share with me about "the contractor"?

____
____
____
____
____

[1]Best approach is to substitute the actual name of the contractor at each appropriate point throughout the interview questions.

to meet with the contract administrator at each site without the contractor's representative in the meeting. In this way he knew they would get a more frank appraisal of both the positive and negative aspects of working with each of contractors.

Contractor Interviews

The best way to get answers to organizational questions about contractors' foodservice programs is to schedule individual interviews with each contender. However, unless required by bidding laws (such as those that apply to some government agencies), there is no reason to interview a contractor whose proposal is not responsive to your RFP. Keep in mind that coming to interviews with potential clients can cost some contractors thousands of dollars in time and travel expenses. It is therefore best not to put a company to any unnecessary expense, since all marketing dollars are eventually spread over each company's total cost of doing business and are charged back to the clients they do get.

During the actual review of contractor proposals, many questions are likely to arise about each proposal. In the case of AU's committee, questions about the proposals helped to determine that only three of the four submitted were responsive to the organization's foodservice needs. Since interviews with all contractors were not mandatory, the committee decided to set up interviews with only those three, reserving the right to call the fourth company in at a later date. The evaluation committee's questions, based on reviews of individual proposals, were immediately sent out so that the finalist contractors could come to the interview prepared to address the real issues of concern to AU. The contractors were told to bring the district manager and a candidate for the AU manager's position to the interviews. After all, it was these people, not the corporate or regional salespeople, who would make or break the AU operations.

CONTRACTOR SELECTION

Based upon the proposal evaluations, site visits, reference checks and interviews, a contractor should be selected following the interview process. The entire methodical process may seem cumbersome and tedious in the beginning but the relative ease of making the final selection should more than compensate for the effort.

In some organizations the decision is immediately relayed to the contractor. In others, the decision of the committee is referred to a higher jurisdiction for approval.

NEGOTIATION OF THE FINAL CONTRACT TERMS

Once AU's new foodservice contractor had been selected, Jones met with AU's legal counsel, to discuss how the contract should be finalized. Because the RFP had been written with the intent that it and the proposal response would become part of the contract, the process went smoothly. It is important that the final contract includes in writing all clarifications, including items requested and agreed to during interviews.

It is important for organizational administrators to be in control of the contracting process. The more responsibility that administrators take for defining the process, the better contractual relationships will be. The best contract administrators are those who manage their foodservice according to the terms of a well-written contract.

TRANSITION PLANNING

Although a signed contract represents a significant commitment, it is not the end of the process unless an organization is retaining an incumbent contractor. In many instances it is necessary to modify a transition plan to meet the dates and conditions of the final contract. An appropriate transition period should provide time for the new operator to interview, place, and train staff; make arrangements with purveyors; and install accounting systems and all the other resources that must be marshaled prior to actually taking over an account. When the transition is from one contractor to another, contract language should provide for them to deal with any existing inventories on their own. However, when the transition is from self-operated to contract foodservice, the organization will have to make provisions. Sometimes the RFP clearly states that the contractor will buy the inventory at some reasonable price; in other cases the company may dispose of the inventory by donating it to a charitable organization.

A transition will take a minimum of 30 days. In most instances, 60 to 90 days provides for the smoothest transition for both the contractor and the organization. One of the most important aspects of any transition will be the communications with everyone involved. Current foodservice staff and employees will respond more positively to change when they are informed.

Exhibit 4-2
SAMPLE REQUEST FOR QUALIFICATIONS LETTER (RFQ)

Foodservice Contractor
Street
City

Dear Contractor:

The ____________________ (Organization) intends to issue a request for proposals for __________ of its cafeteria operations. The cafeterias are located in Rockland, USA. All of these cafeterias currently are self-operated *[or contracted]*. When necessary, all Organization cafeterias can be subsidized up to the limits permitted by the Internal Revenue Service *[or are to be operated on a profit and loss basis, etc.]*. Each facility serves an Organization population of from 700-800 persons. Each has major catering requirements/events throughout the year in support of its sales and customer service efforts. Organization's foodservice program is a very important employee service relative to enhancing the workplace environment, fostering productivity, and presenting a positive image to its customers and guests.

The purpose of this letter is to ascertain your interest in operating one or more of the above cafeteria locations. In order to be considered for receipt of an RFP, you must submit the answers and/or data requested herein to Organization by no later than August 24, 19XX. Due to the fact that Organization wishes to consider no more than four contractors in its RFP process, this prequalification process is necessary. All proposing contractors must be prepared to assume management control of the foodservice operations at the locations on or about December 31, 19XX.

If your company wishes to be considered, please answer the following questions or requests for information:

1. Name, address, and phone number of company headquarters. In addition, please list the names and phone numbers of the person(s) to contact concerning your response.
2. Please indicate that your company is willing to operate all of Organization's location(s).
3. A list of all comparable size and type client foodservice operations within the geographic area or operating region of each facility for which you intend to submit a proposal response. Each listing should include the following information:
   - Name and location of client
   - Name and phone number of client contact
   - Length of time your company has had this contract
   - Type of contract (management fee, profit and loss, et al.)
   - Approximate employee population (if not confidential)
   - Size and number of cafeteria(s) (square feet and number of seats)
   - Hours of operation

Exhibit 4-2 continued

- Service levels (breakfast, lunch, dinner, and catering)
- Menu offerings for each service level

4. A list of three comparable accounts that your company has *lost* over the past three years. Please include the name and phone number of the client contact.
5. A copy of your company's most recent audited financial statement.
6. A detailed description of your catering capabilities as they would apply to one or more of the locations.
7. Background statements and/or resumes for key headquarters or regional *and* area management, line, and support personnel.
8. A statement as to your company's ability to meet Organization's attached proposal response(s) schedule and assume complete operational responsibility for the ________ cafeterias on or about December 31, 19XX.
9. Your response must be received by August 24, 19XX. It should be addressed to:

Ms. Mary McGuire or Mr. Eric Behnke
________________ Organization
444 Cranberry Road Rockland, USA 20850

Any questions should be directed to Ms. McGuire or Mr. Behnke at the above address or call (111) 111-4444.

In preparing your response, you should be aware of the following contract requirements/selection criteria:

1. The contractor must secure and maintain a minimum of $1 million in comprehensive general and product liability insurance.
2. The contractor will be expected to secure and maintain a performance bond of $25,000 for each facility. *[Since performance bonds become a "cost of doing business" there may not be a need for this requirement.]*
3. Organization may, at its discretion, terminate the contract for any reason upon 30 days' written notice. The contractor, however, may not terminate the contract with any fewer than 90 days' written notice.
4. Contractors that have the ability to effectively serve all ________ sites and submit a management fee *[or profit and loss]* proposal that is advantageous to Organization will receive priority consideration.
5. The contractor must demonstrate proven ability to operate facilities similar to Organization's in an operationally and financially effective manner. The prospective contractors will be expected to prove their ability to meet Organization's quality and financial accountability standards.
6. Proposers should be aware that this is not a bidding process. Organization

Figure 4-2 continued

intends to select the contractor that can provide the best-quality food and service to its employees and guests. *[If price is a prime determinant, then this clause will need to be modified accordingly.]*

7. Those contractors selected to submit an RFP response will be asked to propose an incentive plan, based on sales growth/maintenance and adherence to budgeted cost controls.
8. Organization will evaluate the relative strengths and weaknesses of each proposing contractor on a consolidated and individual Organization site basis. All site manager candidates must be interviewed and approved by Organization prior to contract execution and as provided for within the contract.
9. Organization intends to aggressively administer the contract in terms of holding the foodservice company(s) responsible for maintaining all quality standards and financial accountability/audit trail and reporting requirements.
10. The contractor's proposal response and pertinent written correspondence concerning this account will become an amendment to the contract.

Thank you for your consideration of this Request for Qualifications. Once all of the responses are in and have been evaluated, we will notify all submitters as to which companies were selected and if there are any changes to the RFP time schedule.

Sincerely

Mary McGuire
Support Services Administrator

Exhibit 4-3
MODEL RFP

[What follows is a generic request for proposal (RFP) format which should be used as a guide in preparing a similar document for your organization. It should be understood that there will be a number of items that will need to be changed or deleted to fit your specific requirements. In addition, there will be a need to add points in the appropriate section(s) or even add new sections in order to specifically address subjects or legal concerns unique to your situation. Please carefully review and evaluate each point to assure yourself and all concerned within your respective organization that this RFP and the attached contract document truly reflect all critical minimum requirements. All notes which are presented within brackets [] should be deleted once the primary draft has been completed.]

I. General Information

The __________________ (Organization) is requesting management fee *[versus profit and loss versus defined profit or variations thereof]* proposals for its cafeteria operations from qualified foodservice management companies (Contractors). At the present time, Organization is not interested in putting its vending contract out for rebid. The foodservice facilities are located at:

4444 Berry Road
Rockland, USA 80850

177 Mooberry Road
Rockland, USA 80850

1266 Cranberry Road
Rockland, USA 80850

All __________ cafeterias are currently self-operated. All Organization cafeterias are subsidized up to the limits permitted by the Internal Revenue Service *[or are operated on a profit and loss, etc. basis]*. Each facility serves an Organization population of from 700 to 800 persons. Each has major catering requirements/events throughout the year in support of its sales and customer service efforts.

Organization's foodservice program is a very important employee *[could also read student, faculty, staff, patient, inmate, etc.]* service relative to enhancing the work [or living] place environment, fostering productivity, and presenting a positive image to its customers and guests. It is in Organization's best interest to solicit a Contractor(s) that will be able to maintain a high-quality cafeteria and catering program that will be operated in a financially responsible manner. Toward that end, Organization will select the Contractor(s) that is(are) best qualified to meet these goals and objectives.

[Note: This introduction represents a very important summary of the scope of services and quality level required. In this case, "Organization" is asking one or more companies to provide a relatively wide range of services, that is, from coffee and sweet rolls to multiple course meals. Organization is asking only foodservice companies with this range of skills to submit proposal responses.]

Figure 4-3 continued

II. Conditions of Proposal—General

It is Organization's preference that proposing Contractors submit proposals for all the cafeteria facilities. If a Contractor wishes to submit proposals for fewer than all facilities, they must be submitted separately.

[Note: In this case, the cafeterias were in the same location. If your cafeteria(s) are in different geographical areas, you may wish to contract with more than one foodservice company. From Organization's perspective, administering one contract is generally more efficient than multiple ones. There may be circumstances, such as the need to set aside a certain percentage of business for minority and women-owned business enterprises, that would result in more than one contractor being selected. From the contractor's perspective, it also can be more efficient plus allow a more competitive administration and management fee.]

All prospective Contractors must read the Organization contract specifications attached to this RFP *carefully*. Any exceptions, additions, and/or deletions to the terms and conditions presented must be clearly stated within the proposal response. Unfamiliarity with Organization's foodservice contract and operations shall not relieve the successful Contractor(s) from the necessity of furnishing and installing, without cost to Organization, any materials, or performing any labor or service that may be required to carry out the intent of the resulting contract(s).

There will be a mandatory proposing-Contractors' meeting and facilities tour held at the Cranberry Road site on September 20, 19XX at 9:00 A.M. Any contractor considering or wishing to participate must notify Organization in writing of its intent to participate by September 18, 19XX. Contractors are requested to be sensitive to the fact that these facilities are presently self-operated. Organization employees may or may not decide to take a position with Contractor should a change be made.

If any Organization employees should desire employment with the selected Contractor, that Contractor must guarantee those persons will be given priority consideration for comparable positions at the same or mutually acceptable location. In addition, those employees must be given the same trial period, orientation, and training to enable them to have every opportunity to succeed as employees of the new Contractor.

[Note: The preceding two paragraphs are, in effect, a tribute to the persons who, regardless of which contractor is there, have chosen to work at these Organization locations. Whether employed by the Organization or an independent contractor, many of these people as well as the balance of Organization's personnel consider them to be a part of the "family." In most cases, a new contractor is more than happy to hire and retain all of these productive workers.]

At each meeting, there will be an opportunity for each proposing Contractor to receive copies of the current menus and become completely familiar with the kitchen, cafeteria, and catering facilities. In addition, Contractors will have an opportunity to ask questions or seek clarifications to this RFP and the

Figure 4-3 continued

attached contract specifications. Questions may be asked up until the close of business on October 15, 19XX. All questions must be submitted in writing to:

Ms. Mary McGuire or Mr. Eric Behnke
_______________ Organization
444 Cranberry Road
Rockland, USA 20850

Once all of the questions and requests for additional information have been received, Organization will then will publish the same along with the answers. This document will be mailed to all qualifying contractors by October 17, 19XX. Subsequent site visits are encouraged, but they must be arranged at least 24 hours in advance with the foodservice manager *[or administrator]* at each site.

It is in Organization's best interest to provide as much nonproprietary information as possible about its present foodservice operations. It is critical that Organization receive quality, easy-to-compare proposal responses in order to make the best-informed decision. Toward that end, all proposing Contractors are encouraged to ask questions and seek whatever information necessary to accomplish this goal.

Contractors who have submitted acceptable proposal responses will be invited to an interview, which will be held on or about November 4, 19XX. All concerned will be notified as to the exact time and place. Prior to that, on or around October 28–29, there will be contractor site visits. The actual selection and notification of the contractor(s) will be made by November 7, 19XX.

Six copies of each proposal response must be submitted to Ms. Mary McGuire or Mr. Behnke at the above address by 4:00 P.M. on *Friday, October 25, 19XX*. Proposals submitted past this time and date will be considered only if it is in Organization's interest to do so.

Organization intends to have its Contractor(s) assume operational control of the __________ cafeteria and catering operations on or about December 31, 19XX.

This RFP, the Contractor's proposal response, and any amendments and correspondence resulting from this process will be made a part of the final contract.

Organization reserves the right to change the terms and conditions of this RFP and attached contract. Organization will notify all potential Contractors of any material changes.

Organization reserves the right to reject any or all proposals.

All proposing Contractors must adhere strictly to Organization's Code of Business Conduct. Applicable portions of this document will be available for review upon request.

The contract term will be for three (3) years from the date of the first day of operation, with two (2) one-year renewal periods, which may be exercised

Figure 4-3 continued

at the sole option of Organization. Organization may, at its discretion, terminate the contract for any reason upon 30 days' written notice. The Contractor, however, may not terminate the contract with any less than 90 days' written notice.

[Note: There are a number of points listed here that are in the attached contract document as well. It is important to repeat and/or reference all key contractual requirements in order to make sure there is no misunderstanding as to Organization's intent.]

III. Conditions of Proposal—Special

Organization intends to retain the most qualified Contractor(s) relative to the skill levels and expertise required to provide the best possible food and service for its locations. Prospective Contractors should be aware that they are being evaluated primarily on the basis of their experience with comparable cafeteria and catering accounts *and* their knowledge and understanding of Organization's environment. Your proposal responses, therefore, should strive to answer each question as clearly and concisely as possible as they relate to the Organization and its foodservice facilities. Sales promotion pieces and information/data that are not relevant to Organization are strongly discouraged. Organization is most interested in getting to know more about the Contractor, its people at a headquarters, regional, and local level, and its ability to meet and maintain Organization's specific requirements.

Each prospective Contractor shall answer the following questions or provide the information requested as part of its proposal response(s).

1. Please provide a brief assessment of your current concept(s), menu(s), portions, prices, and service levels. In addition, please provide Organization with specific proposals as to what changes and/or improvements should be made in the cafeterias. Sample or representative one-week cafeteria menus that detail portions and prices should be submitted for each facility. Unless otherwise specified by Organization, the Contractor's proposal is to address the foodservice program as it is at present. Any proposed changes should clearly delineate any potential operational and/or financial impact(s) for each location.

   [With respect to facilities such as colleges, schools, hospitals, jails, and other entities, this clause will need to be revised to accurately reflect that particular situation.]

2. Please provide a brief assessment of the equipment and space at each facility and note what, if anything, Contractor would do to enhance or improve what is currently being offered. You should also note if there would be a need for capital equipment or facility improvements that would have to be provided by Organization. A listing of specific improvement recommendations that will involve construction and/or equipment along with estimated costs should be submitted.

3. Please refer to Section 4.2.10 of the attached contract specifications concerning the minimum food and quality standards and indicate what

Figure 4-3 continued

exceptions, additions, and/or deletions you wish to propose. *[These specifications can either be detailed by the organization or the contractors requested to propose them and, if acceptable, become part of the contract.]*

4. It is the goal of Organization to have regular (defined as no less than monthly) promotions and special events designed to relieve the monotony of dining in one facility every day. You should supply a representative sample of ideas used at comparable accounts that would be appropriate for Organization.

   Any ideas for increasing Organization employee *[or student, faculty, staff, public, etc.]* participation will be appreciated.

5. Organization's catering requirements range from coffee and sweet rolls to seven-course formal dinners and receptions. Contractor should provide an assessment of Organization's current catering operations and address how it will be able to meet or exceed what is now being offered. Sample menus, prices, and pictures of this capability should be included. The level of culinary, management or specialty talent expertise available to each Organization cafeteria and/or that specific geographic region for which a proposal is being submitted should be included.

6. Given cafeteria and catering projected sales (see RFP item #11), please submit a management and support personnel staffing chart that details the following information:

   - position title
   - times scheduled to work
   - wage rate or salary and benefits package
   - brief job profile and description

   Please provide resumes for the management candidates you would propose for each facility. [It is understood that these individuals may not be assigned to Organization, but their backgrounds and general skill levels should be representative of what Organization can expect.] If a Contractor has specific candidates in mind for an Organization cafeteria, their attendance at the interview would be appreciated.

   Please indicate if the employees who would be assigned to this account will belong to a union. *[This is a sensitive item which may or may not need to be formally asked.]*

   Please provide a brief description of the practices/methods in place for hiring, training, and retaining foodservice employees in this type of account. [As with any organization, food service contractors are only as good as the people they are able to hire and retain. Wages, benefits and training programs which do not meet local area or industry norms may be an indicator of potentially poor performance.]

7. Please provide as much information needed to demonstrate your Organization's systems and methodology for the following financial and control matters:

Figure 4-3 continued

- Methods of recording, verifying, and reporting cash and charge sales.
- Defined system for cash handling, including the procedure(s) for holding funds overnight and transporting funds to the bank.
- The purchasing, receiving, storage, and inventory control systems in place for food and supplies.
- The system in place for controlling labor costs.
- Your fiscal year and accounting periods definition. In addition, you must provide a statement concerning your willingness and ability to meet specification 4.5.3 in the attached contract.
- Internal audit system. Please note if Organization will receive copies of these audits.

Copies of the forms and/or systems in use should be submitted.

Where appropriate, your response should highlight the areas in which Organization may, at its option, easily audit the operational and financial records in use. Organization is specifically interested in knowing the level of detail that will be submitted with each monthly invoice.

8. Please submit a brief description or a copy of your Quality Assurance program. The description should include the number and types of visits by district/area and headquarters personnel. Please indicate if Organization will receive a verbal and/or written report of the findings and recommendations.

[Note: These eight items can best be described as "quality of thinking" points. It is very easy for contractors to present all of their generic policies and programs as proof that they meet or exceed all normal foodservice industry standards. Organization, however, is most interested in learning how each of the proposing contractors intends to "apply" resources to best meet its requirements. In other words, how well does each contractor know and understand who Organization is, its culture relative to employees and guests, and what it specifically wants to accomplish. The people responsible for evaluating the written and oral contractor presentations will want to keep these points in mind throughout the entire RFP process.]

9. The Contractor is to propose the type and frequency of its oral and written communications that Organization can expect to receive.

10. Please propose the maximum management fee percentage and/or annual dollar amount that will be charged for each facility. If the proposed management fee percentage and/or annual dollar amount will be less for all facilities, please state the amount. Organization reserves the right to negotiate all fixed dollar and/or percentage of gross sales (or costs) fee proposals as part of its Contractor selection process.

    With reference to the proposed management fee or annual dollar amount request, please propose an incentive plan whereby both Organization and the Contractor will benefit from the proper application of management and financial controls.

11. Please prepare a pro forma statement of sales and expenses for the first year of operation. Within the pro forma, the following items and the

Figure 4-3 continued

methodology (per capita spending/average check, projected participation rate, etc.) for computing should be identified:

- Cafeteria sales
- Catering sales
- Food costs for each sales segment
- Labor costs (to include fringe benefits and taxes)
- All other controllable expenses
- Fixed expenses
- Administrative and general (if applicable)
- Management fee (fixed dollar amount or percent of gross sales)
- Organization subsidy (if applicable)

12. Each prospective Contractor, by submission of a proposal response, accepts the terms and conditions set forth within this RFP, the attached contract, any amendments, and correspondence. Exceptions, additions, or deletions to the terms and conditions presented shall be identified by page and paragraph number and listed on an individual sheet with the suggested changes enumerated.
13. Contractors must indicate if there will be any one-time only or periodic expenses involved with the opening of this account and/or relocation of management staff or any other extraordinary expenses that would be charged to Organization. If there are such anticipated expenses, the amount budgeted and complete explanation for them should be provided.
14. Prospective Contractors are welcome to submit any other information that is deemed pertinent for consideration by Organization. Suggestions relative to improvement of this request for proposals process also will be appreciated.

IV. Proposals Format

1. Six (6) copies of each proposal response must be submitted in three-ring binders. The responses should be formatted in the same order as sections 1 through 14 above.
2. All proposal responses must be typed.
3. Each proposal response must contain a cover letter signed in longhand by the Contractor's authorized representative with his or her signature. The name and a statement of authority for that individual should be typed above or below the signature.
4. All proposal responses must be received by Ms. McGuire or Mr. Behnke on October 25, 19XX by no later than 4:00 P.M. in the Rockland, USA office.
5. No oral, telephonic, or telegraphic proposals or modifications shall be considered unless requested by Organization.
6. All requests for information or questions must be answered. If for any reason a Contractor cannot provide the required information, that reason(s) must be stated in the proposal response. Omissions, inaccuracies, or misstatements may be sufficient cause for rejection of your proposal.

Organization sincerely appreciates your interest in providing foodservice for its employees.

Exhibit 4-4
ORGANIZATION MANUAL CONTRACT—DRAFT

1.0 BACKGROUND AND SCOPE

1.1 ____________ Organization[1] (hereinafter referred to as the Company/College/Hospital as applicable) desires to establish a business relationship with a foodservice contractor for providing cafeteria and catering services to its employees and guests. The following contract specifications are designed to communicate to XYZ Services, Inc. (hereinafter referred to as the Contractor) requirements that are important. This document will address issues concerning foodservice philosophy as well as operational and financial responsibilities of both the Organization and Contractor. This document has been developed to enrich existing foodservice that is presently being provided by the Organization. This document is not intended to limit the foodservice Contractor's creativity and excellence in foodservice delivery. The Organization desires foodservice efficiency, accountability and the best foodservice program possible for its employees and guests.

1.2 Individual facilities descriptions are contained in the Addenda. Each facility is described in terms of facility population, makeup of patrons, hours of operation, cafeteria service levels, catering service levels, liquor service and any special instructions.

2.0 PHILOSOPHY

2.1 The operation of foodservice should be guided by the predominant ____________'s Foodservice Philosophy. The Organization maintains that foodservice is an employee service and convenience. As a result, it should provide quality products and service at a competitively advantageous price level. The Organization expects that this type of service will enhance the Organization work *[student/seniors' living, patient healthcare, inmate morale, etc.]* environment, helping stimulate productivity by keeping employees on location and, in general, raising employee morale. To that end, the Organization is willing to underwrite, if necessary, certain overhead and direct costs with the understanding that any savings to the Contractor will be offset by the application of higher food quality, increased service, and/or lower menu prices than would otherwise be possible.

2.2 The Organization is willing to underwrite, within budgeted limits, any operating losses that would be qualified as a de minimis fringe benefit within the meaning of Internal Revenue Code (IRC) Section 132 (e)(2). For this purpose, the operation of an eating facility will be considered de minimis if the annual revenue from such facility normally exceeds the direct operating costs of such a facility. Direct operating costs are defined as (1) the cost of food and (2) the cost of labor for personnel whose service(s) are performed primarily on the premises of the eating facility.

[1] Substitute your organization's legal name.

Exhibit 4-4 continued

[Clause 2.2 should be modified to precisely fit the pertinent operating goals and objectives of your organization.]

2.3 Catering is an important aspect of the Organization's foodservice program. A wide range of catering events with different menu items, service levels and service formats is consistently scheduled for both customer and employee events. The Organization acknowledges the value of its catering programs and the esteem it brings to customers and employees alike.

3.0 RESPONSIBILITIES OF THE ORGANIZATION

3.1 The Organization will provide areas for foodservice operations as specified in the general description of the facilities described unit by unit and included in the addenda that are part of this contract.

3.2 Special or unique expectations apart from the terms and conditions contained herein, for any of the individual units will be clearly outlined in the relevant addenda *[if applicable]*. The Organization will provide, within reasonable terms and subject to its security requirements, adequate ingress and egress for the employees of the Contractor and its suppliers and will permit such employees to have reasonable use of existing elevators, corridors, passageways, driveways, restroom/ locker areas, refuse collection areas, and loading platforms. The Organization will provide heat, lights, heated and cooled ventilation, and utilities as may be required for providing such manual foodservice.

3.3 The Organization will make improvements and alterations that it deems necessary or desirable to prepare the areas allocated for foodservice operations.

3.4 The Organization will repair, paint, redecorate, and maintain as it deems necessary the building structure in areas allocated to the Contractor's use, including the maintenance of water, steam, sewer and electric lines, electrical light fixtures, heating systems, floors and floor covers, the walls and ceilings, any windows and doors, hoods and fire extinguishers provided, however, that the Contractor will bear the expense of repairs necessary when damage is caused by its employees' negligence or willful misconduct.

3.5 The Organization will provide, install, and permit the Contractor to use equipment that the Organization deems necessary for foodservice and related activities such as food processing, or servicing and sanitizing equipment, and initially supply the amount, type, and variety of expendable equipment such as cutlery and cooking utensils required for the service of quality food to the employees of the Organization.

3.6 Given proof of adequate maintenance, the Organization will replace equipment it has provided as it deems necessary, considering the average life of the equipment as well as any extraordinary circumstances.

Exhibit 4-4 continued

3.7 The Organization will be responsible for the cleaning of all walls (over the five (5) foot level), windows, and ceilings to include lamp fixtures (relamping) in the kitchen, dining, and service areas. The Organization will dispose of garbage and waste properly deposited in designated areas.

3.8 The administration and management of each unit cafeteria for the Organization is the direct responsibility of the foodservice administrator or authorized representative. No adjustments in the level of service, hours of operation, menu or prices, or any other matters concerning the delivery of foodservice may be made without the express written consent of the foodservice administrator.

4.0 RESPONSIBILITIES OF THE CONTRACTOR

4.1 General

4.1.1 The equipment and space provided by the Organization to the Contractor will be used only for foodservice and permitted related activities, as provided in this document, unless the foodservice administrator(s) in each case gives express written permission for any other use. The space and equipment are to be exclusively used only for providing foodservice to the Organization staff and guests, and for other functions for which the Organization has granted specific written approval. Any changes in this policy must be approved by the Organization.

4.1.2 The Contractor shall provide, install and maintain all of the equipment specified within its proposal response (include appropriate exhibit) as a means to increase and maintain sales as well as meet the nutritional, sanitary and efficient operational standards specified within this contract.

4.2 Food and Service

4.2.1 The Contractor will procure, prepare and serve nutritious (heart healthy), wholesome, and palatable food and beverages in the Organization's designated cafeteria(s) and dining rooms on such days and at such hours as the foodservice administrator(s) may stipulate. No foods that are beyond the manufacturers/processors established expiration date or time will be served and/or sold.

4.2.2 Hours of operations are to be in conjunction with those periods specified in the addenda or by mutual agreement with the foodservice administrator as meals and break periods.

4.2.3 The Contractor will monitor customer satisfaction with the quality of food and service by conducting no more than quarterly Organization-approved surveys of patrons at all the units. Survey responses will be directed to the foodservice administrator for initial review prior to the Contractor's compilation and analysis process. A summation of the survey results will

Exhibit 4-4 continued

be submitted to the Organization within ten (10) business days of their return. Consistent negative results could be cause for contract termination. The Organization reserves the right to conduct its own independent survey and to utilize comment cards for soliciting immediate employee and guest feedback.

4.2.4 Subject to the detailed provisions stated in this document these specifications, menus, recipes, the quality of food and service, the prices charged, the portions furnished, and all other phases of operations will be subject to the review and approval of the foodservice administrator or designated representative for each unit at all times. All Organization cafeterias under this contract will charge the same prices and offer approximately the same levels of service unless specifically approved in writing by the foodservice administrator. Prices for all major food items are to be prominently posted in the cafeteria.

All prices are to be reviewed at least annually. If it is necessary to raise prices, the Contractor must present pertinent evidence showing that food, labor and other controllable cost adjustments justify such increase. In the event that there are temporary raw product price increases, the Organization and Contractor may elect to impose a temporary surcharge until such time as those prices have returned to their normal levels.

4.2.5 The Contractor will, on a weekly basis, prepare and dispense visual menus covering the food and beverages to be sold. The initial format of the menu must have approval of the foodservice administrator. This menu will be posted in each cafeteria service area and other agreed-upon locations.

4.2.6 The Contractor will staff the units with the optimum number of employees for the efficient operation of the cafeterias and provide the best possible service to Organization employees within the approved budgeted labor cost percentages. Any changes in staffing levels, dollars and/or labor hours will be subject to approval by the foodservice administrator. The Contractor is expected to consistently maintain the existing cafeteria and catering service levels. Changes or periodic reductions in service levels may be cause for contract termination.

4.2.7 It is the goal of the Organization to have regular promotions and special events designed to encourage employee wellness/nutrition and to relieve the monotony of dining in one facility every day and to stimulate/enhance productivity and positive employee image. To facilitate these activities, the foodservice administrator will expect a monthly list of a substantial number of ideas for promotions and special events to be conducted three (3) months hence. The three (3) month lead time is necessary to allow the foodservice administrator and divisional managers to select those activities in which they want their units

Exhibit 4-4 continued

to participate. It is recognized that not all ideas will be used. A minimum of one week of promotion/advertising will be required for each special event selected.

Any materials purchased for promotional purposes and charged to the Organization will require the prior approval of the foodservice administrator.

4.2.8 The Contractor will provide foodservice for special functions on an as-needed basis. These might include meetings with outside groups or staff recognition functions. Prices (to include the basic formula for calculation) and menus for these events will be approved by the foodservice administrator. Catered functions outside the scope of the established menus will require prior approval of the foodservice administrator or designated representative.

4.2.9 The Contractor may accept checks for customer purchases but it does so at its own risk. The Organization will not reimburse nor be liable in any way for dishonored checks.

4.2.10 The food is to be purchased in a competitive fashion by the Contractor for use in the cafeterias and catering events and must meet or exceed the quality specifications set forth as Exhibit (insert appropriate exhibit) *[whether specified by Organization or the Contractor]*. The Contractor will be expected to demonstrate, not less than semiannually, how its purchasing practices result in the Organization receiving the best prices for all food and supply items.

4.2.11 The level of service (menu variety, timeliness, food quality, attractiveness, etc.) shall be equal to or better than that presently existing in the cafeterias or exceed the quality specifications set forth for that cafeteria according to the relevant Addenda *[numbered or identified for each foodservice facility]*.

4.2.12 Unless otherwise requested by the foodservice administrator, the Contractor will provide quarterly written operational analysis reports to the Organization. These reports should address issues that affect the efficiency of the operations, financial results, security, service, food, sanitation, and any other relevant topics, such as health and safety, advancements in foodservice systems and other meaningful foodservice information. Operational issues should include adequate supporting data and recommendations for improving the situations. The Organization will use these reports to make management decisions to effect improvements in the overall quality of employee *[student, patient, inmate, staff, etc.]* foodservice.

4.2.13 The Contractor will furnish all paper, plastic, and other

Exhibit 4-4 continued

expendable items used in the cafeterias/dining rooms in accordance with the existing specifications *[or Contractor proposed and/or that which is mutually determined to be recyclable]* and as permitted by local or state jurisdictions. The foodservice administrator will approve the use of all expendable serviceware.

4.2.14 The Contractor will maintain Organization approved par stock levels of china, glassware, flatware, expendable equipment (including cutlery and cooking utensils), and where applicable, catering decorations not to be less than the quality presently on site. The Contractor will be required to exercise due diligence in the use and storage of these items. The Contractor will be required to replace all lost, pilfered, or broken or damaged serviceware due to Contractor employee negligence or willful misconduct. The Contractor will pay and be reimbursed for all costs, so as to maintain the amount, conditions, and quality level of said equipment as initially furnished to the Contractor by the Organization. The foodservice administrator or designated representative will approve the budget line item for this expense. All such replaced expendable equipment shall be the property of the Organization.

4.2.15 When required for catering events, the Contractor will provide all special serviceware, equipment, and flowers. All costs associated with special serviceware, equipment, and flowers will be identified by the individual catering event and as separate line items on the billing statement. At no time will the expense for serviceware, equipment, and flowers be combined with any other expense categories.

4.2.16 The Contractor will *[will not]* have exclusive rights to operate foodservice in the Organization's facilities.

4.2.17 The Organization retains the right to conduct regular on-site quality audits of the entire Contractor operation. The appropriate quality audit evaluation is contained in Exhibit xxx. *[See Chapter 11 for one possible format]* Failure to maintain a ninety percent (90%) score will require an additional evaluation of the facility within ten (10) days. Failure to achieve a satisfactory score of ninety percent (90%) or greater with the second evaluation may be cause for contract termination.

4.2.18 The Organization from time to time will purchase *[or request that the Contractor purchase]* and dispense alcoholic beverages for special meetings and catering events. The Contractor will be expected, where permitted by law, to assist the Organization in providing this service.

The Contractor must conduct all legally mandated and pru-

Exhibit 4-4 continued

dent training as well as provide adequate supervision to assure the Organization that all laws and industry standards regarding liquor service are being met or exceeded.

4.2.19 The Contractor will, upon Organization's request, cooperate with the Organization's vending contractor in providing customer refunds.

4.3 Facilities and Equipment

4.3.1 The Contractor and Organization will agree to a plan to maintain and repair the equipment (to include the hood, stack ventilation, and fire extinguisher systems) provided by the Organization. The cost of these preventive maintenance programs and repair expenses will be processed by the Contractor and clearly identified as a repair and maintenance expense on both the unit and consolidated income statements submitted to the Organization. The Contractor must provide documentation (to include work performed and costs) for maintenance and repairs on each individual piece of equipment in each facility.

4.3.2 The Contractor will provide and maintain the supply of plastic trays for customer use in the cafeterias. The Contractor will have a supply of paper trays or comparable, available for those customers who wish to take food back to their workstations.

4.3.3 The Contractor will undertake all due diligent and prudent means to prevent any infestation of rodents and vermin in the areas under its direct control. Any evidence of a problem of this nature must be reported immediately to the foodservice administrator.

4.3.4 The Contractor will maintain an effective program of janitorial services that will meet or exceed all local and state health standards. The program will include the periodic cleaning of tables and chairs in the dining room; removal of all waste to designated areas; spot dry mopping/sweeping of the floor in the dining and service areas; cleaning of all the service equipment in the serving areas, floors in the walk-in refrigerators/freezers, and all secured storage areas; the washing and cleaning of all cutlery, dishes, glassware, and cooking utensils, and the cleaning of all equipment in the kitchen. The foodservice administrator or designated representative will approve the techniques and products used in each unit for this purpose.

4.4 Personnel and Supervision

4.4.1 The Contractor will provide professional, competent, trained

Exhibit 4-4 continued

managers and chef-managers. All prospective manager candidates will be subject to the final approval of the foodservice administrator. At no time will the Organization be charged the direct expense of on- or off-site training of managers without the prior approval of the foodservice administrator. Managers are expected to be trained at the Contractor's training centers prior to active management. Managers are expected to be proficient in all aspects of foodservice. These areas include, but are not limited to, operational, financial, and catering matters. The Contractor will specify the costs and techniques for ongoing development and training of these individuals. There will be no direct or indirect costs to the Organization associated with the Contractor's on-the-job training of management-trainee(s) occurring in Organization facilities.

4.4.2 On-the-job training of the Contractor's nonmanagement employees can occur in Organization facilities as long as the Contractor intends to have the trainee(s) remain within a Organization cafeteria for a period of no less than one year.

4.4.3 Managerial and nonmanagerial personnel will not be trained at Organization sites for work at non-organization sites.

4.4.4 Contractor employees will be limited to one meal per day, not to exceed a fixed dollar value of $x.xx per day. Contractor employees will only eat meals on premises and during authorized break periods. Contractor visitors and guests will not be eligible for the Contractor's employee meal privileges. Any such meals are to be paid by or charged to the Contractor.

4.4.5 The Contractor will comply with all federal, state, and local rules and regulations regarding the employment of personnel.

4.4.6 The Contractor will submit a staffing and hours chart for in-house cafeteria and catering foodservice employees. The labor chart will be updated quarterly and submitted to the foodservice administrator.

4.4.7 Any changes in staffing from budget will be documented and approved by the foodservice administrator prior to staffing deployment. Documentation will include reasons and supporting data for the deviation in staffing. Any staffing changes beyond previously approved budgets without prior approval will be paid by the Contractor.

4.4.8 The Contractor will furnish its employees with uniforms. The foodservice administrator will have prior approval over uniform

Exhibit 4-4 continued

style, costs, quantity, and maintenance. The Contractor will be responsible for ensuring that the uniforms are clean and neat in appearance at all times and are returned upon employee termination. Uniforms will be standard to each unit or group of units.

4.4.9 All employees of the Contractor must demonstrate acceptable personal hygiene for foodservice work. The foodservice administrator and Contractor's cafeteria manager will establish policies regarding the use of plastic gloves, hair-nets, fingernail polish, perfume, wearing of jewelry, and other personal hygienic issues. Employees will dress in the agreed-upon uniform and will wear the Organization's identification badge specific to the unit in which the employees are assigned at all times. These badges will be supplied by the Organization. The Contractor is responsible for returning badges to the Organization upon employee termination.

4.4.10 The Organization may require the Contractor to immediately remove any of the Contractor's employees from the Organization's premises for any reason sufficient to the foodservice administrator, but any and all such removals will be made in the name of the Contractor and the responsibility, therefore, will be assumed by the Contractor.

4.4.11 The Contractor will not permit gambling or other unlawful practices of any kind on Organization's premises by its employees.

4.4.12 The Contractor and the Organization will protect each other's confidential information and require that each employee who enters Organization's facilities or has access to such confidential information to execute an appropriate nondisclosure agreement. The Contractor will not permit the use of a camera by its employees and/or guests.

4.4.13 The Organization reserves the right to establish restricted areas that will be off-limits to all Contractor personnel.

4.4.14 The Contractor agrees that no supervisory employees of the Organization will be hired by the Contractor for the term of this Agreement and six (6) months thereafter.

4.4.15 The Organization acknowledges that the Contractor has invested considerable amounts of time and money in training its employees in the systems, procedures, methods, forms, reports, formulas, computer programs, recipes, menus, plans, techniques, and other valuable information that is proprietary and unique to the Contractor's manner of conducting its business. Therefore, the Organization agrees that employees of the Contractor will not be hired by the Organization for the term of this Agreement and six (6) months thereafter (unless

Exhibit 4-4 continued

such employees were formerly employees of the Organization). For the purpose of this prohibition, the Contractor's "employees" shall include nonsupervisory persons who were employed by Contractor on the Organization's premises at any time during the twelve (12) month period immediately preceding termination of the Agreement as well as those persons who have directly or indirectly performed management or professional services on the Organization's premises at any time during the twelve (12) month period immediately preceding termination of this Agreement.

In addition, the Organization agrees that if it violates the conditions set forth in the immediately preceding paragraph, the Organization shall pay to the Contractor and the Contractor shall accept as liquidated damages and not as a penalty for such breach, an amount equal to two times the annual wages or salary of the Contractor employee hired by the Organization or allowed to work on the Organization's premises in violation of the terms of this Agreement.

4.5 Accounting and Financial Control

4.5.1 The agreement between the Organization and Contractor is designed to provide a management fee *[or profit and loss]* financial arrangement for management of foodservice operations outlined in Addendum 1, 2, or 3 within Organization facilities to include, but not limited to the cafeteria, and catering. The Organization and Contractor will jointly agree to an incentive plan (see Exhibit xxx) *[usually negotiated at the time the contract is executed or after six to twelve months operational experience has been gained so that both parties are comfortable with the sales and expenses expectations.]* within twelve (12) months of contract execution that addresses incremental increases in sales and real dollar control of food, labor, and direct expense. Monthly management overhead/profit and administrative fees as presented in Exhibit xxx *[percentage of sales or fixed dollar amount fees that have been proposed and/or negotiated by either party]* will be paid to the Contractor as a percentage of gross sales *[or a fixed dollar amount per month]* with a not-to-exceed annual dollar amount. Gross sales are defined as the total amount generated or accruing from all sales or rentals for cash whether collected or not. Manual cafeteria net sales do not include sales and use taxes, gratuities, or collections from the Contractor's employees.

4.5.2 The Organization reserves the right to audit any aspect of the foodservice cycle (to include all purchasing, financial, and personnel matters) as performed by the Contractor, according to generally accepted accounting and auditing standards.

Exhibit 4-4 continued

4.5.3 The Organization is on a monthly *[or accounting period, academic year, etc.]* business cycle, with the fiscal year beginning November 1. The Contractor will supply financial data in accordance with the Organization's fiscal year/periods cycle. Period income and expense statements will be presented in accordance with or close to the method recommended in The Uniform System of Accounts for Restaurants by the National Restaurant Association. Where applicable, there will be both a summary income and expenses statement for each cafeteria.

4.5.4 The Contractor will forward to the foodservice administrator copies of each location's sales and expenses forecast presented in twelve (12) month *[or accounting]* periods, no later than the date specified by the foodservice administrator. Included in the sales forecast will be projections for sales per menu or service (cafeteria and catering) category, participation counts, total sales, cost of goods, labor, and all other controllable overhead expenses.

4.5.5 The Contractor will prepare weekly summaries and a monthly *[accounting period]* compilation of the cafeteria and catering operations on a per shift basis. These summaries will include sales totals taken at various times during the operating day, customer counts, sales per menu group (if appropriate cash registers are available), food cost (by category), daily labor usage, Contractor's employee meals, and other pertinent operating data, and will be sent to the foodservice administrator no later than the 30th day of the following month. The Contractor must be prepared to explain variances between actual figures and forecasted projections.

4.5.6 All financial reports will be prepared in a simple, consistent fashion and distributed to the foodservice administrator on a monthly basis. These reports will show both budgeted and actual gross sales, sales tax, employee discounts, food cost (by category), and all major expense categories for current month, previous month, and year-to-date. These reports will also include, at a minimum, customer counts by meal period (breakfast and lunch), average check (sales divided by customer count), per capita sales (sales divided by the total number of persons in the building) *[or residence hall, campus,]* and a sales mix (sales breakdown of breakfast items, snacks, entrees, sandwiches, grill items, beverages, and desserts). All reports will be sent to the foodservice administrator no later than the 30th day of the following month. A consolidated report showing the above information for facilities outlined in Addenda *[fill in numbers or identification of each]* will also be included.

4.5.7 The Contractor shall submit monthly invoices to the Organi-

Exhibit 4-4 continued

zation for compensation earned and reimbursable expenses incurred in the preceding calendar month. Each invoice shall show the Contractor's labor classifications, employees' names and corresponding hourly rates during the billing period, the time spent, and task descriptions. Nonemployees, such as subcontractors and consultants, shall not be billed as employees. Items of expense shall be clearly described on each invoice. Supporting data (such as payroll records, vendor invoices, Contractor purchase orders, purchase contracts, and all relevant documentation) shall be furnished for items of expense $100 and over. The unit and quantity of each item of expense based on cost shall be shown on each invoice.

Payment will be made to the Contractor within thirty (30) days of invoice approval by the Organization. Any invoices with substantial errors will be returned to the Contractor for correction prior to resubmittal.

4.5.8 All purchasing that entails the use of purchase or other trade discounts/rebates will be summarized and an annual summary report forwarded to the foodservice administrator. Included will be the discount types (i.e., trade, early payments, quantity purchases, coupon savings). Discounts will appear on the income statement as a credit and a separate line item in "cost of sales."

4.5.9 The costs for contract administrative functions such as management functions beyond those of the general manager and resident staff (i.e., dietitians, purchasing, accounts payable/receivable clerks, software training/support and other accounting functions, et al.) are to be included in the Contractor's administration or overhead fee.

4.5.10 The Contractor will pay, as part of its management or general and administrative fees, all costs for proprietary corporate level services, programs, computer hardware/software (to include upgrades and ongoing assistance), and like materials. Costs for Contractor-related permanent promotion items such as signs, displays, and similar items will be depreciated over a mutually agreed period of time. In the event of contract termination, the Contractor will not be financially liable for the undepreciated value of these items.

4.5.11 The cost of Contractor manuals and other documents that the Contractor considers proprietary are to be included in the Contractor's management or general and administrative fees. The Organization will not pay for materials that are/or will be the property of the Contractor.

4.5.12 Any material and documents developed specifically for the Organization will become the sole property of the Organization and use by the Contractor outside of the Organiza-

Exhibit 4-4 continued

tion must be approved in writing by the foodservice administrator.

4.5.13 The Contractor will maintain an audit trail to back-up all financial and operational reports given to the Organization for a minimum of two (2) years. Such records are subject to an audit by the Organization.

4.5.14 A physical inventory will be taken at least once a month and utilized in the determination of food cost and supplies by category/food group for that period.

4.5.15 The Contractor will provide the working capital for cash banks and beginning inventories.

4.6 Security

4.6.1 The Contractor and its employees will be responsible for receiving and accounting for food and supplies, and for locking all doors, windows, and access points in its assigned area.

4.6.2 All articles found by the Contractor or its employees or patrons and delivered to the Contractor will be turned in to a designated representative of the Organization as lost and found items.

4.6.3 The Contractor will quantify losses of cash and products due to theft and make recommendations for the immediate solution of the problem. Losses due to Contractor employees' actions and/or negligence will not be reimbursed by the Organization.

4.6.4 The Contractor will use generally accepted methods to safeguard cash banks and receipts throughout the accounting cycle. Safes for the unit(s) will be provided by the Organization.

4.6.5 The Contractor's employees will abide with any special requirements for entering Organization buildings and restricted work areas, including those with high security concerns.

4.6.6 The Contractor will notify the foodservice administrator or designate at least twenty-four (24) hours in advance of any visitors that will be touring the unit(s) with the Contractor.

4.7 Sanitation and Safety

4.7.1 The Contractor will obey all federal, state, and local laws and ordinances regarding food handling, safety, and sanitation.

4.7.2 The Contractor will provide medical examinations and/or food handler certificates required by law, and appropriate records for each employee will be kept on file with the Contractor's unit manager.

Exhibit 4-4 continued

4.7.3 The Contractor will not allow persons with obvious illness, open sores or other symptoms to work. Any contagious disease such as hepatitis must be reported immediately to the foodservice administrator or to an executive of the respective division. This should be done before reporting to any persons outside the Organization. The Organization may request testing for contagious diseases.

4.7.4 The Contractor will report fires, hazardous conditions, Contractor employee accident(s), items in need of repair or replacement and security hazards to the foodservice administrator immediately.

4.7.5 The Contractor will immediately notify the foodservice administrator of any sanitarian/Health Department review/inspection. The foodservice administrator, at his/her option may participate during the inspection. The Contractor will submit the complete score/grade report to the foodservice administrator immediately following all reviews/inspection. The Contractor will be expected to correct the problems and respond in writing that all problems have been solved, or issue an appeal, within five (5) business days.

4.8 Energy Conservation and Recycling

4.8.1 The Contractor is encouraged to develop and participate in any recycling programs of its own so long as they do not conflict with existing or future Organization programs. Any revenues that may result from recycling programs are to be credited to the Organization.

4.8.2 When cafeteria space is not in use or when business volume dictates, the Contractor will assume maximum utility/energy cost conservation by turning off or down lights, fans, water, ovens, steam equipment, and other energy-consuming items. The Contractor will be responsible for turning off all nonessential equipment when not in use.

4.9 Assignment

4.9.1 The Contractor's rights and obligations cannot be transferred or subcontracted without written approval from the foodservice administrator.

4.10 Inspection and Complaints

4.10.1 The facilities operated under the contract will be visited by representatives of the Organization for the purpose of inspecting for sanitation, food handling, food portion standards, safety, quality of food and service, or any other valid reason. After each inspection, the Contractor will be advised in writing of unsatisfactory conditions for which the Contractor is responsible. The Contractor will promptly correct such

Exhibit 4-4 continued

deficiencies and communicate in writing the solution to each problem, when it was corrected, and what has been done to prevent recurrence of the problem, within ten (10) business days. Repeated unsatisfactory inspections will be cause for contract termination.

4.10.2 Complaints, comments, and suggestions from individuals other than employees of the Contractor with regard to food, service, or any other reason, will be reduced to writing by the Organization and a copy will be delivered to the Contractor's designated representatives. The Contractor will review these items and their circumstances and will respond in writing to the foodservice administrator as to the solution/corrective action and implementation date within ten (10) business days. It is understood that some complaints will not be valid or that special circumstances may have caused the problem. This information should be communicated to the Organization.

4.10.3 Discrepancies/disputes between the Organization and Contractor are to be settled in a timely fashion. If ten (10) business days have elapsed since written documentation has been sent to and received at the Contractor's regional office by the foodservice administrator, and no acceptable Contractor response has occurred or been received, this will be cause for contract termination.

4.11 Insurance

4.11.1 The Contractor will furnish the Organization with Certificates of Insurance covering worker's compensation, employees' liability insurance, and comprehensive general liability insurance to include liquor service liability in the amount of $1,000,000 per occurrence for each facility plus any other mandated insurance. These certificates will provide for thirty (30) days' notice to the Organization of any cancellations and failure to renew.

4.12 Indemnity

4.12.1 The Contractor will defend, indemnify, and hold the Organization, its officers, directors, agents, and employees harmless from any and all liability for bodily injury, sickness, or disease, including death resulting therefrom, or damage, destruction, or loss of use of any property arising out of or in any way connected with sales, possession, or distribution of any product, foodstuff, or beverage or from any operation in rendering service to the Organization, its employees, subcontractors, agents or their guests or from any act or omission, negligent or otherwise, of the Contractor or any of its employees, subcontractors, agents, servants or any other persons associated with the Contractor, excepting only the employees of the

Exhibit 4-4 continued

Organization whose activities the Contractor does not have the right to control. *[Note: This clause usually results in careful scrutiny by one or more attorneys.]*

4.13 Independent Status of Contractor

4.13.1 The Contractor is an independent contractor and will not under any circumstances be considered an employee, servant, or agent of the Organization, nor will the employees, servants or agents of the Contractor be considered as employees, subcontractors, servants, or agents of the Organization and neither the Contractor nor its employees, subcontractors, servants, or agents have any authority to bind the Organization in any respect whatsoever.

4.14 Termination of Contractor

4.14.1 In addition to the quarterly review of Contractor's performance and normal provisions for termination upon default of the Contractor, the Organization shall have the right to terminate the arrangement if for any reason the Contractor fails to provide continuous cafeteria and catering service in any of the designated locations for two consecutive working days/or the Contractor's labor relations result in picketing at any of the Organization's facilities. *[Note: The last phrase concerning labor relations should be carefully considered.]* Consistently unsatisfactory sanitation and quality audits as well as unresolved customer complaints will also be considered just cause for termination.

4.14.2 Either party may terminate the arrangement or any individual unit at any time without cause by giving proper notice. The Contractor may terminate by giving not less than ninety (90) days' notice to the Organization. The Organization may terminate by giving not less than thirty (30) days' notice to the Contractor.

4.15 Contract Changes

4.15.1 The Contractor will be flexible to accommodate changes with the number of cafeterias in use, (upward or downward), the number of customers at cafeteria locations, foodservice quality, service levels, or pricing and policy changes.

4.16 Performance Bonds

4.16.1 If specifically requested to do so by the Organization's foodservice administrator, the Contractor will furnish a performance bond equal to ______ for each location to assure full contract compliance. Such bond, in the form approved by the Organization, will be submitted to the Organization by the Contractor.

4.17 Responsibility for Tax Assessment and Fees

Exhibit 4-4 continued

4.17.1 The Contractor, regardless of residence, is subject to all applicable federal, state, local, and any other taxes, assessments, and fees that will arise from transactions under this document.

4.18 Compliance With Laws

4.18.1 The Contractor shall comply with all applicable state and local laws, rules, and regulations, and shall obtain all applicable licenses and permits for the conduct of business and the performance of the work called for in this document.

5.0 TERMS OF CONTRACT

5.1 Time Frame and Renewals

The terms of the contract shall run from November 19XX through October 19XX. At its discretion, the Organization retains the option to extend the contract for up to two (2) one-year intervals.

6.0 ENTIRE AGREEMENT

6.1 Contents

This contract, the Organization's Request for Proposal, the Contractor's proposal response, and any relevant correspondence attached hereto represents the entire contract between the parties in respect to the subject matter and supersedes any previous or contemporaneous oral or written proposals, statements, discussions, negotiations, or other agreements. The parties acknowledge that they have not been induced to enter into this agreement by any oral or written representations or statements not expressly contained in this contract. This agreement may be modified, or any provision waived, only in writing signed by the parties.

In witness whereof, the parties hereto have caused the CONTRACT to be executed by their respective proper officers, thereunto duly authorized the day and year first above written.

For: ORGANIZATION

By: ______________________________

Title: ____________________________

Date: ____________________________

For XYZ SERVICES, INC.

By: ______________________________

Title: ____________________________

Date: ____________________________

CHAPTER FIVE

Foodservice Administrator Communications

Sitting down early one sunny spring morning to review his Seattle seminar notes, Jones was reminded of the seminar leader's admonishments that establishing open and honest communications with a selected contractor would be one of the keys to successful foodservice management. In fact, the seminar leader emphasized that communications was the key to serving as a foodservice administrator whether an organization's program was self-operated or contract-operated. One way or the other, Jones realized, he needed to speak "foodservice lingo" with his foodservice management team.

Popping the tight lid on a container of fresh-brewed cafeteria coffee, Jones continued reviewing his notes. Prominently written on a page by themselves were the two basic elements of successful communications:

- VERBAL COMMUNICATIONS
- WRITTEN COMMUNICATIONS

Surprisingly, the vital communications process is often either ignored or deliberately avoided with respect to the foodservice program. When this happens, problems inevitably arise that frequently result in the replacement of one manager (or, if applicable, contractor) with another, assuring the ultimate repetition of the process. Administrators must gain enough understanding of foodservice to communicate knowledgeably about their organizations' expectations and how well the program is meeting them. So far, Jones realized, the educational resources he had at his command included the following:

- Contractors who continued to call on his organization
- Foodservice administrators at other local organizations
- National foodservice trade organizations, such as the National Restaurant Association and the Society for Foodservice Management (See Chapter 14 for more information on these and other groups.)

COMMUNICATIONS GUIDELINES

In the case of contract foodservice, the first series of written communications are the RFQ, the RFP, and, finally, the contract. Jones was aware that contractors' proposals, and even their subsequent self-promoting mailings, were a normal part of the foodservice industry's communication process.

As with life's other lessons, it is important for administrators to understand clearly which forms of communication are appropriate. Foodservice is a highly intense "people" business. An administrator must, therefore, foster a business relationship that acknowledges the givens, tolerates the unexpected, glorifies the triumphs, bears up under and learns from mistakes, and otherwise continues to grow progressively better.

What follows are some guidelines to help administrators establish productive relationships with their own (if self-operated) or contractors' personnel. To begin, a refresher session covering the basic questions that are most likely to arise within the foodservice department/administrator relationship should be held.

Why are we here?

This may seem like a naive question to someone who has worked in an organization for a number of years, but it is not always easy for the foodservice management and staff to understand their roles, especially if they are new. Administrators' first step should be to communicate the nature of the organization. Such explanations should include:

- Organization culture
- Organization goals and objectives

- Division or site functions and how they support the organization's mission
- The foodservice needs of both the organization's personnel and its guests
- Specific site rules, regulations, or practices that will affect foodservice operations
- How the organization's traditions and practices create foodservice requirements throughout the year

What are the department's specific goals and objectives?

The answers to this question should help a foodservice manager learn about the department's specific operational and financial goals and objectives for foodservice. Topics for discussion might include the following:

- The hours of operation, which may or may not have changed
- The service levels now being provided
- Which service levels might be added or deleted
- The current perception of foodservice quality by the organization's personnel and guests
- Facility and equipment considerations
- Security and staff parking considerations unique to the subject organization

How often should we communicate?

While the response "as often as necessary" lacks specificity, its intent is clear. When building a relationship with management staff or contractors, administrators may wish to meet daily with unit managers to answer any questions and discuss problems. As the new team settles into its responsibilities, the requirement for meetings will probably diminish. It is recommended, however, that administrators meet with their foodservice managers at least once a month. If a major problem arises, communication should be immediate. For example, during a routine review of paperwork, it may be discovered that some numbers have changed dramatically from those of the previous financial period. Such changes should serve as a "red flag" to alert the administrator to potential problems. Often a problem is a simple error, but, by bringing such errors to the contractor's attention, everyone will know that the organization's foodservice program is receiving thorough administrative oversight.

What should we talk about?

There are three basic subject areas that will need to be discussed regularly. These include:

- Operational Concerns (i.e., "The lines are too long at noon," "The salad bar always runs out before 12:30 P.M.") and similar issues. (See Chapter 11 for more on how to address these issues.)
- Financial and Operational Reporting (see Chapter 12). Are the sales in line with those of the previous months? Are customer counts up or down? Have the number of complaints in the suggestion box gone up or down?
- Facilities and Equipment (see Chapters 2 and 10). What needs fixing versus what should be considered for replacement in the next fiscal year? What new equipment would enhance service and increase sales? Can the new equipment be cost-justified? What is the payback time? Questions about foodservice's physical plant and equipment are covered in the above referenced chapters. In addition, administrators should anticipate the need to address equipment replacement and facility improvements, as well as remodeling requirements that will require capital funds.

In addition to receiving regular feedback on operational performance, a foodservice manager will need to be aware of periodic or unique events that will positively or negatively impact foodservice sales. Regardless of whether a foodservice is a profit-and-loss or subsidy-funded operation, it is important to share such information in order to help all concerned respond appropriately. (The financial and operational reporting aspects of foodservice will be covered later in this chapter.)

How do I keep from asking dumb questions?

There is no such thing as a dumb question about foodservice. The better informed administrators are about what is happening with their programs and within the local foodservice industry, the more effectively they will be able to evaluate their own programs. This will help assure better results for all concerned.

Whether hiring your own manager or approving a contractor's assigned manager, what selection criteria should be used?

As can be imagined, it would take a fairly thick volume just to detail all of the management traits administrators should look for in foodservice personnel. The following criteria, though, should offer useful guidelines. Successful candidates will have:

- Past foodservice preparation and/or general management experience.
- Past foodservice preparation and/or management experience in comparable cafeteria and catering locations.

- Educational background. Look for formal training in the foodservice industry as well as ongoing attendance at relevant seminars, trade shows, and other programs designed to keep a foodservice manager current.
- Background and tenure with previous employer or, if applicable, current contractor.

  In all instances it is important to look at the length of time an individual has remained in each position. It is obviously not positive if someone has moved every few months from one job to another.

  With respect to contract foodservice, if an individual is to be hired from the outside to manage your facilities, there may be problems with that individual not understanding and being fully trained in the procedures of the contract management company for whom he or she works. Ideally, the individual will have been with the contract management firm a minimum of two years and have management experience with that company at another of its accounts. There are, however, extenuating circumstances under which it will be to an organization's advantage to have the management company hire someone from the outside. For example, if an organization has installed a new system such as cook-chill, it may want the management company to specifically locate an experienced cook-chill management person. The relative newness of this type of technology has resulted in a high demand for individuals with experience. That fact may necessitate the management company hiring from outside its own personnel ranks. Ideally, another member of the proposed management team would be experienced with that company to provide the expertise necessary with respect to systems and procedures for that contractor.
- Knowledge and understanding of the organization in general and own site in detail. Did the individual take the time to become familiar with your organization?
- Ability to communicate.
- Perceivable people skills.
- A pleasant personality. Administrators should ask themselves, "Will this person fit comfortably in our organization?"

What if there are conflicts with a manager that cannot be resolved?

In self-operated situations, it is best to have a pre–agreed time set for review and evaluation of an individual. Finding a replacement is sometimes difficult and time consuming for self-operated foodservice programs. However, it is also true that such conflicts happen more times than most foodservice contractors would care to admit. The difference is the pool of talent that the contractor has to draw from which a self-operated administrator would most likely not have. When conflicts occur, honesty is the best policy. Administrators should first inform their own personnel department or, if applicable, the contractor's district manager about the situation. The district manager may choose to find another manager immediately or ask that an administrator grant a specific period of time during which the conflict(s) will be resolved.

Sometimes I feel bad having to criticize my "eager-to-please" manager, especially in front of other people. What can I do?

This can be a tough situation. It is important to remember, however, that managing an organization's cafeteria and catering program is not easy. Success requires talented, experienced people able to master the (literally) thousands of tasks that must be attended to on a daily basis. When administrators find that they have to criticize a foodservice manager frequently, the cause may simply be that the manager needs more experience in a less demanding environment. It is more difficult in a self-operated program where there may not be a place to put the individual to receive more training. A contractor will most likely have a place to move and/or the resources to train the individual.

Which potential communication problems are most likely to occur?

The most common communication difficulties include the following:

- A breakdown in or absence of one or more communication skills (e.g., listening, speaking, writing, and/or nonverbal communications).
- One or both parties are unable to determine the relevancy of critical factors, and to analyze and act on key data.
- Organization personnel (other than the Support Services administrator) are giving the foodservice staff conflicting or contradictory messages.
- Regular communications are not maintained and/or messages are not responded to on a timely basis.
- There is poor or nonexistent documentation to support decision making.
- The foodservice staff do not handle problems or complaints responsibly.
- Personnel in the organization cannot understand why the foodservice department cannot serve a luncheon for 50 at the last minute.

As Jones reviewed this list, it occurred to him, not for the first time, that the challenges for administrators who oversee foodservice, whether self-operated or contracted, are the sort that are never-ending and, almost certainly, never boring.

FINANCIAL AND OPERATIONAL REPORTING

The foodservice manager will be required to provide a number of financial and operational documents. Many of those reports will be ones good managers already generate and/or are readily available from sources such as cash register tapes. These reports should provide information that will be extremely valuable in helping administrators control the following areas:

- Preparing and conducting budget analyses
- Developing cost-cutting ideas
- Planning capital expenditures

  Records on equipment repairs might show that a certain piece of equipment generates annual repair bills equal to 25 percent of its replacement cost. Given that piece of equipment has a life of about 10 years, it makes sense to replace rather than to repair it.
- Adjusting hours of operation

  Customer counts by the half-hour show that the cafeteria could be closed at 3:30 P.M. rather 4:00 P.M. since most days there are only one or two transactions during the last half-hour.
- Increasing/decreasing service levels

  There has been such a high demand for the coffee cart on the third floor that service hours will be increased and a second cart will be planned for another similar location.
- Planning menu modifications

  The sale of ice cream novelties has declined since the frozen yogurt machine was installed. Perhaps the ice cream should be removed from the cafeteria or a new line of novelties tried.

One of the most critical aspects of monitoring a contracted account or working with self-operated management is conducting the ongoing reviews and periodic audits of foodservice's financial data. Jones knew that he was really going to have to get involved with financial accountability issues, especially since his plans called for working with both contractor- and self-operated foodservice. If he was to achieve his goal of mirroring the two operations and, eventually, determining which was best for AU, he would need to be able to "tackle the dollars." But that lesson would have to wait for another day. He scratched his head and turned his attention to reports on the non-foodservice areas of his responsibility. Somehow, those areas were not getting as much of his attention as they did before he took over foodservice. "Ah well, Jones thought, "I have a good system and trusted staff in place to implement it. All I need to do is keep on top of some of the strategic things for now. Someday I hope we can feel just as confident about our foodservice operations."

QUALITY ASSURANCE AUDITS

Besides the financial and operational aspects of cafeteria programs, administrators will want to review any pending issues that have arisen from previous Quality Assurance audits (see Chapter 11). It is important for administrators to stress to foodservice managers that these audits are not designed to "catch" personnel doing something wrong. Rather, a Quality Assurance audit is an objective means of evaluating the quality of foodservice provided at a particular facility or venue. Whether they are contracted personnel or self-operators, managers should be interested in finding ways of improving service and be receptive to audit outcomes. If this is not the case, administrators should meet with the manager to explain the reasons for conducting an audit and attempt to understand why that manager does not understand the objective nature of the evaluation. (Refer to Chapter 11 for further information.)

A word of caution: If an organization has retained a foodservice contractor, Support Service administrators will find that they communicate primarily with their contractor's on-site foodservice director. In order to foster trust between contract administrators and foodservice management, all comments about foodservice employees, including those regarding dress, hygiene, appearance, and work habits, should be made solely and directly to their managers. The reason is that it is easy for an administrator to sabotage a manager's authority by becoming directly involved with the foodservice or contractor employees. However, if employee activity that is dangerous, unlawful, or against organization policies is observed and these staff members' manager is not present, administrators *should* intervene. This said, when it comes to personnel issues that require more sophisticated handling, administrators should restrict their responses to a memo or phone call placed directly to foodservice managers.

Once again, Jones realized how relevant good communication skills were to administering either a self-operated or a contract foodservice program. He hoped that his previously honed communications skills would stand him in good stead in this new foodservice assignment.

CHAPTER SIX

Sanitation/Legal/ Social Obligations

There are literally hundreds, if not thousands, of issues associated with foodservice. Many of these issues are the same ones that other departments within an organization have to address. There are, however, some concerns that are generally thought to be unique to the foodservice industry. This chapter will address important sanitation, legal (ranging from the Food and Drug Administration, Internal Revenue Service to insurance/liability concerns), and social issues.

In order to learn about his responsibilities vis-à-vis foodservice's sanitation/legal/social obligations, Jones scheduled a private meeting with Yoshi Namura, the dean at a local university's Hotel Restaurant and Institutional Management (HRIM) college and an expert in issues of this type. Fortunately for Jones (and other Support Services administrators), the HRIM professor was able to offer a series of "real-world" case studies that helped point up the serious, consequential nature of foodservice's sanitation/legal/social obligations. Here's what Jones learned.

SANITATION ISSUES

Foodservice primarily consists of two imperfect mediums, food and people. Realistically, there is little chance that scientists will be able to clone, much less raise/grow, perfect food. And, unless George Orwell's vision of humankind manifests itself, there is no chance that the human component will be perfected either. To offset these imperfections, government and the foodservice industry have established a number of laws and safety guidelines pertaining to how foods must be handled, prepared, and held prior to service. Unfortunately, neither the government nor the foodservice industry has been able to keep up with either rapidly changing technology or numerous societal changes, such as sous vide, cook-chill, and an increasing number of vegans and vegetarians. As a result, a number of serious, food-related health and sanitation flaws in the food distribution chain have recently been exposed.

To illustrate his points, Namura first offered Jones a series of current examples of food poisonings and food-borne illnesses that had arisen in U.S. foodservice establishments. Jones, who had always believed the American food supply to be the safest in the world, was nonplussed at first by the educator's discouraging list. He told himself, however, that it was better to face the "ugly" truth than to remain ignorant and later be victimized by it. Here are Namura's examples:

#1

In 1993 the foodservice industry experienced numerous incidents involving *E. coli* contamination of hamburger meat and raw milk. Health authorities reported that people became ill because hamburgers were inadvertently undercooked (i.e., a minimum internal temperature of 155°F was either not achieved or maintained during the cooking process). In one case, though, cutting boards and knives used to process contaminated meat had not been properly washed and sanitized before being used to cut up fresh fruit for a salad bar.

#2

A case involving raw milk was a little more remote but just as dangerous given today's consumers' growing preference for all-natural, unprocessed foods. A local dairy farmer was selling raw milk to neighbors on a regular basis. At the request of several people, he asked a local grocery to sell the milk in its dairy case. Even though the dairy was regularly inspected, because the milk was not pasteurized, some contaminated milk did manage to make it to consumers, resulting in several cases of food-borne illness. This preference and related demand for raw milk are now most prominent

on college and university campuses, though Jones was shocked to learn from the professor that the trend was moving from campuses to corporate dining environments. Raw milk is simply milk that goes straight from the cow to the consumer without being pasteurized or processed in any way. Scientists disagree as to the how and why of *E. coli*'s appearance in this product, Namura emphasized. Given that the bacteria appears in milk periodically, there is a twofold need for industry suppliers to provide adequate testing and for consumers to demand assurances that the products they purchase are truly safe. Jones made a mental note to send a memo to all the foodservice units that products could only be purchased from legitimate, licensed vendors and that no raw milk or raw milk products would be sold at AU.

It should be noted that in all of the recent *E. coli* cases, those affected became quite ill. Unfortunately, a few persons were unable to fight the infection and died.

#3

During the past few years, hepatitis has been transmitted to numerous foodservice patrons by employees who have failed to observe the most basic of sanitation rules: washing hands thoroughly after using the bathroom. In most cases, the infection was passed when foods such as salads (that are normally prepared and served chilled) were contaminated by foodservice employees. In these instances, not only did a number of people contract hepatitis, but many more people were exposed to it, necessitating mass gamma-globulin inoculations as a preventative measure. To say the least, many noncommercial foodservice programs, as well as commercial restaurants, have found it extremely difficult, if not impossible, to restore public confidence after an outbreak of hepatitis. Namura also noted that hepatitis is particularly dangerous for senior citizens.

#4

Another case of improper foodservice sanitation that did not get much national press coverage, but nonetheless was quite devastating, occurred at a hotel in a major metropolitan area. Two small but separate groups of attorneys and accountants simultaneously held dinner meetings at the hotel. Both groups ordered prime rib. When preparing the prime rib the day before, the cook had apparently placed an unclean meat thermometer into the product's center and left the meat sitting out on a counter for a few hours before placing it into a slow–cooking oven at a low temperature. Low-temperature cooking is a popular means of ensuring minimum product shrinkage and making sure that sufficient quantities of rare/medium rare meat portions are available for diners.

Unfortunately, on this occasion, the internal temperature of the prime rib never rose above 130°F. And, since the thermometer was left in the meat throughout the cooking process, sufficient microbial growth occurred to cause severe cases of food poisoning among the two groups of hotel guests.

The resulting negative publicity was certainly bad enough for the hotel. The fact that members of one of the affected groups were attorneys did not help. The eventual out-of-court settlement was said to have been substantial.

By this point during his meeting, Jones had become thoroughly depressed and asked Namura if he could offer anything positive. The response was affirmative, as Namura viewed these incidents as a long overdue wake-up call for the foodservice industry. While food-poisoning incidents remain notably rare relative to the number of safe, wholesome meals served to millions of customers each day, Namura stressed that both government and various foodservice industry groups (organizations representing corporate dining programs, as well as those in hospitals, universities, schools, and others) were aligning themselves with the influential National Restaurant Association to attack the problem head-on.

While somewhat relieved by this information, Jones quickly recognized there were some important lessons he needed to learn. These included the following:

- All of the above examples involved facilities that were, by law, subject to the jurisdiction and overview of local or state Health Departments. Yet, despite regular inspections, serious food-poisoning incidents were still occurring.
- When there was an incident, each foodservice operation was subjected to intense media scrutiny. Without exception, Health Department inspections increased.
- All of the facilities or foodservice programs that have experienced food-poisoning incidents suffered significant damage to their image/reputation, a loss of customer confidence, and negative financial consequences.

Namura's final point was one Jones definitely did not want to hear. Many food-poisoning and food-borne illness cases are never reported. Many times, those who suffer from ingesting bad or contaminated foods attribute their illness to a case of stomach flu. In fact, food-poisoning incidents usually only become publicized when a group of people report the same or a similar set of symptoms to their doctors or local health authorities.

PREVENTION

What Jones and other administrators responsible for foodservice need to know is that food-poisoning incidents are preventable. As with any quality assurance process, preventive measures require administrators and foodservice personnel to pay close attention to the details and assume nothing. Consistent staff training and constant reinforcement on the part of managers and line supervisors is the only true antidote for a problem as serious as this one.

The fact is that most foodservice providers, whether they are self-operators or contractors' directors, know the proper way to hold, handle, prepare, and serve foods. Numerous books and food safety classes/ training courses are also available (See Chapter 14). As noted earlier, a large number of sanitation laws and guidelines have been prepared by the federal government and a variety of state and local authorities. To date, however, there is no single uniform Health Department-enforced food handling and facility sanitation code that governs operators' procedures across the country (See Chapter 11).

Unfortunately, various laws and regulations cause a great deal of confusion among foodservice workers and health inspectors alike. Worse yet, health inspectors, even if from the same department, may interpret and enforce applicable rules differently. This inconsistency of inspections has certainly not helped foodservice providers adopt standardized approaches to ensuring sanitation in their day-to-day operational programs.

There is a solution to this dilemma. Administrators need to work closely with their local Health Departments to make sure that the same strict standards are applied to all their foodservice operations. Some helpful hints to accomplish this goal include the following:

- Administrators should ask their health inspectors or foodservice managers for notification when an inspection is about to take place. When time permits, administrators should accompany inspectors during their tours. Most inspectors will welcome the attention and extra set of eyes provided by administrators who inspect their organization's foodservice facilities more often than the once- or twice-a-year visits Health Department officials make.
- Ask the foodservice provider which procedures are in place to ensure that all food is handled, processed, prepared, and held properly.
- Ask the foodservice provider to review established procedures for ensuring that the kitchen and all food-handling equipment (used both for preparation and service) are being properly cleaned and maintained.
- Ask for and review all training programs and materials that are made available to foodservice management and staff. Administrators should make sure that easy-to-understand training materials are available and that they are studied regularly. (See Chapter 11 for the training and certification process.)
- Make it a practice periodically to walk through foodservice's kitchen(s) at various times on different days. As administrators

become familiar with what to look for in regard to proper food-handling practices and equipment/facility sanitation, they will be amazed at how much a quick walk-through will reveal. In contract situations, foodservice administrators have the right to access kitchen and serving areas at *any* time. Requests to bar administrators or any other authorized organization personnel from foodservice facilities should not be countenanced. However, when foodservice facilities are producing meals or are otherwise busy, administrators need to make sure that they are not obstructing the work flow. Therefore, conversations with foodservice staff should be kept to a minimum, in order to avoid distracting employees from what they need to be doing.

These walk-throughs are designed to help administrators ascertain if foodservice staff are, in fact, performing their duties in accordance with established policies and procedures. This applies to both food handling practices on the part of the staff, as well as equipment and facility sanitation. If not, foodservice management needs to be informed that some inconsistencies have been discovered that will not be tolerated.

Administrators should also know that a number of federal and state food-handling laws exist that apply, primarily, to companies that produce, process, and/or handle foods at the factory or wholesale level. Support Services administrators' concern is that their foodservice managers are purchasing specified foods and supplies from approved sources. Administrators will want to turn a wary eye on requests to purchase food and supplies from "distress" merchandise wholesalers, especially if assurances about these products' wholesomeness and sanitation cannot be confirmed.

Because of the very real threat posed by food-poisoning/contamination incidents, the federal government and various citizen groups have recently increased their efforts to make sure that the food chain produces safe products at all stages.

HAZARD ANALYSIS AND CRITICAL CONTROL POINT

The acronym HACCP stands for Hazard Analysis and Critical Control Point, which is a prevention-based food safety system. HACCP systems are designed to prevent the occurrence of potential food safety problems by assessing the inherent risks attributable to a product or process and determining the steps that control the identified risks. It is not necessary for an administrator to be aware of the details of the HACCP program. It is, however, critical that an administrator be aware of the regulations and insist that either in-house or contract managers demonstrate that they have developed and implemented a HACCP program for the foodservice operations.

The regulations are detailed in the Food Code, 1993 U.S. Department of Health and Human Services, Public Health Service, Food and Drug Administration. The Food Code is available for public sale from the U.S. Department of Commerce, National Technical Information Service, 5285 Port Royal Road, Springfield, VA 22161 or by calling 703-487-4650 and asking for report number PB94-113941AS.

One of the most critical changes in the Food Code is the temperatures at which food is to be cooked and stored. These changes have an impact on every food service operation. Whereas refrigeration units were deemed safe if the temperature was 45°F or less, that standard has now been changed to 41°F. This change could result in the need to increase refrigeration unit capacity to maintain that temperature as walk-ins and coolers are opened and closed throughout the day.

Another change that impacts many foodservice operations is the need to chill cooked foods from 140°F to 41°F or below within four hours. This means that leftovers cannot be placed hot into a walk-in or reach-in to cool over an extended period of time. Some organizations are now installing at least a single blast chiller (see Chapter 10) to assure compliance with this requirement, even though the facility is not a "cook-chill" operation.

There are many pages of standards within the Food Code, not all of which will apply to any one operation. Every administrator responsible for foodservices should address the issue of the HACCP plan with management on a regular basis to make sure that a plan is being developed, implemented, and maintained.

LEGAL ISSUES

As with any business or major industry, there is no shortage of federal, state, and local laws that dictate what an organization's foodservice can and cannot do. Since ignorance is not considered a valid legal defense, administrators need to stay abreast of all issues that might impact foodservice. What follows is a short listing of just a few legal considerations unique to foodservice. This list is not inclusive, and readers are encouraged to seek out the resources listed in Chapter 14 to learn where additional information can be obtained.

The IRS

It may seem a little strange to be concerned about the IRS in the context of noncommercial foodservice. The IRS, however, takes an interest in how much, if any, employer subsidy is provided to support an organization's foodservice. The ruling applies normally to corporate cafeterias, but also to faculty clubs, corrections facility staff dining rooms, doctors' dining rooms, and any other free or reduced price meal service. If free, the value of the meal usually must be included in gross wages for the purpose of calculating F.I.C.A. taxes. If meals are provided free or the subsidy exceeds a certain amount, it could be considered a de minimis benefit and be subject to the usual payroll taxes. The IRS offers some very specific regulations regarding the value of meals provided at an employer-operated dining facility. The value of meals provided to employees may, in some instances, incur taxes for the employees, since the meals will be considered a benefit. The value of the meals is *not* taxable to employees as a benefit, however, if the sales (gross revenues) cover all "direct" costs of providing these meals. To avoid creating a situation in which on-site meals are deemed to be taxable, the IRS stipulates that *all* of the following criteria must be met:

- The facility must be owned or leased by the employer.
- The facility must be operated by the employer or by a third party under contract to the employer.
- The facility(ies) must be located on or near the business premises of the employer.
- The meals (which include food, beverages, and related services) must be provided during or immediately before or after the employees' workday.

The IRS goes on to define direct [foodservice] operating costs as "(1) the cost of the food and beverages, and (2) the cost of the labor for personnel whose services are performed on the premises of the facility."

While few in government wish to admit it, the purpose of this tax legislation is to prevent corporations and other organizations employing a significant executive contingent from writing off all or major portions of extravagant dining room operations.

Many government and not-for-profit organizations are subject to federal and state taxation rules. The status-determining issue here is whether an income source is "related" or "unrelated" to an organization's primary mission and/or not-for-profit tax status. Within the past few years, more than one organization has had state and/or federal tax officials come knocking on their doors, seeking to collect sales and income taxes on "unrelated" income generated over the past two or three years. As readers may know, most tax authorities have no sense of humor and will use whatever means are necessary to collect what they believe to be due. Some examples of what might be construed as receiving "unrelated" business income include the following:

- A hospital, in an effort to cut costs and raise revenues, engages in a marketing program to attract outside groups to utilize its foodservice facilities for meetings and catering events.

- A college, located near a major seasonal tourist attraction, rents out its residence hall rooms to budget-minded tour groups.

- A private high school's foodservice department, in an effort to provide year-round employment and extra income for staff, provides lunches to a number of summer day camps in the local area. In addition, this foodservice submits proposals for and receives contracts to provide catering at concerts and semiprofessional football games held at the local civic stadium.

Staff tips are another foodservice-derived source of taxable income that should be of concern to the numerous corporations and not-for-profit organizations that provide restaurant and catered table-service for which a gratuity is either expected or is automatically added to customer bills. In most instances, tips are then allocated to the appropriate personnel and paid to them either in cash or by check. A few things to remember about tips include the following:

- Employees receiving tips must report them as income to the IRS.
- Employers are liable for paying their share of the FICA tax on tip income.
- Employers may have to withhold a certain percentage of tip income for state and federal income tax purposes.

Sales Tax

The best thing to say about sales tax laws is that they are a veritable crazy-quilt of rules, regulations, exceptions, and personal interpretations. The sales tax interpretation issue has become even more complex recently as state and local governments attempt to garner as many tax dollars as they can. The following examples may assist administrators in understanding the potential complications.

The State of California passed what has lovingly been referred to as the "Snack Tax." Up until that time, all packaged, ready-to-eat foods, such as potato chips, nuts, and trail mix, were exempt from state sales tax. Then the California legislature decided that these items *should* be taxed, whether they were purchased in grocery/convenience stores, snack bars, cafeterias, or from vending machines. As a result, numerous foodservice cash registers had to be reprogrammed to compute automatically the tax on a very limited classification of items. The subsequent confusion for both foodservice operators and customers was unbelievable and, as a result, the "Snack Tax" was later rescinded by the legislature.

In some jurisdictions, if a government agency provides foodservices, then no sales tax is charged. However, if a foodservice contractor provides the same services for employees of that government agency on a "cost plus management fee" basis, the meals are considered taxable. For example, in California, inmate meals prepared by self-operated staff are not taxed. The same meals, prepared by an outside contractor, are taxed.

Since many tax authorities are resistant to the idea of waiving taxes owed due to an honest misunderstanding or omission, it will be prudent for administrators to check regularly to make sure that their organizations must either continue to pay or are still exempt from paying local and/or state sales taxes.

Tax issues are nothing to fool around with or make gross assumptions about. It is both essential and cost-effective to check with an attorney or accountant familiar with relevant tax laws to ascertain if all or a portion of an organization's foodservice income might be subject to taxation.

Liability Issues

Most administrators in companies, government entities, and noncommercial organizations are aware of general liability and workers' compensation issues. There are, however, some liability and legal issues that are unique to foodservice that may require attention. While an attorney should be consulted, here are a few liability issues to consider:

- Product Liability. Organizations that provide their own foodservices need to make sure that their insurance policies cover product liability in regard to the preparation and service of food. Sometimes, there is a need to categorically state that food is to be prepared and served at specified locations only. The preparation, transport, and service of food to an off site location belonging to another entity may result in an unanticipated liability suit.

When foodservice is contracted to an outside company, administrators must specify and be assured that the contractor is carrying a predetermined minimum amount (usually from $500,000 to $1 million) of product liability insurance.

- Liquor Liability. The service of alcoholic beverages carries a number of important obligations. One obligation is the need to carry a liability insurance policy that covers the service of alcoholic beverages (the rates will depend on the type of liquor, size of the organization, and the level[s] of service provided). As an example, the service of wine or beer with meals will require a different sort of liability insurance coverage than that necessitated if a foodservice is providing a full-service bar in a nightclub-type of setting.

  Personnel assigned to work at a function where liquor will be served need to meet all applicable local and state regulations. More important, service staff need to be familiar with appropriate guidelines and have a mandate to control the sale of liquor to minors and persons who are visibly intoxicated.
- Workers' Compensation Insurance. In most states, all employers are required to carry adequate workers' compensation insurance for their employees. When a contractor is providing foodservice, the client-organization has the obligation to assure itself that the proper type and amount of insurance for all of the contractor's employees is being carried; it is a given that foodservice programs can generate a variety of accidents. It would be advantageous to all concerned to have a comprehensive workplace safety program in effect.
- Vendor Liability. Most foodservice organizations deal with a large number of product and service vendors. In some cases, vendors may not have been properly screened before contracts were signed. In these instances, it is often only after an accident occurs that an administrator discovers that the organization is potentially liable for damages, regardless of who was at fault. Personnel from vendors, including delivery people from local area restaurants, should be prescreened and questioned as to the types and amounts of insurance coverage their employers carry and if their policies are current.

Regular and Special Licenses

It is a rare foodservice program and/or facility that does not require some form of license to operate. Most foodservices, in fact, are required to have business, Health Department, and/or restaurant licenses. Others are additionally required to maintain health cards/permits for each employee. The purpose of these licenses, whether they have to be paid for or not, is to allow local Health Departments access to and lawful control over foodservice operations to ensure compliance with all local and state mandates. The purpose of health permits is to make sure that all foodservice staff have received a minimum level of training and education in the areas of proper food preparation, handling, and sanitation procedures.

SOCIAL ISSUES

Depending on local economic conditions, state or local ordinances, voluntary guidelines, or an organization's sense of social responsibility, there are a number of ways a foodservice provider can operate in accord with popular sentiments, such as by recycling. In general, foodservices generate the following products that can be recycled:

- Corrugated cardboard boxes
- Scrap paper (if not stained by food)
- Aluminum foil (if clean)
- Aluminum cans (if clean and flattened and labels have been removed)
- Glass bottles (if clean and separated by color)
- Tin cans (if clean and labels have been removed)
- Plastic containers #2, #4, and #6 (if clean and labels have been removed)
- Polystyrene foam (check local ordinances; does not always require cleaning)
- Used cooking fats and oils

Before embarking on a recycling program, it will be important for an organization's foodservice to ascertain the following conditions:

- Are one or more companies locally available to collect the materials?
- Do any of the materials have a significant financial value? If yes, is

there a process in place to monitor how these items are distributed for recycling and whether all income is being received?
- Has it been determined who will provide and maintain (including cleaning) the collection container(s)?
- Is it necessary to document the number or total pounds of materials being recycled versus the amount being sent to a landfill?

Some foodservices that recycle do so for reasons other than social responsibility. Money earned from the sale of recycled goods is generally directed to a local social service agency or employee welfare fund. There is, however, an additional, residual benefit in the fact that most organizations find their solid waste removal bills become lower once they begin recycling, as there are fewer items going in the garbage.

While not exactly recycling in its traditional sense, some government jurisdictions still permit foodservice providers to sell their food garbage to hog farmers. If so permitted, a foodservice staff must take care to not mix any other garbage, especially glass, metal, or other inorganic materials, in with the food waste.

Charitable Donations of Excess Food

Depending on the type of foodservice program an organization operates, leftover foods may be available on a daily or occasional basis. Until recently, much of that food was thrown away, as there was no other established use for it. With the growing and critical need to feed the homeless now present in many communities, many foodservice providers have offered to or have been asked to donate their leftover foods.

Many organizations' attorneys and risk managers note a serious liability concern, however, if donated foods were to become contaminated and/or one or more persons were to file claims suggesting they were made ill by donated leftovers. It has only been over the past few years that many social service agencies have developed waiver of liability agreements that basically hold the organizations donating leftover foods harmless in the event there is an incident of food-borne illness.

Political/Social Correctness

Some organizations, especially colleges/universities and numerous other noncommercial entities, due to their purpose/philosophy and/or clientele, are highly sensitive to the politics and social activities of the companies with which they do business. Therefore, it is incumbent upon such organizations' foodservice providers to respond accordingly. Some examples of this situation encountered during the past few years include the following:

- A small but vocal segment of a major university's student body became agitated when they learned that a certain fast-food restaurant had been granted a lease in the student union. The agitated students wanted the lease rejected because the fast-food company's president and principal stockholder had taken a dogmatic public stand in the pro-life/pro-choice debate.
- A zoo operated by a local government declared that it would not purchase meat from companies that imported beef from Argentina. The zoo management's rationale was that Argentine ranchers were cutting down local rain forests to create more range land on which to raise cattle. Interestingly, the same zoo's managers were distressed when they later learned that the wooden beverage "stirrers" they were purchasing were made from trees from those same Argentine rain forests.
- Numerous organizations, including universities and government entities, have declared that they would not do business with any organization actively involved in South Africa until its apartheid system was completely dismantled.

Managed Health Care

Many organizations, seeking to lower health care costs and have a more productive labor force, have entered into managed health care programs. Some of these programs go so far as to include having the foodservice program assure that low-fat, low-sodium, healthful meals are available in the cafeteria. Jones mused that it was rather odd that AU spent thousands of dollars on annual physicals, fitness programs, and other attempts to help its executives maintain a healthful lifestyle but sent those same people to the executive dining room to feast on elaborate classical food preparations loaded with fat and sodium. He made a mental note to contact the Human Resources department to determine how they might coordinate the cafeterias and executive dining room into the corporate-wide health and fitness plan.

Jones had noted that the nutrient content of menu items was posted at some foodservice facilities he had visited. One thing he knew for sure: he could not afford to hire a full-time registered dietitian. He had been pleasantly surprised to learn of at least two less-expensive ways of providing this health education service.

- Foodservice software is available that will calculate the nutrient content of food once the recipes are entered into the system. In fact, Jones had learned, there are systems that will control the production planning, maintain the inventory, provide current food cost data by menu item, and analyze the nutrient contents. Jones chuckled to himself. "Who knows, someday the software might just cook the meals, too!"
- There is also the option of using an outside dietary consulting service. On a contract or retainer basis, it is possible to have a registered dietitian review menus periodically to assure healthful content and to provide customers with the nutritional information necessary to make healthful choices. Most foodservice contractors have staff dietitians who are available to provide those same services.

As always, Jones was amazed at the direction his new foodservice assignment had taken him—so much to learn, so many different elements. A foodservice administrator just might be described as the ultimate "Jack-of-all-trades"—better yet, "Jack-of-all-knowledge."

CHAPTER SEVEN

New and Remodeled Facilities

Jones was about to get a very unpleasant wake-up call as he prepared for an "emergency" meeting with AU's facilities and maintenance director, Michele Larkin. Jones knew Larkin in a casual, say-hello-in-the-hallway sort of way, as they both had been with the organization for a number of years. Larkin had literally worked her way up the ladder, as her first job had been to repair and maintain refrigeration units. Jones had not, however, had an occasion to work directly with her. That was about to change, because Larkin was heading up the planning team for the new office and foodservice complex AU was planning. The telephone message Jones received setting up the sudden appointment, though, specifically noted that this meeting was to deal with some recently discovered problems with foodservice's existing production facility.

When Larkin arrived for their meeting, Jones was embarrassed to discover that his order for coffee and fresh fruit had been forgotten by foodservice's catering staff and he would have to once again draw refreshment from the community coffee pot in the office next door. What's more, Larkin's news did nothing to improve his disposition.

A recent building inspection by AU's liability and workers' compensation insurance carrier had uncovered some significant problems. Unfortunately, a number of these had been found in foodservice's main production kitchen. As Larkin started reading her list of foodservice's shortcomings, Jones began taking notes:

- All of the steam pipes in the kitchen were wrapped in asbestos insulation. Since the kitchen was a major user of steam, the asbestos would have to be removed eventually—definitely at the time of remodeling.
- The steam equipment (including the boiler, pipes, kettles, and steamer compartments) was in terrible shape. It would appear that Larkin's predecessor had decided to save money and disconnected the water softening system used to feed the boiler. As a result, massive mineral buildups in the pipes and equipment had occurred.
- The grease trap (part of the kitchen sewer system) had "fallen off" the maintenance list. As a result, the grease interceptor became clogged, overflowed, and had recently run off into the city's sewer system. The city already indicated that it would be charging AU for the cleanup, as well as levying some stiff penalties for the resultant environmental violations. Larkin suspected that the grease trap, a nasty cleaning job, did not accidentally fall off the Maintenance Department's "to-do" list.
- Many major pieces of kitchen equipment, such as all of the refrigeration, freezer units, and ice makers, had been sporadically maintained over the past three years. Only recently had this become apparent, as maintenance work orders from the kitchen had tripled. The lack of regular preventive maintenance was a conscious cost-cutting measure, Larkin asserted.
- A number of structural problems, including broken floor tiles and damaged walls, had been uncovered. Jones was surprised to learn that foodservice's storeroom door had been recently knocked out of alignment by a fork lift truck, thereby making it impossible to close and lock it at night. No one had bothered to report this problem, and the health inspector was losing patience with AU's slow reaction to fixing foodservice's wall and floor problems.

Jones thanked Larkin for her "stimulating report," adding, "We might as well cut to the bottom line." Her response was not surprising. "The kitchen and much of its infrastructure is now beyond the ability of our department to justify any more repair dollars. Dana," Larkin said sadly, "your main kitchen needs to be gutted and completely remodeled."

Jones decided that this latest piece of news was going to require his most creative, intensive management plan. He first asked for and received permission from Vice President of Employee Services Bell, to form a foodservice task force. Along with the permission came a budget approval for the funds necessary to hire whatever outside help Jones thought necessary to assist the task force in reaching the best possible conclusions about foodservice remodeling and facility-planning options.

To begin, Jones once again got on the telephone to ask his counterparts at other local organizations which individuals they would recommend for the task force. Without exception, Jones' sources recommended that he put together a balanced mix of internal and external resources. His list included outside consultants and representatives from AU's:

1. Maintenance Department,
2. Purchasing Department,
3. Budget and Finance Department,
4. Human Resources Department,
5. AU's food committee chair,
6. an industrial architect,
7. a food facility consultant,
8. a foodservice management consultant,
9. Foodservice director.

Fortunately for Jones, the sort of architect he was seeking was already under contract to Larkin's department. Jones agreed to a not-to-exceed budget transfer amount in order to work with the architect. The architect recommended a food facility consultant, but Jones rejected the choice after discovering that the person's prime experience was in designing school kitchens. Jones next placed a call to Harry Daulton and asked the recently retired director if he knew of any kitchen or foodservice management consultants the task force should consider. Ever agreeable, Daulton called his old industry contacts and came up with a few names for Jones.

Jones next put together a short Food Facilities Consultant Request for Qualifications (RFQ) letter and sent it out to the recommended consultants (see Exhibit 7-1 at the end of the chapter and on disk). When the responses came back, he was somewhat astounded to find that they indicated a wide range of expertise, including replies from some persons who seemed to think that they were far more qualified to help AU than their backgrounds suggested. As a result, Jones was able quickly to cut the possible candidate list to two management consultants and three kitchen planners.

The more Jones listened to the consultants during the interviews he conducted, the more he realized that there was more to learn about foodservice facility reconstruction than he could assimilate within the current project's time frame. After interviewing each candidate, Jones hit upon a novel idea. The selected foodservice management consultant would also take on the responsibility of co-chairing the task force to make use of that person's specific expertise.

The first task force meeting was scheduled to start at 11:30 A.M. and Jones, on the strength of foodservice's solemn promise to avoid screw-ups, ordered a catered lunch. The meeting was called to order and introductions were made, including brief descriptions of each person's background and reason for being on the task force. Jones introduced the foodservice management consultant last and then asked that individual to take over the meeting.

For the next two hours, task force members were immersed in all of the intricate details of what it takes to plan, design, construct, implement, and maintain a smooth-running foodservice facility. With the management consultant taking the lead, the discussion focused on the following tasks:

- The need to develop a clear mission statement which would then be used to prepare all appropriate operational and financial objectives.
- The simultaneous demand for a comprehensive assessment of the facilities and equipment and an organizational needs assessment relative to present anticipated growth or downsizing for the subject sites.
- The needs assessment/market research that will be used to validate customer preferences with respect to food choices, services levels and prices.

Initiate the process of preparing the operational program by:

- Preparing the menus that will be offered in or at each facility or service point (such as catering).
- Projecting the level(s) of service that will be offered in or at each facility or service point. Identify potential staffing impact of each service point.
- Projecting the anticipated locations and number and type of vending machines required.
- Ascertaining how the facilities and overall program will be managed. In addition, identify opportunities and costs associated with branding (such as Taco Bell), staffing requirements and wage/ benefits costs. If required, prepare a pro forma statement of

income and expenses for the proposed foodservice program (this is for the purpose of determining overall feasibility and, if applicable, the potential payback if loans are to be amortized).

Jones and his fellow AU task force members all acknowledged that what the consultants and architect said made sense. What they were not prepared for was the level of detail they were expected to master about AU's expectations for its foodservice program. To sum up, the task force was going to have to address a lot more issues than just remodeling foodservice's existing kitchen and building a new one across Highway 61 on the new campus. In fact, Jones was startled to learn that AU might not even need two kitchens!

The last half-hour of the first task force meeting was spent identifying the predesign process and handing out assignments for each task force member to complete before the next meeting. The consultant noted that the ultimate goal of the task force was to prepare a foodservice program document that clearly states what AU wants. The end product will then be given to the architect and food facilities planner to design the space and specify the furniture, fixtures, and equipment necessary to meet the program's requirements. The task force's initial action plan was organized as shown in Exhibit 7-2 and on the accompanying disk.

THE ACTION PLAN

Mission Statement and Operational/Financial Objectives

The major concern is what, exactly, an organization wants from its foodservice in regard to its mission statement. What role is foodservice to play in the organization? Some of the issues that will drive the foodservice mission statement include, but are not limited to, the following:

- Is foodservice to be a quantifiable employee benefit? If the answer is yes, and bargaining units are involved in determining organizational expenditures, foodservice's status could be an issue at the bargaining table.
- If not a benefit, is foodservice to be a convenience or service?
- Is foodservice expected to contribute to the organization's efforts to improve productivity?

Exhibit 7-2
ACTION PLAN

ASSIGNMENT	*ACTION PERSON*	*DATE*	*COMMENTS*
1. Develop mission statement along with operational and financial objectives		5/5	Research to include interviews with key executives
2. Conduct comprehensive facility/ equipment assessment		5/10	Primary focus to be on work and cost required to fix kitchen problems
3. Needs assessment relative to present and anticipated growth or downsizing at the two subject facilities		5/15	Meet with strategic planning team and foodservice management team
4. Market research		6/4	Management consultant to utilize market research firm to help frame questions and provide computerized cross-tabulations of the results
5. Menus		6/15	If all requested service levels were provided, here are the menu items that should be offered
6. Service levels requested		6/21	In tandem with the menu and market research results, this represents the "ideal" level of service for each facility
7. Vending		6/23	Number and type of machines that will be needed to supplement cafeteria service as well as provide service in remote locations
8. New Facility Management A. Self-Op versus Contract B. Branding Opportunities C. Staffing Requirements D. Financial Results Pro Forma		6/30	Management consultant to prepare discussion paper outlining pertinent issues, pros/cons and probable cost impacts
9. Program document or goals and objectives with respect to operations, facilities and equipment		7/2	Entire team to accomplish as part of half-day workshop

- Is this an organization that requires or recommends that its employees adhere to strict meal breaks?
- Are there security and/or safety reasons that make it advantageous for people to stay on-site during mealtimes?
- Are there conditions/situations that would suggest or prudently dictate that the company/organization subsidize its foodservice program?

  Before attempting to answer this question, it is important to define exactly what a subsidy is and how it might be accounted for in most organizations. There are several sorts of subsidies. Direct subsidy is generally defined as those dollars paid to offset the difference between foodservice sales and expenses. This is the amount of cash necessary to make up the difference between what is taken in at the cash register (whether in cash or as charges) and the cost of food, labor, and other controllable items. Indirect subsidies are costs associated with the occupancy of a facility (such as rent, building/equipment maintenance, security, utilities, insurance, and property taxes) and management/administrative overhead charges (such as those for human resources, purchasing, and contract administration support).

There are no hard and fast rules that dictate how any one organization should define its subsidy. Some organizations expect their foodservice programs not to require any subsidy, as well as to generate a certain percentage of profits to offset indirect costs. Other organizations simply expect foodservice to break even or stay within IRS guidelines relative to how much subsidy can be budgeted on a year-to-year basis. In either case, subsidy is usually an expense that has to be actively managed.

At this point, Jones asked himself, "Why do I have to be concerned with subsidy as part of a facilities planning process? Isn't that an operational issue?" There are numerous answers to Jones' questions. A few key ones to consider follow:

- A design that requires inefficient foodservice staff levels or activities will generally result in a higher-than-necessary labor cost.
- A too-small service area (servery) will result in congestion and slower patron throughput. If it takes too long to get food, patrons will become discouraged and start to seek alternative choices

(such as vending machines, brown bagging, or going off-site to a local commercial facility).

- A kitchen or servery that is too large or has too many physical partitions (such as walls or doors) will create blind spots and cause inefficiencies, as it is more difficult for management to supervise employee activities.
- Insufficient cash register stations will mean that customers will have to wait longer than they should to check out, thus further discouraging participation. Inappropriate register placements result in an inability to downsize; or, achieve better staff productivity by being able to move a register to another more convenient location during specified slow periods.
- A dining room that cannot hold all of the people who want to eat will also stifle participation. Therefore, sales and patron satisfaction will go down.

Needs Assessment and Market Research

The foodservice management consultant next asked Jones to help establish an employee profile. The purpose of such a profile is to allow the task force to get a good fix on what is currently happening with an organization's foodservice program. Therefore, the management consultant and Jones needed to ascertain the current level of participation, average check, sales mix, and sales per hour being recorded by AU's program (see Chapter 12). The management consultant then asked Jones for a employee profile that he could use to help establish a market analysis that would allow him to determine appropriate menus and service levels.

With the help of the head of AU's Human Resources Department, Jones was able to provide the consultant with a clear demographic profile of AU's workforce, including gender, age, ethnic background, and salary ranges. "So," thought Jones, "with the profile information on cafeteria use and the organization's economic/demographic profile compiled, it seems we should have sufficient information to proceed. Right?" Wrong. The management consultant's next question let Jones know this part of the planning process was still not done.

"Okay, now, who actually uses AU's cafeteria on a day-to-day basis?" When Jones admitted that he couldn't answer that question, the foodservice consultant explained that it was vitally important for the task force to learn which potential customers were and which were not using the current cafeteria and why. The management consultant added that before the design process for the planned second facility could even start, the task force needed to know what the practical capacity of the entire foodservice program should be. "Once we have that information and integrate it with the company's growth and population projections for the two sites, we should be able to construct an accurate projection of what the market for your two facilities will be." (The methodology for conducting this market research is presented in Chapter 13.)

With the successful completion of the consultant's market research and the compilation of the other required information, the task force met again to share and analyze its findings.

Facility/Equipment Assessment

AU's maintenance director, the architect, and the food facility designer had found the kitchen and infrastructure to be in just as bad a condition as suspected. In practical terms, a major refurbishment would be required. While not requiring a total demolition, the group agreed that the kitchen would have to be completely shut down for anywhere from four to six months while renovation work took place. The trio's "rough" cost estimate for this work ranged from $950,000 to $1 million. The estimate included the purchase and installation of new refrigeration, ice-making, and steam-related food production equipment.

At this point, both the maintenance director and the consultant raised the question of whether it would be necessary to operate two full production kitchens that would be located within three blocks of each other.

The consultant explained that there are numerous examples of organizations operating a single, centrally located kitchen whose production is used to support (i.e., is sent out to) one or more satellite dining facilities within a defined geographic region. The management consultant explained that it was simply a matter of appropriate planning and making sure that AU's management, administrators, and foodservice management all fully appreciated the implications of the decision.

Progress Report

The next meeting item was a report on the market research results, and the findings were quite revealing. Much to Jones' amazement, an astounding 50 percent of AU's employee population indicated that they rarely, if ever, patronized the cafeteria. The primary reasons those surveyed listed included the following:

- Prices were too high.
- There were not enough items on the menu reflecting customers' ethnic preferences.
- The cafeteria was too far away. Survey respondents said that it was impossible for them to walk to the cafeteria, get their food, pay for it, find a place to sit and eat, and return to their workstations within the organization-allotted 30-minute meal breaks.
- It was "just as easy" to brown-bag meals and purchase beverages from the vending machines. Vending's beverage prices were cheaper than the cafeteria's, anyway.
- There was a high level of dissatisfaction with service in the headquarters cafeteria, based on the perception that service staff "bent over backwards to serve the suits." Also, according to some survey respondents, service staff allegedly provided larger portions to men.
- The food was too greasy and not healthful to eat, especially, as one AU worker said, "when you sit at a desk all day."

Without ignoring foodservice's positives, the task force decided that there were some shortcomings that definitely required rectifying prior to initiating the new facility's design process. The AU team members in particular expressed a great deal of concern that the absence of solutions to the problems defined by the recent research might lead to a number of false assumptions driving how the new and remodeled facilities should be designed. All group members agreed that what they did *not* want to do was use the current program as a model since it contained a number of inherent flaws.

With a much clearer idea of the importance of knowing the who, what, and why of AU's potential foodservice customer base, the task force was able to structure what should always be the first component of a foodservice design development process: the operational program.

THE OPERATIONAL PROGRAM

Simply stated, the operational program is the foundation from which architects and food facility designers can "begin" their work. A program should provide a clear statement of what the planners believe is necessary to effect a successful foodservice program from both an operational and a financial perspective. Such a plan, however, does not necessarily mean that a complete program will be realized, as there are usually space and/or capital dollar constraints that eventually force compromises or program deletions. Nevertheless, it is considered best to base a foodservice development program on the premise that "If we could have a perfect foodservice program, this is what we would do." The reason for this assumption is that it is easier to make realistic compromises in light of an optimum whole as opposed to considering the worth of individual program pieces.

A good program document consists of two important parts: the first depicts an operational scenario, while the second defines specific design elements and ties all of the elements together in a cohesive, easy-to-understand narrative. Once created, the program document, all pertinent meeting notes, and final plans should become part of a permanent project file. The operational scenario will address, but not necessarily be limited to, the following subjects:

- The Menu. Without a doubt, the menu is the most important planning consideration, as this determination will affect all subsequent space and equipment requirements.
- Projected Food Production Requirements. Depending on the anticipated size of a foodservice facility and estimated number of potential patrons, it may be necessary to calculate the type, size/capacity, and amount of production equipment that will be required. This process is called a "menu explosion."
- Proposed Service Levels. These levels will be based on the menu and the method(s) chosen to prepare and serve food to patrons. Oftentimes planners focus on cafeteria or dining room requirements, but fail to pay attention to such components as catering (service of from five to 500 meals, some or all of which must be presented some distance away from the kitchen).
- Proposed Preparation/Processing Mix. Rarely will a foodservice program operate so that every menu item served is prepared from scratch (i.e., production begins with its raw ingredients). Today, in fact, there are literally thousands of commercially prepared products that have won the approval of foodservice customers. In addition, for programs whose labor costs run higher than others in their local market, the use of prepared items is almost essential as a cost-cutting measure.
- Hours of Operation. Generally speaking, the tighter a foodser-

vice's peak load service times, the more service and seating spaces will be required. If the peak service time (generally, lunch periods) can be extended over a longer time period (by scheduling or the patrons simply adjusting their meal/break times to avoid the rush), operations will be easier to conduct and foodservice staff will function more efficiently.

- Location(s). If an organization has just one foodservice location, a need to "load in" as many service and menu components as space and dollars permit will exist. If, however, there are multiple foodservice locations, especially those that are generally accessible, it may be appropriate to create separate foodservice identities at each facility. This will permit patrons to choose the type of menu and service level they find most appealing on any particular day.

  An example: On a given day, AU's current cafeteria might offer a variety of traditional cafeteria choices, such as hot entrées, prepared salads, and grill items, while the new facility (once opened) could feature a salad bar, pizza-by-the-slice, and a Mexican food concept.

  In sum, the ultimate financial success of any remodeled or new foodservice facility will depend on planners determining an effective mix of concepts, menus, and service levels that are in proportion to the anticipated market demand.

- Storage Requirements. The amount of storage required is contingent on several factors, including:
  1. The menu relative to how much fresh or raw product will be prepared on site versus purchased in a refrigerated or frozen state.
  2. Where the facility(s)/foodservice program is located in relation to local population centers and food distribution points. As a rule, the greater the distance, the lower the delivery frequency will be. Therefore, it is sometimes necessary for foodservices situated in isolated areas to keep on hand as much as three to four weeks' worth of anticipated inventory. Those school, government, and social service agency foodservice programs that qualify for U.S. Government Surplus Food Commodities require even more storage space than other foodservices, since they generally receive their allotments in bulk, quarterly shipments. If foodservice's storage space is insufficient, these products will have to be stored off-premises in costly private facilities.
  3. The purchasing practice or philosophy of each particular orga-

nization. Many government entities put their food and supplies requirements out for annual or semiannual bid, with shipments to be received monthly or less often. In other cases, including most contractor-operated facilities, managers will be reluctant to tie up cash in inventory, so there will usually be more frequent deliveries and faster inventory turnover.

4. The need to react to emergencies. If major weather problems or a catastrophe were to occur, foodservice's ability to receive deliveries is likely to be severely hindered for a number of days. Depending on the department's location, such as in a hospital, prison, or university campus in a remote area, foodservice will probably need to have sufficient quantities of food on hand to feed the normal population, as well as to provide emergency assistance to the community at large.

- Administrative Support. It is easy to forget, but the people responsible for managing and supporting a day-to-day foodservice program need to have office space. This is especially true of large programs in general and those that do significant catering business (such as booking events, scheduling rooms/staff, and billing).
- Space Flexibility. This need must be accommodated in catering spaces and central production kitchens, as well as by designing service and dining areas that can be expanded or consolidated in accord with shifting capacity requirements. Generally, most organizations have a need for "blank" or "flex" space in which to stage/organize large-scale events.
- Technology. This concerns the need to ascertain if any new technological improvements in food production or processing should be incorporated into a new or renovated foodservice operation. Recent examples of this sort of innovation include cook-chill systems, conveyor broilers and ovens, computerized point-of-sale cash registers, and information management systems. (See Chapter 10 for more detailed information.)

BEGINNING THE DESIGN PROCESS

Once the design parameters are in place, architects and kitchen facility planners can initiate the design process. While no single approach to new or renovated facility planning is used by all architects and kitchen planners, here is a general overview of what their efforts will create.

1. The kitchen planner creates one or more bubble diagrams showing the various food production, storage, and service components. Each bubble represents a specific function, rather than space and adjacency relationships.

2. Using the program document, which may already include the menu explosion, and bubble diagrams as a basis, the kitchen planner will prepare square-footage requirements for each component.

3. If designing a new building, the architect will incorporate the kitchen planner's square-footage requirements into the overall building "footprint." If renovating an existing building, the architect will need to ascertain if the amount of space specified by the kitchen planner can be economically applied to foodservice use.

4. At this point, there may be a need to start downsizing or compressing the planned foodservice facility into a more practical space. Simple dollar and cents calculations of anticipated construction costs per square foot may dictate that plans for a new or renovated facility will be too expensive.

5. All of the input gained up to this point will become the basis for the first of several schematic plans. At this point, administrators are at the stage where specific components (i.e., space and equipment) begin to appear in specific locations within a logical flow pattern. When this stage is reached, administrators' primary concern should be to make sure that adequate space has been allotted for each operational function and that all required and "nice-to-have" adjacencies have been identified.

6. If not performed as part of the programming phase, this is when the menu explosion process should take place. It is sometimes necessary and/or prudent to extend the menu explosion process to include dry, refrigerated, and freezer storage requirements. Doing so will give architects and kitchen planners the clearest possible idea as to how much square footage and/or cubic footage will be needed to support foodservice when it is operating at its anticipated maximum capacity.

7. The final major portion of the schematic plan process is identification of all the resources that will be needed in terms of management/support staff space, external and internal communication needs, and computer requirements. The communications and computer requirements are especially important as there is generally a need to provide a conduit/chase and/or hardwired connection to various components.

8. At roughly this point, most architects will request that the schematic plan and cost estimate be formally approved before the actual design development process is initiated. In other words, now is the time for administrators to speak up if they have any concerns regarding the

amount of allocated space, its configuration, equipment layout, or flow patterns.

9. The design development process is where architects and kitchen planners begin to design the kitchen's specific layout, make the final equipment selections (by manufacturer name and model number), and determine all of the requisite mechanical, electrical, and plumbing connections. The sets of drawings submitted by these professionals will represent what the architect believes to be different completion percentages. Usually, the client is asked to review and approve drawings and cost estimates at the 50 percent, 90 percent, and 100 percent levels. Larger projects will usually require still more submittals.

10. It is when the process has reached the estimated 50 percent completion level that input from foodservice management and administrators becomes most critical. For the client, it is important that the design schedule permits sufficient time for all concerned to review thoroughly the drawings and to check them against what was originally presented and agreed to in the programming document and/or menu explosion process. It is also at this point that the kitchen planner will be expected to produce a "spec" book comprised, in essence, of a series of equipment "cut sheets" taken from equipment manufacturers' catalogs. With these cut sheets, administrators and their planning team will now be able to form a good idea as to the type and size of equipment envisioned for their new or renovated foodservice facility.

In foodservice situations, where it is essential to make sure that the equipment and space will work reliably under "normal" operating conditions, it is sometimes wise to lay out that portion of the space on a bare floor and use tables and other furnishings to represent the various pieces of equipment. Experienced foodservice managers, cooks, and other staff can quickly tell if a needed piece of equipment is missing or is located in the wrong place. Something as simple as whether the french fryer should be installed on the left or right side of a griddle can have a significant impact on service speed and staff efficiency. There are also several other factors that now need to be considered and/or explored with foodservice's design team:

- Are competent, factory-authorized service centers located nearby that can perform "warranty work" and other repairs? That rotary oven from France Dana Jones would love to install in AU's renovated kitchen may be the best there is, but he needs to know whether it will be necessary to get replacement parts from France.
- Does it make sense to specify the purchase of "like" types of

equipment (i.e., steamers, ovens, griddles, broilers, mixers, slicers, refrigerators, and ice makers) from a single manufacturer so that fewer service agencies will have to be dealt with? This practice would *not* be advantageous when, for example, a company has a high-quality, unique piece of equipment that can be a cost-benefit to the organization and cannot be obtained from one of the major manufacturers. For example, if most of the basic equipment will come from manufacturer X except that the best-quality dough rounder is produced by another company, it would not be in the best interest of the organization to buy a lesser quality machine from manufacturer X just to consolidate service.
- If need arises, does specified equipment have sufficient flexibility to be used for other purposes?
- Does the equipment specified have the *proven* capability to produce the products called for on the menu? For example, if a floor mixer will be used to mix bread doughs, as well as cake mixes, the bread dough mixing function will require a mixer with a stronger motor and drive mechanism than is usually found in models used solely for cake mix blending.
- Does all equipment meet local, state, and national code requirements such as the Underwriters Laboratory (UL), National Sanitation Foundation (NSF), and the National Fire Protection Association (NFPA).

11. Once the drawings have reached the 100 percent completion phase, architects will, once again, ask for their clients' approval. Once they have gained this approval, architects and kitchen planners will then develop a comprehensive set of construction documents. As a rule, client-organizations will find most of the documents too technical and specialized to understand fully. However, opportunities should be provided to review the equipment list against the list of items specified and their number to make sure that no omissions or substitutions have been made.

12. Once the actual construction process at the new or remodeled facility(ies) has been initiated, administrators often perceive that there is little for the organization's foodservice management team to do. This is not always true.

- Administrators need to stay involved in order to monitor if the project is falling behind or running ahead of schedule.
- Oftentimes after foodservice's equipment package has been let out to bid, administrators need to participate (proactively, if nec-

essary) in any discussions of major equipment substitution requests. The kitchen planner's portion of the construction documents usually specifies one or two particular brands/models of foodservice equipment, and then adds the phrase "or equal." *Please treat this phrase with caution.* The "or equal" options can sometimes cause a great deal of debate because the person making the decision does not understand what is or is not "equal." It may appear on the surface that a device to chop food is a device to chop food. However, some machines have multiple features; others may have restricted capabilities and, if selected, could potentially cause a large number of ongoing operational headaches. A case in point was the purchasing agent who decided on one large dough mixer over the one specified to save about $150. The mixers had the same mixing capacity, but the expensive one had a movable bowl while the cheaper one had a stationary bowl. The staff had to use a step ladder and multiple lifting steps to empty and clean the bowl, resulting in increased potential for workers' compensation claims and increased labor every time the mixer was used. The item was truly not "or equal" and the savings were more than lost in the first month of operating time.

- When a remodeling project is underway, administrators should always anticipate "surprises," such as a hidden electrical conduit being uncovered or drain pipes that prove to be nonexistent. Such "surprises" can cause project delays or necessitate last-minute design changes. While these changes are necessary, if made without adequate consideration or planning in regard to the entire project, they will result in major design and/or operational problems later on.
- Again, with remodeling projects, it is sometimes necessary to cease operations and close down all or a portion of a kitchen. In other cases, equipment (such as a walk-in refrigerator) situated in an existing location will have to be dismantled and moved to a new location long before opening. This means that administrators will have to be prepared to shut down a kitchen as soon as this project phase begins or ensure that foodservice can continue to operate without major equipment.
- When situations such as the above occur or when a facility must be completely shut down during construction, the need to provide an interim foodservice program will arise. Without a kitchen, this will represent a major challenge to a planning team, one that suggests the need for an administrator to work closely with food-

service management personnel, as well as the architect, kitchen planner, and building contractor, to seek out the most cost-effective ways of providing interim meal service. Several options suggest themselves. In one case, an organization successfully provided an interim program through the rental and installation of mobile service carts. In another instance, the foodservice provider rented a tent, leased a field kitchen from a local caterer, and provided two meals a day for three months to an organization's employee population. No matter which option administrators favor for their organizations, it will be critical to begin planning the logistics of an interim foodservice program as soon as it is clear that facility construction or renovation will cause a disruption in the permanent program.

13. When a renovated or new building is almost complete, contractors will conduct a "punch list" tour of the facility. (A "punch list" is a checklist of the items installed during construction.) It is usually the responsibility of the kitchen planner to handle the kitchen and servery portions of the punch list. It is important for administrators to understand that most punch list processes are specifically intended to make sure that all pieces of equipment are as specified and are as shown on the construction drawings. The person doing the punch list, however, may not actually ascertain if the equipment works or if it was properly installed. In this case the responsibility for checking equipment condition and installation falls to the facilities designer and equipment manufacturers/sales representatives under the direction of the foodservice manager.

One way to avoid unnecessary problems when opening a remodeled or new facility is to have the kitchen planner specify that representatives from each manufacturer must be present to demonstrate that the equipment is in proper working order. This means that the manufacturers must send one or more representatives or technicians on-site to demonstrate how to use and maintain their piece(s) of equipment. Administrators should expect that any installation or manufacturing flaws will be exposed at this time, so that timely repairs can be made. It is a good idea to videotape these demonstrations for later use in training staff. The kitchen equipment contractor should provide operation and maintenance manuals that describe how to operate and provide maintenance, as well as list the service agencies for warranty work.

14. Once a facility is in full operation, break-in or training time for staff to become familiar with their new or remodeled environment must be allocated. Determining when to schedule this training and how long it

should last is the responsibility of foodservice management. An organization's planning team may also want to phase in the operation of a new or remodeled kitchen over a period of time, rather than trying to open it and go to full production in one day.

15. The final piece in the planning process, the "postoccupancy evaluation," is, perhaps, the most important. Within 30 to 60 days of a new or renovated facility becoming fully operational, the entire planning team should visit the facility to evaluate how well the design is working, whether all of the equipment is performing as specified, and if there are any operational problems that need to be resolved. Most of this evaluation process should be based on observations and discussions with the foodservice staff members who work in the area(s) of concern or with the new piece(s) of equipment.

It would be a rare new or remodeled kitchen that did not have one or more flaws come to light as the result of a postoccupancy evaluation. However, should equipment be found not to be working as specified, administrators should notify the manufacturer(s) of the need to fix or replace the item(s) while they are still under warranty. Other times, problems have been caused by foodservice staff not understanding the new flow patterns or work processes designed in the programming phase. When this concern appears, it is up to foodservice management to ensure that service staff do not take it upon themselves to make process or procedural changes until they fully appreciate how those alterations could negatively impact the new program as a whole.

The final advantage of a postoccupancy evaluation is that it will prove useful in the future as a tool for planning other new or remodeled foodservice facilities. Therefore, all documentation concerning the planning and design phases must be securely stored for successor managers and administrators to refer to if they should have any questions as to the original design's intent.

Exhibit 7-1
FOOD FACILITIES CONSULTANT REQUEST FOR QUALIFICATIONS (RFQ) and FEE PROPOSALS

THE PROJECT: *Organization* Facility Renovation and New Headquarters Construction

ORGANIZATION CONTACT: Mr. Dana L. Jones
Support Services Administrator
Address:
Phone:

PROJECT COORDINATORS: To Be Selected

ARCHITECT: To Be Selected

SCHEDULE:

Release RFQ	September 12, 19XX
Responses Due	October 10, 19XX
Cut List	October 15, 19XX
Fee Proposals Due	October 25, 19XX
Interviews	October 28, 19XX
Designer Selected	November 1, 19XX
Organizational Meeting	November 9, 19XX
First Schematics Submitted	December 9, 19XX
Schematic Review Meeting	December 15, 19XX
Second Schematics Submitted	January 19, 19XX

Balance of schedule to be determined by architect

SCOPE OF WORK:

Organization intends to develop a central commissary kitchen to support its existing and future facilities within a 25 mile radius through the year 2010. A site at or near Organization's headquarters campus will be selected by November, 19XX. This kitchen must provide for five major functions:

a. Food processing/production in a yet-to-be determined cook-chill system.
b. Preparation of baked goods.
c. Packaging and distribution of bulk and certain individually portioned foods and baked goods prepared on site.
d. Receiving, warehousing and distribution of all foods and supplies for all Organization facilities within a 25 mile radius. This would exclude items such as milk and certain types of produce that would be delivered direct to each facility.
e. Central administration office for the foodservice management team.

Space and efficient systems for the preparation and/or processing, packaging, storage and disbursement of a variety of foods are all critical elements. In addition, the opportunity for preparation and packaging design flexibility as well as future expansion of the production and storage areas is equally important.

Exhibit 7-1 continued

The facilities designer will be expected to work cooperatively with the Organization's project coordinator and the selected project architect and Support Services administrator. The Organization's foodservice management consultants will have responsibility for providing the operational portions (to include the menus and population projections) of the foodservice program document.

Specifically, the facilities designer will be expected to accomplish the following:

1. Develop a space program/schematic design for the kitchen, bakery, warehouse, employee facilities, offices and dispensing/shipping areas. This program must consider adequate circulation, work areas, staging/dispatch areas and freezer/refrigeration space.
2. Provide cost estimates for all furniture, fixtures and equipment associated with the project.
3. Make three on-site presentations of schematic design(s) and cost estimates to the Organization's task force and architect.
4. Prepare the final drawings and detailed specifications for the kitchen, including mechanical, electrical and all other necessary functions.
5. Provide all necessary shop drawing approvals, architect/ building contractor coordination, installation supervision and/or punch list services.
6. Assist the Organization in arranging manufacturer's on-site training in the use of all major equipment and systems.
7. Within 30 days of kitchen opening, inspect the kitchen and meet with the foodservice management team and task force to assess the kitchen design and equipment performance. The consultant will be expected to assist in making any corrections and/or assuring equipment manufacturer cooperation with start-up and training.

SPECIFIC PROPOSAL RESPONSE REQUIREMENTS:

The RFQ responses should be presented in the same order as the request for information presented below.

1. Firm Background/Description
   Please provide the following information:
   A. Size of the firm (identify number of professional and support staff personnel by title).
   B. Scope of services offered (provide a brief explanation for each).
   C. Average number of projects completed over the past three years.
   D. Total dollar value of projects completed over the past three years.
   E. Number of current projects.
   F. Firm ownership classification (corporation, sole proprietor, etc.)
   G. Does your firm have more than one office? If yes, please list all locations.
   H. Please list all firm and/or principal professional society and association memberships.

Exhibit 7-1 continued

I. Provide proof of adequate liability insurance.

2. Specific Experience
   Please provide a list of successfully completed *comparable* (in terms of size and/or scope) projects over the past three years. A brief description of each project along with the names and phone numbers of the architect(s) and client contact(s) *must* be provided. Consultants must have a minimum of three comparable projects in order to be considered for this assignment.
3. Personnel
   A. Please provide the names and complete resumes (to include project and educational background) of the persons who will have any significant involvement with this assignment. The person who will supervise and have overall responsibility for this project should be identified.
   B. If invited to the interviews, samples of past central kitchen projects must be presented.
4. Schedule
   With reference to the schedule on the cover page of this RFQ, please provide a proposed phase-by-phase work schedule for this project. All on-site visits must be separately identified as to who will attend and approximate length of visit. Assuming timely responses from the Organization, the consultant will be required to adhere to the schedule agreed upon.
5. Selection for Interview/Cut List
   It should be clearly understood that this is a Request for Qualifications. A maximum of four firms will be selected from the respondents for interviews. A design firm will then be selected from those interviewed.
6. Qualifications Response Submittal
   A. Three copies of your response must be submitted to Dana Jones by no later than 4:00 P.M. on October 10, 19XX.
   B. One copy must be received by the project coordinator no later than 4:00 P.M. on October 10, 19XX.
7. Fees
   Those notified on October 15, 19XX that they have been selected for interviews must submit a fee proposal no later the 4:00 P.M. on October 25, 19XX.
   A. Please provide a listing of the hourly billing rates for all professional and support staff projected to work on this project.
   B. With reference to number four above, a phase-by-phase fees proposal should be submitted. The fees quoted should reflect the guaranteed maximum the Organization will be charged *including* all reimbursable expenses.
   C. All fee quotes must remain firm through the completion of the project.
   D. Please quote the hourly fee(s) which will be charged if additional assistance is required.
   E. The precise scope of work and final fees agreement will be subject to the review and approval of the project architect and the Organization.

CHAPTER EIGHT

Noncafeteria Entities

One warm morning shortly before the July 4 holiday, Jones found himself once again hurrying to a meeting with his boss, Vice President Patricia Bell. Mentally reviewing the meeting's agenda, which included an examination of foodservice's noncafeteria entities, Jones thought, "I know Patricia wants to discuss our catering services, particularly our ability to support the training conferences that were scheduled after Harry Daulton's departure last March." These annual conferences were attended by key distributors from around the world, and required meticulous support services to ensure that all attenders had their needs looked after and were free to concentrate on business. Thus, to prepare for his meeting, Jones had made a thorough assessment of current catering resources, as well as all the rest of foodservice's noncafeteria entities, to evaluate their management efficiency and to suggest ways they could be improved to meet the organization's strategic goals.

Jones walked quickly toward the vice president's office, thinking that it was about five years ago that AU had determined that it was less expensive to provide meeting spaces and dining services for all the extended training and sales meetings it held throughout the year at organizational headquarters. Housing for meeting attenders was arranged by contract with several nearby hotels. All foodservice, however, had always been provided in-house. That decision had netted AU substantial financial savings over the years, in addition to decreasing staff's travel time and time away from families.

However, due to the periodic and ongoing scheduling of these meetings, foodservice was now facing the challenge of making its program interesting and unique for each group of attenders. In the past, when controlling expenses had been less of a priority, AU had held its meetings at commercial resorts around the country, where commercial chefs would prepare menus of different regional cuisines. This foodservice variety had always elicited high marks from meeting attenders. In order to maintain program quality and diversity, Harry Daulton had brought in local restaurant chefs each of the past five years to add a "special touch" to foodservice during each meeting session.

By networking with other foodservice administrators, Jones had been given the opportunity to tour foodservices at several local organizations. Most of these operations offered several types of catering, as well as operating other noncafeteria foodservice entities. During his tours, Jones had been exposed to some new ways that foodservice could provide cost-effective hospitality outside of cafeterias to organizational employees, visitors, and dignitaries. This new information had helped him prepare his meeting notes, including suggestions for improvement of AU's own noncafeteria entities.

CATERING

Catering requirements at different organizations vary—from the elaborate staging of dinners and receptions for VIPs to providing simple coffee and baked goods service for employee meetings. As a result, foodservice catering departments face a wide variety of requirements and potential problems. Jones, for example, had recently experienced one of the many "catering pitfalls" that can arise in any organizational structure.

Recently at AU, a vice president's secretary had called Jones to complain because she was denied lunch service for a meeting her boss was holding. When the foodservice administrator looked into the situation, he discovered that the catering department had a standing policy requiring 48-hour advance notice for all meal orders and 24-hour notice for beverage service. Jones also ascertained that the complaining secretary had called the kitchen at 10:30 A.M. the day the service was required.

It turned out that last-minute catering orders like this one were a common practice for this vice president's secretary and that the new catering staffer had simply followed instructions she had been given during training: "Catering requests must be in 48 hours in advance." She had not been given Harry Daulton's rules of exception, which exempted calls from the upper executive offices. Daulton's law of survival was to have kitchen staff drop everything and prepare last-minute functions for senior executives' meetings. He then always overstaffed (i.e., had more workers on hand than were necessary for regular production) in order to accommodate such situations. In other words, Jones had realized, AU was subsidizing the whims of its senior administrators.

At the end of the week, when Jones casually brought up this catering problem with the subject AU vice president, he was surprised to learn that this executive was unaware of the late orders. What's more, the vice president had told Jones that the executive secretarial staff had known about the disputed lunch meeting for weeks and had had ample time to make catering arrangements. It was then that Jones began to understand how critical it was that catering policies and restrictions be communicated and enforced throughout an organization. The vice president with whom he had conferred agreed to take the matter up with the secretarial staff to assure that they would follow the catering policies drawn up for the good of the organization.

Afterward, Jones made a mental note to address the catering manager's overstaffing practice by conferring with the interim foodservice director to draft a new catering staffing policy. "We can't go on building 'hidden' costs into our catering program," he thought to himself. "What a waste!"

Another element of concern had surfaced during Jones' resolution of his initial catering problem. Only days ago, he had learned that AU's finance group had taken a liking to a local commercial catering company and was using that firm for all of its business-related catering. "We are subsidizing our foodservice, then paying an outside vendor to do catered events? Something is wrong with a system that allows or results in that type of behavior," Jones mused. Thinking the situation over, he realized that the issue had arisen from two causes. "First of all," he asked himself, "why does company policy allow the use of outside vendors when we already have our own subsidized foodservice program? Second, and perhaps more important, what is wrong with our in-house catering to cause some of our people to use outside catering suppliers?"

Jones decided to seek out the cause of this conundrum. His first order of business was to determine the catering needs of various organizational groups and then to assess AU's foodservice to determine, whether, in fact, it could provide the level and quality of catering services needed. In all cases, if the first answer is that individual tastes alone are creating the demand for outside vendors, then organizational policy needs to be changed (particularly if costs need to be controlled/reduced). If, however, the on-premises catering program is of insufficient quality in any area, then catering performance must be improved before members of internal departments can be directed to use it exclusively. It is also possible that the in-house catering staff will not be able to provide for some major events, whether due to size of the group or lack of qualified staff. It is important that the daily staff meet the daily needs. It may be most cost-efficient to use outside caterers for occasional special catering events. The decision must be made on a case-by-case basis and the foodservice administrator, in consultation with the foodservice manager, should have the final vote on when to use an outside caterer.

In order to ensure and maintain the best possible catering performance, some organizations form employee committees to speak on behalf of the needs of different user groups and to assess the performance of in-house service. Others prefer to hire outside consultants to assist them in the evaluative process. An outside, objective opinion will be especially helpful when strong emotions or opinions emerge over whether the in-house catering services being offered are meeting expectations and/or standards. Given his current lack of foodservice expertise, Jones decided to seek outside help, but also to recommend the formation of a catering evaluation committee with representation from each of AU's major departments. Building consensus on legitimate catering needs and performance standards with the help of an outside "expert/mediator," Jones decided, would be his recommendation to Bell.

With this decision in hand, Jones next turned his attention to the second largest noncafeteria component of AU's foodservice program: its executive dining room.

THE EXECUTIVE DINING ROOM

Whether to maintain or close an executive dining room is often a question foodservice administrators find themselves facing in the 1990s. Jones' superiors had decided that the benefit of being able to hold effective working lunches and meetings with "outsiders" in private, controlled conditions outweighed the negatives of ongoing subsidy and the image of elitism created by their executive dining facility.

However, between the Internal Revenue Service's de minimis rules mandating that subsidies over a percentage of the actual cost be distributed among employees for tax purposes and the widespread need to operate as cost-effectively as possible, more and more organizations are asking themselves whether to continue providing executive dining services. Whether they take the form of a corporate executive dining room opened as a perquisite for high-level executives, a faculty club, or a doctors' dining room, the wait-served, limited-access executive dining facility almost always requires a substantial subsidy. Though Jones knew that AU's foodservice would have to continue operating its current, loss-making executive dining room, he had prepared several recommendations for Bell that he believed might result in more efficient operation of this facility. Jones' suggestions included the following:

- Increase the potential customer base by granting executive dining room privileges to all vice presidents.
- Change the menu to a daily fresh sheet with three unique entrées. This would increase the variety and, if planned correctly, decrease kitchen labor.
- Assure that at least one of the entrées was truly a low-fat, healthful option that would be compatible with AU's healthful lifestyle program for all of its employees.
- Allow the executive dining room to be used for more outside catered events.
- Change from full linen service to linen placemats and napkins. This would reduce laundry expenses, maintain a gracious dining experience, and expose the beautiful cherrywood tables.

CARTS/KIOSKS

As a result of the consultant's recommendation, Jones' organization had begun operating several food and beverage dispensing carts. These mobile service points can provide flexible, albeit limited, food and beverage service at remote locations on a corporate or academic campus or in busy hospital corridors, arena concourses, or other places with high traffic volume. It should be noted that over the past few years carts have evolved from relatively unattractive metal and plastic holding and selling units into contemporarily decorated, self-contained merchandising units highlighted with brass and mahogany trim, and capable of dispensing a wide variety of hot and/or cold foods and beverages. Carts, which are obviously less expensive to purchase and operate than fixed sales points, also provide greater sales flexibility. This is because mobile units can be relocated when traffic flow shifts due to new construction, a reorganization of departments, or other changes that cause foodservice's potential customers to congregate in different patterns.

Recently, mobile serving carts have been designed to be effective merchandisers of different foodservice in-house products and/or regional/national branded items. For example, Jones had just learned from a colleague that branded product suppliers such as Dunkin' Donuts, Taco Bell, Subway, and Pizza Hut are now beginning to sell a small dispensing unit that can be restocked daily from local stores. Another convenient, cart-based serving option, one that Jones was prepared to recommend to Patricia Bell, was a "breakfast" cart stocked with fresh-brewed coffees, bottled juices, fresh-baked pastries, rolls, and muffins, which could attract considerable business at AU's high-volume, morning traffic location(s). Adding a soft-serve yogurt dispenser on that same cart, Jones figured, would enhance sales in both the morning and afternoon, thus decreasing the amount of time it would take the cart to pay for itself.

One key to successful cart operation that Jones had learned from networking with other foodservice administrators in his area is to ensure that a plan for restocking, cleaning, and storage has been devised before actual purchases of mobile units. Having a reliable source of adequate energy and water is critical, both to maintaining ongoing operation and to performing daily cleaning. In addition, foodservice must designate a space to which carts can be taken for periodic thorough cleaning. The department's ability to resupply its cart(s) during each sales period is another requirement for success, as a cart that is out of product is of no value to anyone. Finally, for both security and aesthetic reasons, carts should be purchased only if they have been designed so they can be secured in place or in a storage closet after serving hours.

In order to back his recommendation with a choice of suppliers, Jones had compiled a list of cart manufacturers who were able to custom-design any type of cart to meet the specific needs of different operators. "Now, if our VP is ready to spend a little money to make some new revenue, we're in business with carts," Jones told himself.

COFFEE POTS (PLUS) IN WORKSPACES

The issue of whether to permit coffee pots operated by employees or organizational departments in workspaces seems to be an innocuous concern to all but foodservice professionals. In fact, however, this one issue can determine the success or failure of an organization's employee cafeteria. If organizational rules allow individuals or departments to use refrigerators and microwaves in their work areas, a foodservice is likely to experience even greater trouble. Most obviously, this is because when employees are allowed to make their own coffee in work areas, they have one less reason to visit the cafeteria. If these potential customers stop visiting the cafeteria during their morning or afternoon breaks, they will not purchase the donuts, cookies, and other impulse or "add-on" items whose sales help keep cafeteria operations on-target financially. Another major factor is the loss of the high-profit coffee and soft drink sales.

Thus, when coffee makers, as well as refrigerators and microwaves, are available in work areas, an organization may, in effect, be subsidizing its own cafeteria while simultaneously competing with it by providing employees with free storage space and utilities. Food in the workplace results in fire and safety hazards, and problems with pest control. Should an organization deem that employee-accessible microwaves and refrigerators are desirable, however, the best place for this equipment is in the cafeteria, if for no other reason than it will be regularly sanitized. When a foodservice manages equipment holding employee-owned food or beverages, the best (and most common) policy to follow is that any foods, brown bags, or other items left in a refrigerator after 2:00 P.M. on Fridays will be thrown out by either custodial or foodservice staff.

Jones first understood the need for such a policy after the local Board of Health's registered sanitarian began to point out the potential health hazards that can arise when foods sit too long in a refrigerator. After that conversation, Jones added a statement to the organization's policy manual noting that AU was not liable for any products stored in the cafeteria's employee refrigerator, said piece of equipment having been provided solely for the convenience of employees. The sanitarian had also advised Jones that the employees' refrigerator should never be used to support foodservice activity, since the department had no control over who accessed that refrigerator. Janitorial and pest control services also increase when there is too much food stored and heated in work areas.

Disturbed by the potential negative effects of employee-run coffee makers and food-storage equipment, Jones had prepared for the meeting with Bell by writing a policy for her consideration. With both financial and health concerns weighing on his mind, Jones had decided to recommend that coffee pots be banned in work areas and that refrigerators and microwaves be accessible to employees only in foodservice cafeterias.

MOBILE CATERING TRUCKS

Another competing noncafeteria entity of which Jones (before his appointment to administer foodservice) had been completely unaware were the independently owned commercial catering trucks that Harry Daulton had referred to as "roach coaches." According to Harry, these catering trucks were self-contained businesses that solicit trade by driving up to the doors of local office and industrial buildings to offer employees anything from coffee and donuts to prewrapped sandwiches. Prior to receiving his foodservice orientation from the former foodservice director, Jones had had no idea that several of these trucks operated on AU's campus without either licensure or control. Over the past years, he had seen such catering trucks parked by various AU workplaces and had assumed (erroneously) that they were company-owned or, at least, company-controlled. He was particularly concerned when he realized that many of these vehicles did not have insurance and that AU would be liable for any accidents, food-borne illness, or other problems arising from their presence on AU property. He had all he could do to control what was AU's. He certainly did not need anyone else's foodservice problems.

Today, mobile catering trucks still fill a real foodservice need in the warehouse districts of many larger cities. This is because warehouses usually have too few employees to support a cafeteria, and "neighborhood" retail foodservice outlets are often few and far between. However, some mobile operators in every major population area are sure to have taken up the practice of driving onto the private campuses of large, local commercial and institutional organizations. These unauthorized entrepreneurs often find receptive customers among those workers (and others) who do not want to or do not have time to walk to the organization's cafeteria(s). Having assessed the situation at AU, Jones recognized that there were several factors that he needed to consider before he suggested a policy concerning these vendors:

- Mobile operators compete with organizations' authorized cafeteria programs. This means that while an organization is spending money to subsidize its cafeteria(s), some of its employees may be acting at cross-purposes by supporting uninvited, outside commercial vendors.
- In many areas of the country, mobile catering truck operators are not licensed or inspected for compliance with sanitary food-handling techniques nor do they carry adequate insurance. If mobile

catering trucks are not licensed or inspected and an organization knowingly permits them to operate on its property, it is the organization that becomes potentially liable for any problems resulting from the sale of foods prepared under unsanitary or unsafe conditions.

- An organization receives no fees or sales percentages from the operation of these mobile units on its campus.
- While it is possible to forge an agreement with one mobile catering truck operator to come onto a worksite and sell products in return for a sales percentage returned to the organization, these operators are difficult to supervise and monitor. However, such an agreement may represent a solution to the foodservice needs of individuals based at isolated organizational facilities, assuming, of course, that the authorized vendor maintains appropriate sanitation controls and liability insurance. The other alternative is for the organization to offer mobile service on its own.

Given the significant investment AU was making in improving and expanding its foodservice operations, Jones had decided to recommend that no mobile operators be allowed on campus during weekday working hours. "We may require some of our people to spend a few more minutes getting to our foodservice facilities," Jones reasoned to himself, "but considering the investment we're putting into our program, any other policy would be directly counterproductive." In addition to the current nontraditional foodservices, Jones had some ideas about new and expanded services that he had learned about from his new foodservice administrator friends. He would at least bring these ideas up with Bell for consideration. Those ideas were as follows:

- The company store was currently located in the basement of the administrative building. There was relatively little patronage, which had caused some talk of closing the operation. Jones wanted to propose an alternative. The empty space adjacent to the current cafeteria would be an ideal location for a combined convenience store with gift items bearing the AU logo, cards, and other items. He also envisioned a small line of typical sundries, cards, wrapping paper, convenience foods, and similar products. Everyone, at one time or another, left the building at lunch to pick up some essential items. Why not save them the trip, since if they did not have to go out they might buy lunch and get back to work on time? He thought the idea had merit and was going to seek

Bell's approval to do a cost/benefit analysis of such a move. Visitors were often taken to the cafeteria and might like the opportunity to buy a hat or tee-shirt with the company logo. Employees with their identification badges could be given a corporate discount on certain items in the convenience store. For sure, they would want to sell postage stamps and have a mail collection box at the store. The more he thought about it, the more he liked the idea. But, ever the conscientious Support Services administrator, Jones knew that both the market potential and the financial feasibility would need to be studied carefully before a decision was reached.

- How many times had he or his wife had to stop and pick up last-minute dinners because of their work schedules? Not to mention a birthday cake for a child's party, a dessert to serve to dinner guests, cookies to send to school for the Valentine's Day party, and sandwich fixings for school field trip lunches. The list was endless. Jones wanted to consider the potential of introducing retail deli and bakery sales in the cafeteria. Daulton had said that the facilities were underutilized and that the existing staff could produce the products. Again, Jones wanted Bell's concurrence that the idea merited an assessment of the market demand before proceeding.

If he could begin to build revenue that generated a net reduction in the current subsidy, he could begin to feel successful about his new foodservice responsibility. Besides, he honestly had to admit that he was beginning to like the somewhat "entreprenurial" feeling he got from administering foodservice. Jones wondered what Bell would have to say about his ideas.

CHAPTER NINE

Vending

It was now mid-August, and Jones thought he was beginning to understand the intricacies and scope of AU's foodservice operation. Then, out of the clear blue sky on a sultry Tuesday morning, Jones received a notice from the Contracts Department that the vending machines contract AU had with a local vending company was due to expire in 90 days. "Do you want to renew this contract?" was the only memo attached to a 2-page document that Jones found a challenge to read. Jones knew that the easy thing would be to send a return memo saying, "Sure, renew the contract under the current terms and conditions." "However," Jones mused, "doing the easy thing might also be a one-way ticket to failure." Before making any hasty decision on the vending contract, he figured that he had better spend some time learning more about vending machines.

VENDING BACKGROUND

Vending machines have been glowingly referred to as a "24-hour-a-day silent sales force" by the companies that sell and maintain them. The customers who use them regularly or periodically more often refer to these machines as "mechanical monsters" or "one-armed bandits that don't pay off as often as those at casinos." The truth about vending machines lies somewhere in the middle of these two schools of thought.

Despite some customers' hesitation about and/or frustrations with using them, vending machines are an excellent way of supporting and complementing a manual foodservice program. Depending on the number of people occupying and visiting a site/building, vending can also provide a source of revenue (in the form of gross sales or commissions) to support cafeteria operations and lower or even eliminate departmental subsidy. On many college and university campuses, for example, the revenue from vending often supports residence hall activity programs, athletic departments, and other auxiliary services. Some organizations, such as government entities, permit vending revenue to go toward the employee welfare fund.

Vending machines are defined as card-, coin-, or paper money-operated equipment that dispense either products or services (such as the information provided by bank machines). Contemporary vending machines are most often electronically operated and, depending on the products offered, may require water and drainage hook-ups. Some also offer products that customers will heat up in microwave ovens.

Each organization's philosophy or mission statement should contain some reference to vending. For example, a corporate guideline might specify that vending is to be a nonsubsidized employee service. In reality, where a number of organizational sites/buildings all operate within the same campus or geographic area, some vending locations serving relatively low population levels will, in fact, be subsidized by the others (if only via a lower-than-average commission structure, if not by direct payments to cover sales' shortfalls versus expenses). Overall, however, organizations rarely if ever should expect to have to subsidize vending programs specifically, unless they have a very small population base.

Vending machine technology is ever evolving. Machines continue to offer more features and capabilities (such as those that can produce a freshly baked pizza or fresh-made french fries). Given that most new machines operate via high-tech electronics, maintenance and repairs are generally quite complex, requiring specially trained technicians.

Organizations that own and operate their own vending programs do so for the following reasons:

- Vending can be an extremely profitable enterprise. In organizations in which there is significant support for vending machines, ample justification exists for purchasing the equipment and hiring the skilled personnel necessary to fill and maintain machines on a regular basis.
- There may be no foodservice contractors or vending companies in the local area that have the expertise and machine inventory necessary to build and sustain a successful program.

Another aspect of contracted vending services' financial performance is the potential to earn revenue in the form of commissions. Commissions are generally offered if certain criteria are in place. Enough potential vending business should exist to generate sales that will cover or exceed a contractor's variable (products and labor) and fixed (taxes, depreciation, insurance, etc.) costs of doing business. As with any business, the better the sales volume, the lower the costs as a percentage and the greater the profit margin. In essence, commissions are a form of profit sharing. Commissions are sometimes provided as a percentage of anticipated total vending sales for all machines/product types. In other cases, a vending contractor will offer commissions based on the anticipated sales volume for each product type. As an example: hot beverages and cold post-mix drinks have relatively low product costs, so the commission payment may be higher than that offered for cold foods such as sandwiches, fresh fruit, or salads. Cold foods usually have a higher product cost and a limited shelf life, so their waste factors can be extremely high.

Commissions or net income from vending can be integrated into foodservice's overall profit and loss statement or recorded separately. Depending on how individual administrators choose to account for vending revenues, commissions can be deposited into an organization's general bank account as "incidental revenue" or be given over to an employee welfare or activities fund.

To help administrators maximize the financial performance of a foodservice's vending component, the following questions need to be answered:

- How many machines of each product category are located in the facilities?
- Where are machines of each product category located? Are the majority of machines located in central, easy-to-access, or heavily trafficked areas? If not, how expensive would it be to relocate these machines?
- How much in monthly sales is each machine generating?
- Are money-changing machines available? If not, are individual vending machines capable of accepting and making change from $1 and $5 bills?

Should an organization choose not to self-operate its vending program but to turn its operation over to an outside vending management company, expect certain minimum financial criteria to be applied. For instance, most vending management companies will require a minimum level of sales be guaranteed before they will install and maintain a vending machine in a client's location. What's more, even those organizations that elect to self-operate vending may find it advantageous to use this option to provide a service option in locations where a manual foodservice operation would require a much higher subsidy.

GETTING STARTED WITH VENDING

Due to the cost of vending machines and the technological training necessary to maintain them, as well as restocking schedules and accounting for collected cash, most organizations choose *not* to own their own vending machines. Instead, most enter into a contract with vending management companies to provide, maintain, stock, and handle cash from the machines.

Many vending contractors are willing to pay a percentage of sales as a commission to client-organizations. The commission percentage usually depends on the number of persons (potential customers) and the size of a particular workplace, class building, residence hall, or other location, as well as the actual or anticipated sales volume. These commissions represent important revenue, as they may be applied against a cafeteria subsidy or used to pay for other programs/services. For instance, one organization uses its vending revenue to provide two scholarships each year for the children of employees who are attending college. Another one uses its vending funds to aid several local families during the holidays each year. Yet another organization has used vending revenue to offset the cafeteria subsidy incurred by offering manual foodservice to second-shift employees. As mentioned earlier, the use of vending income is limited only by the policies and mission of your organization.

TYPES OF VENDING MACHINES

The vending industry has made considerable technological progress over the past 10 to 15 years and now offers a wide array of machines.

Some machines produce a hot, fresh-brewed cup of regular coffee, decaffeinated coffee, or tea, along with requested portions of sugar, sweetener, and milk (or milk substitute). Today, these machines can even provide a full range of gourmet coffee beverages, such as cappuccinos, lattes, and espresso drinks. Some hot liquid machines vend a variety of soups. However, if the use of private coffee pots is widespread in various parts of a facility or if a free coffee program exists, these units would probably not be profitable.

Jones recalled a fellow foodservice administrator relating a situation that might have some appeal to AU. That person's company had allowed coffee pots in the workplace for several years and wanted to remove them, primarily for sanitation and fire prevention purposes but also to support the cafeteria/vending operations. In order to "ease employee reaction," the company had installed vending equipment that offered hot brewed coffee, bouillon, and hot chocolate. The coffee was on "free-play," that is, no charge, and the other liquids were given regular pricing. It was anticipated that the subsidy cost would be less than the costs of cleaning the old coffee stations. The real surprise was that the machines actually broke even, due to the sales of the other beverages. During a couple months, there was even a small profit.

Cold beverage machines come in two types. The first, and most prevalent in the vending industry, is a unit that simultaneously mixes syrups with carbonated water and ice to produce sodas. The second type of unit, most popular with the buying public, simply dispenses from four to six kinds of canned drinks of the kind available for purchase in grocery stores. Vending management companies prefer that their clients install the first type of machine because of its lower product cost and higher potential commission/profit margin. It should be noted that vending customers generally prefer canned soda machines. However, depending on the area in which your organization operates, local regulations or expectations may require foodservice to establish a process for recycling empty soda cans. In some instances, there will be the opportunity to offer both types at different price points so patrons have a choice.

Another issue arising from the operation of cold beverage machines is the source of the machines and product. Some entities, such as college residence halls, are going directly to soda distributors and/or bottlers and negotiating higher commission rates in return for exclusive rights to provide that product. This arrangement results in the exclusive use of one brand's products at a given location. An example of this would be if all cold beverages would be supplied by Coca-Cola, PepsiCo, Royal Crown, or another company that provided the machines. Some canned juice vendors also enter into these exclusive right agreements.

Candy/snack merchandisers are window-display units that can offer a wide range of snack (chips, cookies, crackers, etc.) and candy choices at an equally wide range of prices. These machines can also be used to merchandise sundry items such as combs, panty hose, aspirin, or other pocket items.

Hot/cold food merchandiser units come in a number of variations, all of which are used to merchandise and sell ready-to-heat items (foods that need to be microwaved after purchase) and cold foods. Product selections usually range from chilled entrées and sandwiches to hamburgers, pizzas, hot dogs, and breakfast sandwiches that customers can rethermalize in microwave ovens. These machines can also hold chilled "side" items such as salads, fresh fruit, yogurt, and cheese snacks, to name just a few.

Ice creams freezer units are designed to dispense three to four varieties of ice cream novelties, including bars and sandwiches.

Though most people are personally familiar with cigarette machines, they are rapidly becoming "extinct" as more and more organizations declare their facilities to be nonsmoking areas. Given cigarettes' relatively high sale price, these vending machines (if they are to be installed at all) should be equipped with a dollar bill acceptor.

Wherever foodservice operates hot/cold food merchandisers, a condiment stand and microwave ovens should be conveniently located nearby. A well-stocked condiment stand will offer napkins, serviceware, straws, and, of course, condiments (including catsup, mustard, mayonnaise, and relishes) appropriate for the hot and cold foods offered. In some instances, it is wise to insert single-service condiment packets within food packages. Mayonnaise and mustard packets should be packaged along with a prewrapped sandwich and catsup and mustard provided with a hot dog. This is advantageous because without this control, there is a tendency for these convenient condiments to make their way to picnics, camping trips, school lunch bags, and a variety of other places not related to the sale of product in the vending machines. In addition, to lend convenient and potentially profitable support to a condiment stand, some vending companies are now providing coin-operated microwave ovens.

$1 and $5 bill changer machines act as support units for vending machines. Vending companies have found that sales increase dramatically when a bill changer is located near product machines. However, many food and drink machines are now equipped with their own $1 and $5 acceptor mechanisms, thus precluding the need for separate changer units.

A blood pressure tester is one example of the many new "service-vending" machines that can attract new customers to a vending area. Other such units include video cassette machines and postage stamp machines.

VENDING PROGRAM SPECIFICATIONS

When administrators prepare specifications for their vending programs, they will want to make sure that a selected vending contractor will supply new and/or recently refurbished machines. However, no matter who is managing a vending program, all vending units should have electronic coin mechanisms installed as standard equipment.

Having reliable, state-of-the-art coin and bill acceptor mechanisms is important because numerous studies have shown that the vast majority of customer/client service calls are placed due to problems with coins and/or the mechanical device that accepts them. Modern electronic mechanisms dramatically reduce these types of service calls because there is less chance that coins will jam in them.

When an out-of-order vending machine results in people losing money, customers will usually choose to stop using all the machines. The net result of nonfunctional vending equipment will be reduced service to customers and lost revenue. That's why it is vital to have a system that makes the refund process easy and hassle-free for customers and the personnel in charge of the machines. If the number of refunds is high, there may be a need for more regular service calls plus an easy means of contacting the vending provider to fix the out-of-order machine(s).

VENDING MACHINE SELECTION AND PLACEMENT

Administrators should consider several points when selecting and placing vending machines at building sites. A list of the criteria generally used in these situations should include the following:

- Sufficient facility population (including visitors/students).
- Duration of time when a majority of the available population uses a site where vending equipment is located.
- Facility location and anticipated walking distances and traffic patterns to/from population concentrations.
- Availability of floor space and utilities (as well as proximity to other facilities/services such as rest rooms).
- Ability to provide security coverage. In remote areas, vending machines are subject to vandalism and theft. There may be a need to install electronic alarms as well as make sure the areas are well lighted.
- Proximity to cafeteria or other manual foodservice facilities (if any) and their hours of operation.
- Proximity of local restaurants/convenience stores.

Deciding which type of vending machines should be placed within a facility will largely depend on whether a cafeteria operates on campus and how large employee and visitor populations are on an average day. It is critical that machines be conveniently placed in main traffic locations if they are to be convenient for employees, as well as financially successful. When these criteria are respected, a candy/snack merchandiser(s) and cold drink machine(s) at a minimum can be installed in almost every facility. The facility's population level and customers' manifested demand for other types of products will dictate which additional machines should be selected. For instance, there may be minimal demand for a snack merchandiser in an office building with a cafeteria, but a very high demand in one without. Snack vendors, on the other hand, are often very popular in college residence halls where night owls are likely to look for snacks at all hours.

Since most vending equipment is expensive, whoever is in charge of the program, especially an outside contractor, will generally want to conduct a survey and/or install certain machines on a conditional (trial) basis before beginning a full-fledged program. Most vending management groups have weekly sales-per-product averages that must be consistently realized before they will be assured that it is financially feasible to install a costly machine permanently. Also, please note that those required averages will go up proportionately if commissions must be paid to clients or if the installation of other pieces of non-revenue-generating equipment (such as microwave ovens or bill changers) is required. It is important to remember that if a client-organization does not wish to subsidize any single vending unit, management or employee requests for additional machines must first be cost-justified according to these criteria.

SAMPLE VENDING CONTRACTS

A sample vending contract has been included on the enclosed computer disk and in Exhibit 9-1 at the end of this chapter. As with the sample foodservice contract presented in Chapter 4 (Exhibit 4-4), this document is designed to serve as the basis for negotiations with a selected vending supplier. Most of the clauses are self-explanatory or have already been explained in Chapter 4. Some of the key vending contract points to take into consideration include the following:

- Be sure that the contract specifies clearly how many machines, which types and where machines are to be installed.
- Minimum product selections and minimum fill levels should be specified in appropriate addenda.

- If applicable, the conditions under which a machine may be either relocated within or removed from a location should be stated.
- The use of state-of-the-art electronic coin and currency acceptor mechanisms should be required on all equipment.
- Expectations for the availability of and promptness of response by service personnel should be presented, with special care given to the availability and speed of support when vending equipment is being used most heavily.
- If applicable, the percentage and potential dollar commission structure proposed should be specified. Generally, these figures are determined via a competitive bid process. However, there are some instances in which the rate of return is fixed to avoid any contractor buying business, then raising prices to cover the commission. In some cases, the returns are fixed at a low rate and the contractors are asked to propose the lowest possible merchandise prices.
- The selected vending supplier must agree to meet all of the client's insurance and security requirements prior to be being permitted access to sites/facility.

The last element Jones knew he had to consider was the commission structure. The old contract gave a flat commission on all combined vending sales. In discussion with his peers, Jones learned that, given the wide range of profit margin on different products, it might be better to consider asking for different commission rates on different products. Beverage machines generally yield the highest commissions, with cold food machines generally at the bottom of the list. He made a mental note to review the previous year's vending report and apply a varied commission structure to determine whether AU would have benefited from such a program.

The process for auditing vending performance is relatively simple. Periodically, administrators will need to survey all locations where vending equipment is located to make sure that whoever is serving as operator is meeting the terms and conditions of the signed contract. Some of the more important points to be evaluated include the following:

- Are machines being maintained in a clean, sanitary condition? Both interior surfaces and exteriors should be inspected.
- Do machines contain product varieties specified, as well as sufficient quantities of each type of item?
- Are all available products still within their freshness "pull" dates?

The above checks will have to be done when machines are being serviced or with the assistance of a contractor's representative who has a key to open vending units. In many cases, cold food vending machine(s) may be under the management of foodservice's cafeteria operator. This is often an efficient arrangement when foods are to be provided for second- and/or third-shift staff.

- Do machines have properly installed and operating electronic coin and bill acceptor mechanisms?
- Does the condiment stand have the specified type and number of napkins, straws, serviceware, and, if applicable, catsup, mustard, and similar items?
- If the vending operator's responsibilities include maintaining the area surrounding machines, are the condiment stand(s) and microwave oven(s) clean and/or in good working order?

If any deficiencies are discovered, administrators should submit their findings in writing to the vending operator and immediate resolution should be anticipated.

"Well," thought Jones, "as I see it, in regard to our about-to-expire vending contract, we have three choices:

1. Buy the machines and operate them ourselves. Somehow, that doesn't seem like the smart thing to do at this time. If AU already owned the machines, then that might be the way to go. However, buying or leasing the machines and assuming all of the responsibility for servicing and filling them would require skills that neither we nor our cafeteria staff currently possess.
2. Solicit proposals from a variety of vending contractors and keep the vending program separate from manual foodservices. If our manual foodservice remains self-operated, this would probably be our most viable option.
3. Renew the current supplier's contract for the short term so that if we put manual foodservice out to contract the two could be wrapped into one contract with one provider."

Given the complexity of foodservice (as Jones was beginning to recognize), the third alternative seemed to be the most efficient route for AU to take. "That's it. I will recommend to Patricia Bell that we make the vending contractor report to our manual foodservice management." People at another corporation had told Jones how much easier it was to supervise one rather than two separate foodservice contractors.

Exhibit 9-1
SAMPLE VENDING CONTRACT

[What follows is a generic vending contract format that should be used as a guide in preparing a similar document for your organization. It should be understood that there will be a number of items that will need to be changed or deleted to fit your specific requirements. In addition, there will be a need to add points in the appropriate section(s) or even add new sections in order to address subjects or legal concerns unique to your situation. Please carefully review and evaluate each point to assure yourself and all concerned within your respective organization that the contract and attachments truly reflect all critical minimum requirements. All notes presented within brackets [] should be deleted once the primary draft has been completed.]

1.0 BACKGROUND AND SCOPE

1.1 ___________ (hereinafter referred to as the Organization) is soliciting proposals to provide vended foodservice to its employees and guests. The following document outlines contract specifications for providing vended foodservice. For the purpose of this document, vending is defined as a distribution method for food and beverage products using coin-operated machines.

1.1.1 The contract specifications discussed in this document are designed to communicate to the foodservice vending company (hereinafter referred to as the Contractor) requirements that are important for improving vending foodservice to the Organization's employees and guests. It is the intent of the Organization to offer a quality line of food items and related merchandise for prices at or below that found in the local area on a 24-hour-per-day basis. The vending Contractor will be responsible for providing and maintaining quality foodservice and public relations to all Organization employees, visitors, and guests.

1.2 Individual facilities descriptions are contained in Exhibit xxx. Each facility is described in terms of

- Facility population
- Population demographics
- Organization/Foodservice administrator's name
- Hours of cafeteria operation
- List of current and/or required vending machines, condiment tables, change machine(s), and microwave oven(s) by location, and any special instructions

2.0 VENDING PHILOSOPHY

2.1 The operation of the Organization vended foodservice should be guided by the philosophy that the Organization maintains that vended foodservice is provided as an employee convenience. As a result, it should provide quality products and service at a competitively advantageous price level. In Organization facilities where there

Exhibit 9-1 continued

are cafeterias, vending is to complement the products and services offered. In Organization facilities where there is no cafeteria, vending is to offer a wider range of products and services. Toward that end, the Organization is willing to provide the space and utilities necessary to accomplish this objective. The Organization is not, however, willing to subsidize or underwrite any direct costs of operations.

3.0 RESPONSIBILITIES OF ORGANIZATION

3.1 The Organization will provide the Contractor with suitable space for the placement of the agreed-upon vending machines and areas for the consumption of vended items where applicable. Additional ancillary equipment, such as condiment tables, change machines, and microwave ovens provided by the Organization, are listed in Exhibit xxx.

3.2 The Organization reserves the right to review, inspect, evaluate, and request changes in the operation and condition of vended foodservice at any time with respect to the quality and quantity of food served, prices of all food/beverage items, and generally with respect to safety, sanitation, and maintenance of vending machines and ancillary equipment.

3.3 The Organization shall furnish without cost to the Contractor all necessary utilities and service connections for the operation of said vending machines.

3.4 The Organization shall furnish the services of its maintenance staff, as required for the proper installation and maintenance up to the wall or floor connections for said vending machines and equipment, utilities (including plumbing and wiring), and their use in operations thereof.

4.0 RESPONSIBILITIES OF CONTRACTOR

4.1 General

4.1.1 The Contractor shall furnish all food, beverage, supplies, equipment specified and all management and labor necessary for the nutritional, sanitary, and efficient operation of the vending program included in this document.

4.1.2 All vending machines and currency changers (these may be built-in bill acceptors in the vending machines) will be kept in proper operating order and at appropriate fill levels at all times.

4.1.3 Unless otherwise indicated in Exhibit xxx, the Contractor shall install and maintain, at its expense, vending machines, currency changers, condiment stands, and microwave ovens that are adequate to provide vended food and beverage service for Organization employees and guests. The Organization will exercise the right to approve the products and locations for all machines, and to add or remove locations as necessary. The Organization will not be responsible for loss or damage to

Exhibit 9-1 continued

vending machines, their content or related equipment resulting from any cause whatsoever.

4.1.4 The Contractor will provide to the Organization, on a quarterly basis, a complete and updated listing of all vending machines by type and placement. In addition, the Organization is to receive route fill schedules, and maintenance and cleaning checklists.

4.1.5 The Contractor shall obtain at its own expense any permits, licenses, or bonds required by this agreement, any federal, state, municipal, or county ordinance or regulations and shall pay at its sole expense all taxes lawfully assessed in connection with the delivery of vended foodservice.

4.1.6 All prices and portions of food and beverages in the vending machines must be approved by the Organization's foodservice administrator prior to the time they go into effect in the machines. The Organization acknowledges that manufacturers periodically reduce or increase portions of packaged items, which results in a corresponding wholesale price adjustment. At the time such a price adjustment is required and approved, the Organization will expect documentation and sufficient research to show to the Organization that no other comparable product is available or would be acceptable. Sufficient lead time (a minimum of 14 days) will be required to communicate changes to employees prior to implementation.

4.1.7 Unless otherwise specified in Exhibit xxx, the Contractor shall supply machines for holding cold food that can be prepared in a microwave oven. The Contractor shall also supply the microwave oven and condiment stand.

4.1.8 The Contractor will reimburse employees of the Organization and guests for money lost through equipment malfunction, nondelivery of items, or stale or spoiled products. The Organization will establish and approve the procedure for employee and guest reimbursement. The Contractor will be expected to cooperate with the manual foodservice contractor in providing refunds where applicable.

4.2 Facilities and Equipment

4.2.1 The vending machines installed pursuant to this document will remain the property of the Contractor, which shall have the right, at any reasonable time and on no less than fifteen (15) days' notice, to remove and replace any machine as mutually agreed.

4.2.2 At the onset of this contract, all vending machines shall be factory new within 24 months, of modern design, automatic with modular fronts, uniformly painted, and equipped with the latest electronic coin *[and/or $1 and $5 bill acceptors]* mecha-

Exhibit 9-1 continued

nisms that accept combinations of nickels, dimes, and quarters. Manufacturer logo beverage machines may be used with the approval of the Organization. All vending machines and currency changers shall be equipped with tamper-proof counters and electronic coin return mechanisms.

4.2.3 The machines shall be designed, constructed, and installed in accordance with the standards of the National Sanitation Foundation, the National Automatic Merchandising Association, and Occupational Safety and Health Act. These machines shall be operated in compliance with the requirements of the state and local health codes.

4.2.4 The Contractor will provide maintenance coverage of all machines on an 8- to 24-hour basis, and will provide the Organization with a summary of any service/maintenance calls, and records of repair on a quarterly basis. The maintenance coverage will be on a two (2)-hour response time basis.

4.2.5 The Contractor shall remove coins from machines at regular intervals. The Organization reserves the right to have a representative present and verify the count at any time.

4.2.6 The Contractor will provide the Organization with a summary of service schedules (including money pick-ups).

4.2.7 The Contractor is responsible for cleaning machines (front, tops, behind, underneath). In addition, the interiors of all equipment must be kept in a sanitary condition.

4.3 Vending Specifications

4.3.1 Minimum specifications for vended food items are listed in Exhibit xxx.

4.3.2 The Contractor will document the types and portions of items to be vended, including entrees, subject to approval by the Organization.

4.3.3 No fresh, packaged, or prepackaged food products will be sold beyond the established expiration date or time at which the product is no longer fresh and saleable.

4.4 Personnel and Supervision

4.4.1 All Contractor personnel shall be subject to Organization regulations regarding personal behavior as well as access to/and use of Organization facilities.

4.4.2 The Contractor will comply with all federal, state, and local rules and regulations regarding the employment of personnel.

4.4.3 The Contractor, at its cost, will furnish its employees with uniforms. The Organization will have prior approval of uniform style. The Contractor will be responsible for assuring that the

Exhibit 9-1 continued

uniforms are clean and neat in appearance at all times. Uniforms will be standard to each unit or group of units.

4.4.4 All employees of the Contractor must have acceptable personal hygiene for vended foodservice work and shall wear identification badges specific to that unit. A Contractor's name tag is acceptable identification if the Contractor's employee enters through a specified lobby/entrance where a Organization representative can verify his or her employment status. Any Contractor's employee that necessitates unrestricted movement throughout the Organization facilities will require a Contractor's badge and also be in uniform. The Contractor's badge will include the individual's picture, an authorized signature, and an expiration date. These Contractor employee identification badges will be supplied by the Organization.

4.4.5 The Contractor will not permit gambling or other unlawful practices of any kind on Organization premises by its employees.

4.5 Accounting and Financial Control

4.5.1 All correspondence pertaining to vending services shall be directed to the Organization. There shall be no verbal deviations whatsoever from this document without the prior written approval of the Organization.

4.5.2 The Organization reserves the right to audit any aspect of the financial records regarding vended foodservice, as performed by the Contractor, according to generally accepted accounting and auditing practices. The Contractor shall make said books of accounts, supporting data, and document available for inspection and reproduction. The Contractor will maintain an audit trail to back up all financial and operational reports given to the Organization for a minimum of two (2) years. These reports will be subject to an audit by the Organization.

4.5.3 The Organization is on a monthly business cycle with the fiscal year beginning [insert date]. The Contractor will supply vending sales information, which will include sales by product (machine) type and location, cost of sales, cost of labor, and total commissions payable for each product (machine) type. It will pay the Organization monthly *[or accounting period]* commissions of an amount equal to [XX] percentage of total and/or by product categories, whichever is the greater of gross *[or net if sales or use taxes are to be deducted]* food and beverage vending sales. Within fifteen (15) days of the end of the month, the Contractor shall submit to the Organization a statement for the operation of the vending during the preceding period.

4.5.4 Collection of cash from vending machines is the sole responsibility of the Contractor.

Exhibit 9-1 continued

4.5.5 The Contractor shall maintain accurate, complete and separate books of accounts according to accepted standards of accounting, reflecting its operations of Organization units, together with appropriate supporting data and documents.

4.5.6 The Contractor shall provide such special reports covering its operation as may be requested by the Organization.

4.5.7 On request of the Organization, the Contractor shall meet with the Organization and review each period statement, explain deviations, discuss problems, and mutually agree on a course of action to improve the results of vended services.

4.6 Assignment

4.6.1 Vending may be subcontracted, but the Organization reserves the right to review and approve the selected vending Organization, its contract with the Contractor, and any aspects of operation/maintenance of vending machines.

4.6.2 In the event that all or a portion of the vending is subcontracted, it is fully understood that the Contractor is responsible for administration of that subcontract. It is the Contractor's responsibility for reimbursing employees of the Organization and guests for any money lost through equipment malfunction, nondelivery of items, or stale or spoiled products.

4.6.3 The Contractor shall indemnify and hold harmless the Organization from any loss, damage, expense, or liability that may result by reason of any infringement, or claim of infringement of any U.S. patent, trademark or copyright by any equipment or process utilized by the Contractor with respect to performance of its obligations.

4.7 Inspections and Complaints

4.7.1 The vending services discussed in this document will be inspected for sanitation, food handling, food portion standards, safety, quality of food and service, or any other valid reason. After each inspection, the Contractor will be advised in writing of unsatisfactory conditions for which the Contractor is responsible. The Contractor will promptly correct such deficiencies and communicate in writing the solution to each problem, when it was corrected, and what has been done to prevent recurrence of the problem, within ten (10) business days. Repeated unsatisfactory inspections will be cause for contract termination.

4.7.2 Discrepancies/disputes between the Organization and Contractor are to be settled in a timely fashion. If ten (10) business days have elapsed after written documentation has been sent to and received at the Contractor's regional *[or headquarters]* office by the Organization, and no acceptable Contractor

Exhibit 9-1 continued

response has occurred or been received, this will be cause for contract termination.

4.8 Insurance

4.8.1 The Contractor will furnish the Organization with Certificates of Insurance covering workers' compensation, employees' liability insurance, and comprehensive general liability insurance in the amount of not less than $1 million per occurrence plus any other mandated insurance. These certificates will provide for 30 days' notice to the Organization of any cancellations and failure to renew.

4.9 Indemnity

4.9.1 The Contractor will defend, indemnify, and hold the Organization, its officers, agents, and employees harmless from any and all liability for bodily injury, sickness, or disease, including death resulting therefrom, or damage, destruction, or loss of use of any property arising out of or in any way connected with sales, possession, or distribution of any product, foodstuff, or beverage or from any operation in rendering service to the Organization, its employees, or their guests or from any act or omission, negligent or otherwise, of the Contractor or any of its employees, agents, servants, or any other persons, excepting only the employees of the Organization whose activities the Contractor does not have the right to control.

4.10 Independent Contractor

4.10.1 The Contractor is an independent contractor and will not under any circumstances be considered an employee, servant, or agent of the Organization, nor will the employees, servants, or agents of the Contractor be considered as employees, servants, or agents of the Organization and neither the Contractor nor its employees, servants, or agents have any authority to bind the Organization in any respect whatsoever.

4.11 Termination

4.11.1 In addition to the quarterly reviews of the Contractor's performance and normal provisions for termination upon default of the Contractor, the Organization shall have the right to terminate the arrangement if for any reason the Contractor fails to provide continuous vending service in any of the designated locations for two (2) consecutive working days/or the Contractor's labor relations result in picketing at any of the Organization's facilities. *[The last portion of this clause should be carefully considered.]* Consistently unsatisfactory sanitation as well as unresolved customer complaints will also be considered just cause for termination.

Exhibit 9-1 continued

4.11.2 Either party may terminate this arrangement or any individual unit at any time without cause by giving proper notice. The Contractor may terminate by giving not less than ninety (90) days' notice to the Organization. The Organization may terminate by giving not less than thirty (30) days' notice to the Contractor.

CHAPTER TEN

Equipment and New Technology

One morning in May, while going through the programming process described in Chapter 7, Jones commented to the members of his task force that he was absolutely astounded how expensive it was to build or refurbish and equip a foodservice facility. The construction and equipment cost estimates prepared by the architect and food facility planner were "positively scary," Jones said, envisioning AU's capital projects personnel becoming apoplectic at the projected costs. To prevent this humbling scenario, he decided that it was time to do some more homework on the subject.

He first faxed a request to his food facilities consultant and foodservice management consultant requesting books he could study and local foodservice operations he could visit to acquire more information about kitchen equipment. As luck would have it, a major food equipment show was scheduled to take place in Chicago during the third week of May. Sponsored by the National Restaurant Association, this show not only features equipment, but also more food and supply items than can be found at any other industry gathering. (Information on this and other resources can be found in Chapter 14.)

In order to get a better handle on AU's current foodservice equipment situation, Jones set up an appointment to meet with Harry Daulton's replacement, and the two consultants in order to conduct another kitchen and servery walk-through. This time, the inspecting team would focus its attention on assessing the state of the equipment. Jones outlined the discussion points this inspection team would consider:

- Does AU maintain repair and service records for each piece of equipment? If not, does the foodservice department maintain a record of breakdowns, how long each took to fix, and cost impact? Also, have any records been maintained citing why equipment broke down?
- Is there local repair and maintenance service available?
- Do we know what each piece of equipment cost, who it was purchased from, and when?
- Which process or procedure is used to purchase and/or justify each major equipment acquisition? Has a cost/benefit analysis been performed prior to the purchase of specialty pieces of equipment, such as the new conveyor pizza oven and the four-head espresso maker recently suggested for the new foodservice facility?
- How easy or difficult is each piece of equipment to operate? Specifically, what do the foodservice staff like and dislike about each piece?
- Which local or state codes dictate which equipment is appropriate for use in a foodservice facility?
- Lacking, or in lieu of, mandated requirements, are there foodservice industry standards that suggest minimum equipment performance standards or useful life?
- What is the difference between capital equipment and smallwares?
- How are smallwares being purchased and accounted for now?

After compiling this list, Jones paused, thinking, "That last point may well be the most important." Basically, he wanted to know if there was a way to manage AU's capital and smallwares assets better. He decided that he had best reorganize his list and concentrate first on ascertaining the difference between capital items and smallwares. Fortunately, this first piece of information was available from AU's purchasing department. Jones learned AU defined its capital items as follows:

> "If an item has a purchase price in excess of $500 and it is intended to be a permanent fixture, it will be classified as capital equipment.
>
> If the purchase price is in excess of $500 for any one piece of equipment, regardless of its useful life, it will be considered capital equipment."

The memo went on to define smallwares as:

> "All those items necessary to support the preparation and service of food with a per piece value of under $500." Smallwares include such items as pots, pans, serving utensils, china, glassware, serving platters/bowls, carving boards, and related items."

Instinctively, Jones already knew the answers he was going to get to his original question on managing smallwares. Can we buy new capital items? His prior conversations with Michele Larkin regarding the poor condition of the foodservice's equipment and production facility provided proof of a valid need for new equipment. The purpose for the second walk-through and discussion was to establish a process for dealing with equipment purchasing, maintenance, and replacement issues in the future.

EQUIPMENT PURCHASES

Most organizations look at food equipment purchases in two ways. The first consideration is whether a piece of equipment is to be replaced with a like or comparable item. The second consideration comes into play when a new, additional piece of equipment is being requested for a variety of reasons. Since most organizations have a Purchasing Department that has specific procedures, the following information will focus on those specific to foodservice. In general, the purchasing process will follow this sequence:

1. If foodservice needs to make a replacement purchase, the department should secure a statement and/or documentation that the equipment being replaced is beyond repair and/or has become prohibitively expensive to maintain.
2. Telephone calls or visits must be made to the food facilities consultant or to local equipment suppliers to determine which equipment is available and the potential purchase/installation costs. This information should be used to prepare a capital equipment appropriation request. In some cases, the Purchasing Department will actually secure bids at this point. In others, submitted estimates will be used to secure approval.

   Given that many organizations prepare their capital expenditure budgets up to two years in advance, Support Service administrators need to anticipate which pieces of foodservice equipment might need replacing and new purchase requests. A related concern for administrators is the reality that it can take from six to eight months or longer to get a capital budget approved, and more time yet to initiate the actual purchasing process. In either case, unless equipment replacement and new purchasing plans are made early enough, foodservice will suffer a negative operational and cost impact while the paperwork wends its way through the process.

3. Once equipment has been ordered, it will probably be necessary to coordinate the removal of the old pieces and installation of new ones with the Building Maintenance department. In some cases, the work will have to be done when the kitchen is closed; otherwise, the food preparation/service process will be disrupted. No work should be done that would adversely affect the quality and safety of the food.

   Unless the equipment being replaced is headed for the junkyard, there will be a corresponding need to ascertain its current market value and dispose of it in accordance with the organization's established procedures. In many cases, there are legitimate charities that would appreciate receiving such equipment even though it no longer has a useful life at an organization's foodservice.

4. Prior to regular use, an equipment supplier or installer should demonstrate how the equipment should be used. A separate demonstration should be given to the maintenance staff who will have responsibility for repairing the unit once its warranty has expired. If a training videotape is not supplied with the equipment, it is an excellent idea to prepare your own video. It can be used as a training tool in the future for all new foodservice and maintenance personnel.

5. If foodservice wishes to purchase a new, additional piece of equipment, some cost/benefit justification will likely have to be provided. For instance, it might have to be shown that the equipment will either enhance sales or its use will allow staff to be more productive/efficient. In either case, foodservice management will need to prepare some form of analysis that will permit upper management to make an informed decision. An example of a cost/benefit analysis follows.

Item:	Espresso Machine
Purpose:	Enhance sales/offer patrons a new service
Direct Cost:	$4,500 (estimated installed price, including plumbing and electrical modifications)
Indirect Costs:	Maintenance shop will remodel existing counter, facia, and signing prior to installation at an estimated cost of $1,200. Electrical utility costs will increase by approximately $20 per month, based on manufacturer's estimated power usage on a per hour basis.
Justification:	The popularity of espresso and related coffee drinks in this geographic region is readily apparent. A recent employee survey revealed that 65 percent of the current building population, or 1,050 persons, would purchase an espresso drink one or more times per week if available.
Cost/Benefit Basis:	Current average daily coffee sales (2,800 cups) @ $.50 = $1,400
	Assume: 25 percent loss to espresso station or avg. daily sales = $1,050
	Espresso sales (800 cups,[1] which represent 700 current coffee drinkers and 100 new patrons @ $1.45 avg. purchase) = $1,160
	New sales = $810 per day[2]
	Product cost = $182.25
	Labor cost = 224.50
	Benefits = 56.00
	Supplies = 18.00
	Management = 80.00

[1] Although 65 percent of the survey respondents indicated that they would purchase an espresso drink one or more times per week, 25 percent was discounted to effect a more conservative customer volume projection.

[2] Foodservice management believes that patrons will probably buy more pastries (in the morning) and cookies/biscotti (in the afternoon) than at present. These additional sales were not factored into this payback analysis.

	Overhead[3]	=	75.00
	Total		$635.75 per day
	Daily Profit	=	$174.25
Payback:	Machine Cost	=	$4,500
	Install Cost	=	1,200
	Total Cost	=	$5,700
	Daily Profit	=	$ 174.25
	Payback Period	=	33 Days

[3] Includes electrical power cost allocation of $20 per day plus $10 reserve for equipment maintenance.

In any payback analysis, the rule of reason must apply. That is, everyone must be convinced that there is a good likelihood that the projected number of patrons per day will actually dine with foodservice, and that staff will be able to serve those customers within the peak and off-peak service times as anticipated. In the case of AU's proposed espresso machine, the labor portion of the analysis assumed that there would be as many as four staff persons working at the new station at peak times. Two persons would take orders and collect money while the other two (baristas) would prepare the espresso drinks. During slow or off-peak business periods, two of the staff would be assigned to other functions (such as serving as cashiers during lunch).

There are, of course, many other reasons to consider purchasing new or replacement pieces of foodservice equipment. New, more modern preparation and cooking equipment can create additional staff efficiencies, improve food quality and consistency, and offer more energy efficiency. In some cases, such as conveyor ovens, deep-fat fryers, and coffee brewers, foodservice equipment has become automated to the point where a simple press of a button will control all processes. This means that such equipment can either free a cook to do some other task or that a person with limited foodservice training can be employed to operate the equipment.

Here is an example of a much larger equipment purchase that could result in significant labor savings and productivity improvements:

Item:	20-foot flight dishmachine with a 24-module/6-slide capacity tray accumulator with all appropriate stainless steel sinks, disposer, and work tables

Purpose:	Permit dishwashing section to be operated by fewer employees at both peak and off-peak times
Direct Cost:	$120,000 (estimated installed price)
Indirect Costs:	While the old equipment is to be removed as part of the installer's contract, maintenance will refinish and paint walls, install new light fixtures, and do general repairs at an estimated cost of $1,750. It is not anticipated that electrical utility bills will increase.
Justification:	During peak meal periods, trays are being returned to the cafeteria at the rate of eight per minute or 480 per hour. With the present conveyor system, a total of six employees must work in the dishroom. Three employees must pull trays off the mechanical transporter, break them down, and load dishes into various racks prior to being washed. One employee loads the racks into the machine while another one unloads the racks after they come out of the final rinse process. The sixth employee then transports the dishes, glassware, and serviceware to various service points. Once the peak period activity diminishes, some of the dishwashers are assigned cleaning tasks in the kitchen, but there is usually a daily two- to three-hour period where there is little or no work for any of the dishwashers to do. The reality is that these staff were hired to work through the peak period, but must be given a full eight-hour day or they will quit.
Cost/Benefit Basis:	A flight-type dishwasher would allow a number of dishes to be placed directly on the belt while cups, glasses, and flatware would still be placed in racks. Because of the tray accumulator and a more efficient layout and design, one employee would

be able to pull and break down the trays instead of the three it currently takes. The employee formerly loading racks would now be placing plates directly on the conveyor belt for washing. Two of the tray-puller positions would thus be eliminated.

An annual labor savings of $33,800 would be generated by eliminating the two positions. This was calculated:

Hourly wage = $6.50
Taxes and benefits = 25%
Hours per week = 40
Weeks per year = 52
Net Savings = $16,900 x 2 =
Total Savings = $33,800

Payback: Total Investment = $121,750
Payback Period = 3.60 years

Lifespan: Estimated 15+ years

EQUIPMENT REPAIR/MAINTENANCE ISSUES

A wide array of equipment is available for use in small, medium, and large foodservice facilities. An equally wide array of manufacturers now offers a multitude of equipment models, some with a dazzling list of optional features. This section presents the most vital points of information about various types of foodservice equipment as well as some of the things administrators will need to look for if they intend to prevent their utility and repair bills from going sky high.

While there are few rules of thumb in this area, experience has shown that refrigeration units (both refrigerators and freezers) and ice machines can be the most temperamental, thus requiring the largest amount of maintenance attention. Depending on the location, whether hard or soft water is available, and the anticipated level of abuse, other equipment can be equally vulnerable to service problems. By category, here are some examples of typical foodservice equipment and related service concerns:

Refrigeration Equipment

- New environmental regulations require foodservices to ensure that its equipment uses a nonfluorocarbon refrigerant. To meet new cold food termperature standards (see Chapter 11) refrigerators may need additional horsepower.

- More energy-efficient/better-insulated freezers and refrigerators are being built. They will not operate efficiently if foodservice staff leave the doors open for long periods of time. If it is necessary to leave refrigeration unit doors open, heavy-duty clear plastic or vinyl air curtains should be installed.
- There are units that have alarms that will sound in the event the optimum temperature range is breached. Many newer units can now be monitored by computer. In this way, management can compile a 24-hour-a-day record of temperature recordings. Any major variations can be immediately checked and appropriate action taken to prevent harm to patrons.
- Refrigeration units are not designed or intended to be constantly filled to capacity. As in home refrigerators, there must be sufficient room for air to flow evenly around food items being chilled. When filled to capacity, the refrigeration equipment has to work much harder to maintain optimum temperatures. The excess wear and tear on the equipment will usually result in higher utility bills and more required maintenance.
- Refrigeration equipment usually operates 24 hours a day. Therefore, the original equipment must have quality parts and installation. Regular, planned maintenance of the equipment is an absolute requirement if expensive repair bills are to be avoided.
- Refrigeration units, their motors, and condensation units generate a terrific amount of heat. Where these units are placed and their ability to utilize heat recovery systems will be the key to energy- and cost-efficiency.

Ice Machines

- There are two types: those that produce cube ice and those that produce flake/crushed ice.
- The appropriate size of an ice maker must be carefully calculated before purchase. Most foodservice operations not only use ice for drinks, but as a means of cooling foods and/or for display purposes, such as on a salad or dessert bar. In the case of the latter two functions, 100 pounds of ice can be potentially used just prior to meal service time. Additional ice may be required during the meal period to replenish or freshen the presentation.

- As with steam and coffee-brewing equipment, there may be a need to soften and/or filter the water. Impurities and mineral buildups are two of the major reasons ice machines break down.
- The following advice applies to all ice and refrigeration equipment. The temperature of the surroundings will have a tremendous impact on the efficiency of the equipment. In many older facilities, kitchen temperatures can approach 100°F or above. When this occurs, the equipment has to work that much harder. Eventually, it will break down.

Ovens

- New, more powerful microwave ovens that have both convection (fan) and browning units are now available. While microwave ovens are not extensively used in high-end specialty production kitchens, they are essential for small batch cookery and cook-to-order situations. In addition, wherever convenience products and/or chilled preplated meals are extensively used, microwave ovens are almost essential for regular and/or small batch use. Some users still complain that microwave ovens do not heat evenly; some parts of the food remain cold, while other parts become superheated. Since microwave radiations disperse randomly, it is necessary to keep these ovens clean, so that only the desired food items will be cooked or reheated.
- Convection ovens (ovens in which heat is circulated by a fan) have been around for a long time. In these ovens, the even dispersal of heat not only speeds cooking time, it also helps achieve a consistently baked/roasted product. To maximize heating efficiency, the ovens should be kept clean. To avoid expensive service calls, foreign objects (including aluminum foil and plastic wrap) should be kept clear of fan units.
- Rack and revolving rack ovens are generally found in large production kitchens. In many cases, they appear to have replaced the old rotary (ferris wheel-style) oven that can still be found in some large production kitchens. Cooks like rack-style ovens because they are easier to load and unload than rotary equipment as there is no need to handle individual pans of product. Where cook-chill or cook-freeze technology is in use, rack-style ovens are most efficient because the same rack heated in the oven can be placed into a blast chiller for cooling.

With respect to repairs and maintenance, these ovens must be loaded and unloaded in accordance with manufacturers' specifications. Forcing racks into the holding brackets may result in expensive repairs and oven downtime.

The most efficient ovens, especially when items such as pizza and cookies are going to be baked throughout the day, are the conveyor types. These ovens are generally set at one temperature. Their conveyor lines are timed so that desired products are baked consistently every time. As with other ovens, staff need to keep these units clean. With a conveyor belt, a number of working parts driving the belt can become jammed if foreign objects are placed in them or if racks/trays are loaded carelessly.

In smaller kitchens, it is sometimes necessary to use ovens for both roasting and baking. Since roasted meats have a tendency to splatter juices and fat, there is always the possibility that bakery products such as breads, muffins, and cookies will pick up a "meaty taste" if the oven has not been thoroughly cleaned between uses. That is why many larger kitchens have two sets of ovens: one for roasting and baking meats, fish, and the like, and the other strictly for baking bread and dessert products.

- Cook-and-hold ovens were originally developed to slow-cook large cuts of beef such as prime rib. Slow cooking reduces shrinkage (and loss of net weight) and improves flavor as less moisture is removed. In addition, the cooking process can proceed unattended. Special built-in temperature probes placed in meats indicate to the oven when it should go into a holding mode. Therefore, cooks need not be present to take meats from the oven and place them into some other hot holding unit.

  Some cook-and-hold ovens are now portable, which can be extremely helpful if a foodservice needs to support satellite locations and/or stage catering events. Due to their portability, there is a good chance that these ovens will be subjected to a lot of banging around, which will drive maintenance and repair costs upward if not controlled.
- Traditional roast-and-bake ovens that use conventional heat are still available today. Many chefs and cooks believe that these are still the best heating equipment and have a place in most kitchens. In general, it does not cost much more to include a traditional oven as part of a range or grill top combination.
- Conduction heat (via air, water, or steam) is a relatively new technology that is being used for traditional baking, cooking, and

rethermalization of bulk and preplated foods. Since it is newer in technological terms, this equipment is more expensive and there is little history available to indicate what type of service calls it might incur.

- Combi-ovens are among the newest innovations to hit the food-service industry and, to many, they are a stroke of genius. Simply stated, a combi-oven cooks food by dry, convection, or steam heat. When appropriate, foods can be cooked with any combination of heat sources in these units. Many foodservice operations that have combi-ovens have eliminated the need for steamers but not the need for soft water or deliming. Given that combi-ovens are multifaceted pieces of equipment, service concerns center on potential hard water deposits and foreign objects entering fans. The person operating this sophisticated piece of equipment should have adequate training before being permitted to "solo" on the controls.
- When large volumes of the same or similar products, such as pizza, are to be prepared, it is generally cost and operationally efficient to purchase equipment especially manufactured for that purpose.

Deep-Fat Fryers

- There are two types of fryers: pressure and open vat. Both types can represent major fire hazards, as they utilize extremely hot fat/grease that is highly flammable and can cause serious second- and third-degree burns if not handled with care.
- Some deep-frying equipment has become highly automated. Fry cooks simply have to push a preprogrammed button for certain items (such as french fries, chicken, and fish) to be cooked repeatedly at a grill or fast-food station. Once the product is in the basket, it automatically drops into the fat. When the preset cooking time has expired, the basket lifts up automatically.
- In the past, frying fat would have to be drained and strained as often as twice a day to filter impurities from the fat and clean the cooking vessel. If the fat was not cleaned, the flavor of the food would deteriorate and the fat's useful life would be reduced by half.

  While it is still necessary to drain and filter the fat manually on some basic deep-fat fryer models, there is now a better way.

Many deep fryers come with an automatic filtering system. During operation, the fat is constantly circulated through this filtering system, eliminating the need to drain and clean daily. The equipment only requires major cleaning when the fat is replaced. It is important to note that frying fat will eventually "wear out" and begin to break down (smoking and/or an off or rancid odor are two indicators).

If foodservice personnel follow set procedures, there is usually a certain day of the week when the fat is changed and frying equipment is cleaned. If a need arises to change fat more often, it might be due to the purchase of lower-quality fat that is breaking down more rapidly or because the frying temperature is set too high. Finally, used cooking fat and oils are recyclable. In fact, most jurisdictions insist that the fat be picked up by recognized rendering companies. It must not be poured down the drain or dumped in with the rest of foodservice garbage.

Most fryer maintenance problems are due to two primary causes. First is the improper draining, cleaning, and/or loading of new fat. Spills and spatters can cause control panel problems. The second is not shutting the equipment down or off when it is not in use. This will cause fryers to break down earlier and more often than would normally be the case.

Broilers

- There are a wide variety of electric, gas, wood, and charcoal-fired broilers available for use in kitchens today. Broiling, in essence, is a high-speed cooking method. Rotisseries, which either slow or fast broil food on a spit or wheel-type apparatus, have become very popular, as the process generally does not char the food. The speed of cooking will largely be determined by the amount of heat applied and how close it is to the food. Some heat sources, such as mesquite wood, generate a very high temperature that can place a lot of heat-stress on a broiler's working parts, and ventilation hood system, as well as the equipment located nearby. Most service problems are caused by the high temperatures and/or inadequate cleaning.
- As with ovens, there are automated conveyor broilers that can cook specific products (according to shape, size, and thickness) to the desired degree of doneness. Administrators have undoubtedly

heard one fast-food hamburger chain extolling the virtues of its "flame-broiled" hamburgers. With some specific exceptions, conveyor broilers can only be justified for high-customer-volume operations where patrons are purchasing the same items. The equipment can be staff-intensive, as there is a need for a loader and at least one person on the other end pulling the product and finishing the preparation process (such as placing a hamburger patty on a bun with lettuce, tomato, and assorted condiments).

In terms of maintenance, conveyor broilers can be a challenge to keep clean, since there is a constant need to make sure that working parts are adequately protected from accidental damage.

Grills or Griddles

- A grill is a smooth, flat metal surface heated by electricity or gas, which is used mainly in cook-to-order operations, even though this equipment has plenty of uses (such as the preparation of scrambled eggs, pancakes, french toast, hamburgers, and grilled sandwiches) in high-volume production kitchens.
- There are grooved grill models that cook products as if they were on a broiler grate, but leave less fat/grease remaining in the food.
- Many fast-food restaurants have adopted a clam-shell grill that cooks food from the top as well as the bottom. With this equipment, there is no need to turn product(s).

With all these various griddle designs, staff must strictly follow manufacturer's instructions for cleaning and maintenance. The actual grill/griddle surface is the most expensive part of the equipment and requires specific cleaning and maintenance to last up to or beyond its anticipated working life.

Woks

- Once found only in Asian restaurants, woks have gained popularity in many noncommercial foodservice settings because they offer one of the best ways to cook food to order quickly without a lot of fat or grease. They also offer an excellent opportunity to promote fresh foods that can be prepared to order.
- Since woks are designed to cook foods quickly at high temperatures they generate a lot of heat. In high-use instances, it is expe-

dient to have running water available as a coolant to keep them from overheating.

Steam Equipment

- Equipment of this type consists of the aforementioned combi-ovens, tilting skillets, kettles, and compartmented equipment.
- Steaming is generally considered a very efficient and healthful (because little or no fat is necessary) means of cooking both small and large quantities of food. In many foodservice situations, this can be a critical selling point to patrons sensitive to which foods they will eat and how they are prepared.
- Because steam is water vapor, there is a need to make sure that the steam used for cooking is both clean (from a fresh, potable water source) and free of heavy mineral deposits. The equipment used for steaming must be clean.

Miscellaneous Equipment

A well-equipped kitchen will require more equipment than has been discussed so far. Depending on the type of operation, the menu, the number of persons served, and other factors, a number of other equipment pieces may be required. Here is a short list of such items:

- Mixers. Small ones are table-mounted, while large units are floor-mounted. Most mixers are designed to allow foodservice staff to add attachments that perform grinding, grating, and slicing functions. In terms of longevity, belt-driven units reportedly do not hold up as well as those with gears.
- Slicers. Small ones fit on a table, while larger ones are mounted on wheels or are free-standing floor units. Their purpose is to provide many uniform (portioned controlled) slices of meat and cheese. Automated units not only operate very quickly, but can also handle more than one product (such as meat and cheese) at a time.
- Choppers. There are both table-top and free-standing models of this equipment. Their primary use is to produce large quantities of raw ingredients for immediate or imminent use. Food processors are used for basically the same purpose in small batch production situations.

There are still other types of cooking and preparation equipment available. This section has simply described the major pieces that are usually the most expensive to purchase, require special installation, and/or are critical to the food preparation process. There is, however, one additional piece of equipment that is generally the most expensive to buy, yet receives little or no attention: the dishwasher. This machine, the staff charged with operating it, and the process of cleaning and sanitizing cannot be taken for granted. The selection of the proper chemicals used for cleaning and sanitizing dishware and the manner in which the dish machine is operated (including regular cleaning and preventive maintenance) are of critical importance. Specifically, administrators should pay attention to the following:

- There are two kinds of dishwasher: high- and low-temperature. The high-temperature machine requires a minimum wash temperature of 150°F, while the rinse cycle must operate at a minimum of 180°F. The low-temperature type, with the aid of chemicals, operates both the wash and rinse at 150°F.
- Dish machines range in size and capacity from single-tank machines that handle one rack at a time to flight-type machines that can wash 10,000 or more dishes per hour.
- Some dish machines utilize a lot of energy to operate and a great deal of water. As a result, they can add a lot of waste to the local sewage system. Given current environmental concerns, this could add a higher than necessary expense to an organization's sewage bill.
- Because of their extensive water usage, there is a need to use soft water or carefully monitor the amount of mineral buildup in dish machines if expensive repairs are to be avoided.

A few final thoughts on equipment.

Foodservice equipment is not inexpensive. Good equipment costs more than mediocre or bad products, and plenty of choices are available at all three levels. It is important for administrators to remember the following when purchasing equipment, as well as when making sure that the people who use it are handling it properly:

- The more sophisticated the equipment, the more training will be required to operate it. This is not a hard and fast rule, but it is a good one to follow, unless experience dictates differently. If the equipment, such as mobile ovens and heated or refrigerated carts, is designed to be moved from place to place, the purchase specifications should reflect this fact by requiring stronger, more durable components.

- If there are circumstances under which certain individuals (such as students, inmates, or patients) will have access to the equipment, controls and key working parts (such as connecting hoses, knobs, handles, and related items), these will have to be "securable." In these situations, equipment should have built-in control devices that require a key to operate or a locking panel that prohibits unauthorized use. In addition, there are certain pieces of equipment which by law cannot be operated by minors due to the potential for serious accidents.
- The best piece of equipment is only as good as a conveniently located and competent service agency. If the repair person has to purchase an airplane ticket or the replacement part needs to be sent from a factory in Asia, it may be prudent to reconsider the wisdom of purchasing it.
- Remember, most foodservice equipment comes with a warranty. It is surprising how many Maintenance departments fail to keep this in mind when attempts to make repairs are undertaken. Most warranties clearly state that only authorized service personnel may fix equipment during the warranty or guarantee period. Unauthorized work will void the warranty either in full or in part.
- The more features (sometimes referred to as bells and whistles), the more there is a chance something will break down.
- Be careful when considering the purchase of used equipment. Think of it as being similar to purchasing a used car posted with an "as is" warranty.

EQUIPMENT MAINTENANCE RECORD KEEPING

Because foodservice is not part of most organizations' primary missions, many administrators do not perceive the need to spend the time or effort required to track equipment maintenance costs carefully. Given the cost of new foodservice equipment, to say nothing of the loss in sales and/or efficiency when there are breakdowns, it is best to follow this relatively easy, inexpensive way to track each piece of major capital equipment. Whether equipment records are maintained manually or as part of a computerized maintenance management system, the information shown in Exhibit 10-1 should be tracked.

If properly maintained, these records will prove invaluable when the

Exhibit 10-1
EQUIPMENT MAINTENANCE RECORD

Item: ____________ Asset #: ____________ Manufacturer: ______________________ Serial #: __________

Date Purchased: ______________________ Purchased from: ______________________

Warranty Period: ____________________ Installed by: ______________________

Serviced by: ______________________ (Internal) ______________________ (External Company)

Date	Maintenance Request	Reg. #	Repairs By	Time	Invoice #	Time $	Parts $	Total $ Cost	Running $ Total

Equipment Type: (circle one) Electric Gas Steam Other

time comes to consider future capital expenditures. For each piece of equipment, there is a point when its repair costs start to exceed its useful value. When this occurs, ample justification and documentation should be readily available.

EQUIPMENT BREAKDOWN AND ABUSE

Besides normal wear and tear, extenuating circumstances can add unnecessary downtime and equipment maintenance costs. While not found in all cases of equipment failure, here are some things administrators should look for:

- If there are places where floor tiles or walls (corners and other areas) are broken or cracked, it usually means that equipment has been carelessly handled. Flatbed carts, pallet jacks, fork lifts, and the persons assigned to use them are just some of the probable causes of the damage.
- Many kitchens require use of a wide variety of transport and service carts. If they do not have wall bumpers and corner guards installed, carts will do damage to the walls, as well as an equal or greater amount of damage to themselves when collisions inevitably occur. In the case of refrigerated and heated carts, fixing or replacing this equipment will require a significant financial outlay.
- Improper chemicals (i.e., those not specified by the manufacturer) are perhaps being used to clean the equipment. Their use can cause pitting, discoloration, and weakening of the structural integrity of the equipment.
- The equipment may not be cleaned and maintained in accordance with the manufacturer's specifications. Maintenance personnel may not be following the manufacturer's recommended repair and maintenance procedures.
- Foodservice staff may not receive adequate training in the care and use of the equipment. As damage occurs, there is an immediate need for management to react to avoid further incidents.

SMALLWARES

Smallwares are defined in the introduction to this chapter. In some organizations, they are referred to as "expendables" which can give some people a completely wrong idea about the acceptability of indiscriminate breakage and careless handling. If not managed along with other costs, smallwares expenses can become a major financial burden for a foodservice. In some organizations, smallwares costs do not show up on foodservice's financial statements. Therefore, it is a good idea for administrators to track smallwares costs or usage as if they were line items on financial statements.

Most organizations' foodservice departments require a minimum amount of cooking utensils, pots, pans, plates, bowls, glasses, cups, and related service items in order to function. Since foodservice occurs at peak times, it may mean that a particular piece of serviceware will be used only once a day. Therefore, it is a good idea to have on hand one to two-and-a-half times the amount (the anticipated number of patrons) necessary for a specific meal period. The amount of serviceware required will be still greater in operations doing a high level of catering than those with only a manual cafeteria. Within the ratio presented, it is anticipated that from 25 percent to 30 percent of the available serviceware will be held in reserve, so replacements will be immediately available.

Whether smallwares are used for cooking or to provide service to patrons, it can be terribly frustrating and time-consuming for staff if they have to constantly search for or wait for items to be washed before they can be pressed into service again. In some cases, the lack of an adequate backup inventory can become very expensive, as purchasing disposable serviceware incurs a very high cost.

Besides tracking smallware replacement costs (both in dollars and as a percent of food sales), it is a good idea for administrators to conduct a semiannual or annual inventory to determine if, in fact, foodservice's management team is maintaining required par stock levels. Par stock levels are determined by the number of persons to be served and experience with how quickly things will either become broken, lost, or worn out.

NEW TECHNOLOGY

"There have been a number of new advances in food production, holding, and service technology. What's more, some equipment that people call 'new' may have been around for a long time and just been improved or, in other cases, been wrapped in a more attractive package. That said, the reality is that there are very few foodservices that have not already or will soon have ample reason to introduce equipment incorporating the most up-to-date technology. If not for competitive reasons, then the simple need for efficiency and increased productivity is the usual incentive. The ongoing need to prepare, hold, and/or display foods safely has pushed a number of foodservice operators into considering how current technology can meet increasingly stringent safety standards."

Over lunch in AU's cafeteria, Jones reviewed this assessment from Dean Namura of the local university's Hotel and Restaurant & Institutional Management School. He had already been briefed by his consultants about some of the wonderful new equipment and processes that were being introduced in kitchens around the world. Jones had a concern with this information, which he had shared with Namura: "I need to be able to separate the fads from the enduring trends. I don't want to have to face my boss in five years and admit that AU's new kitchen and foodservice facilities are already out of date." Namura laughed at Jones' remark, because his university had just gone through such an analysis after the decision had been made to centralize foodservice production for the entire campus into one very large, extremely expensive kitchen.

Knowing that he was not alone in his search for the most appropriate foodservice technology motivated Jones to learn more about what was happening in this area of the foodservice industry. Since he had just been to the National Restaurant Show in Chicago, he got out the large stack of equipment brochures and educational seminar outlines he had picked up and reviewed their contents with renewed interest.

Here's what Jones learned:

- "K Minus." This term defines a facility that has *no* kitchen. A number of schools, senior citizen centers, rest homes, and hospitals have decided that it is more efficient and just as effective to have all or major portions of their daily menus prepared and provided by outside sources. Therefore, these organizations receive cooked foods in refrigerated or frozen states in either bulk or preplated forms. In essence, all that is left for the foodservice staff to do is to place entrées or hot items into an oven, assemble the rest of the ingredients, and the meal is ready.

  One hospital has set up purchasing arrangements with a number of food processors to provide specific menu items (prepared to its specifications) on an as-ordered basis. Since some of the hospital's specified food items are made elsewhere in the country, a local wholesale grocery concern is used as a warehouse and delivery outlet. Food items are delivered to the hospital in ready-to-serve portions. Items are then assembled on trays, per patients' orders, and transported to nursing stations prior to scheduled meal service. Another hospital is using the same purchasing format, but each nursing station has a par stock inventory of various food items from which patients can select.

- Cook-chill. This is a technology that has been around for several decades but is now finding new applications. Hospitals and airlines were the first to use cook-chill equipment, but its use has been expanding dramatically into organizations where foodservice needs to prepare food for large numbers of people in multiple locations in the safest, most efficient manner possible. Briefly, cook-chill is a production process whereby just-cooked foods are rapidly chilled (generally within one to two hours) to an internal temperature of 38°F or below. The rapid chilling leaves little or no opportunity for harmful microbial growth. There are three basic types of cook-chill "chilling" technology.

  Tumble Ice Water Baths. Administrators unfamiliar with this equipment should imagine a huge washing machine full of ice water. Next, picture a large kettle full of spaghetti sauce that is being pumped into heavy plastic bags, which are mechanically sealed, given an identification tag, and placed into the ice water bath. When cooked, the sauce had a temperature of 180°F. After being placed in the tumble chiller, the internal temperature is quickly reduced to 38°F. Once this process is complete, the bag of sauce is removed and placed in a refrigerator at no more than 32°F until it is needed. Under normal operating conditions, the bag, the sealing process, and the quick chilling technique will permit the spaghetti sauce to be held for up to six weeks.

  Blast Chill. If foodservice staff were to take that same spaghetti sauce and place it in a 2.5-inch deep steam table pan, they could then place it in a blast chill refrigerator. A blast chill refrigerator looks like the commercial refrigerator found in most kitchens. The difference is that blast chill equipment has a high horsepower motor that permits cooked food to be chilled to a temperature of 38°F in two hours or less. Since the food has not been bagged, its effective shelf life will be approximately five days.

  It is important to note that it is not necessary for a foodservice to have a tumble-chill system in order to hold food in heavy-duty plastic bags. These same bags can be placed in pans or on trays and into the blast chiller to get similar cooling results.

  Sous Vide. This is a French term that literally means "cooked under vacuum." With sous vide preparation, foods are prepared and placed in heavy-duty plastic pouches (such as Cry-o-vac) and slow cooked at lower than normal temperatures in a vacuum chamber. At that point, products are either blast chilled or frozen. If chilled, they will have a shelf life of approximately 20 days. If frozen, most items will retain full quality for up to a year. Many hotel food and beverage departments and other foodservice operations often purchase products that have been prepared using sous vide methodology. There is an excellent chance that more than one sous vide technology product has been served and no one in the group was aware of it. While certainly more expensive in terms of food cost, sous vide products eliminate the need to employ a highly paid chef or cook if only a few people are to be served or there is a need to serve a large number of persons in a very short period of time. This latter situation recently occurred at an organization that wished to serve a five-course meal to a group of over 500 people seated in a tent. While four of the courses were single choice, guests were offered three entrée choices: fish, chicken, and beef dishes. The challenge for the foodservice department was to provide three high-quality entrée choices at the proper temperature to that organization's guests.

Given the circumstances, foodservice decided to purchase sufficient quantities of the three choices from a local supplier of sous vide products. Using a bank of gas range tops installed for this purpose, the staff was able to plate the ordered entrée choices by simply opening the appropriate pouches whose contents had been brought to the proper serving temperature by immersion in boiling water. Since rethermalization took only five to six minutes, other foodservice staff monitored how fast each product was being selected and made the appropriate adjustments. By the end of the meal, there were a total of 12 leftover entrées, which were given to the staff for their meal. The balance of the unheated sous vide inventory was left under refrigeration and run out (used as daily specials) over the next few weeks at various catering events and through the executive dining room.

At the end of this chapter, Exhibit 10-2 provides a series of questions and answers concerning cook-chill technology. These may be printed out in various formats and used in presentations to educate staff, colleagues, and others about the use of this technology.

- Robotics. A number of initial robotic applications have been introduced to foodservice operations. The first introduction has been the use of robots to deliver food carts to remote locations, usually in hospitals. With a high number of floors/wards to deliver to, robots offer these foodservices a natural opportunity to cut back on the large number of personnel previously required just to deliver and retrieve meal carts three times a day.

In larger, more sophisticated foodservice operations like airline kitchens, robots are now used to handle large volume repetitive motions, such as filling portion cups with juice or condiments.

- Irradiation. While not a process that would normally be performed in even the most advanced production kitchens in the United States, irradiation is used to "cleanse" foods and spices of harmful bacteria. Even though it has been used in Europe for a number of years without incident or problems, some U.S. environmental groups have expressed the belief that the process is, in itself, contaminating the food. The federal government, however, believes that irradiation will help extend the shelf life of food, as well as ensure its safety. The previously noted outbreaks of *E. coli* infestation would not have occurred if the affected meat had been irradiated. Irradiation is a technological and social issue that administrators need to monitor.
- Computer Technology. Information is power. The saying is perhaps trite, but in the world of foodservice, there is an ongoing need to have timely, operational, and financial data on which to base future management decisions. Here are just a few of the computer-powered information services now available for general foodservice use.

  Production Management Systems. These are software programs that generally include modules for creating menus, maintaining a raw and finished products' inventory, maintaining a recipe file, recipe adjustments set to specific production requirements, ingredient assembly, nutritional analysis, labor and food costs monitoring, and other common functions.

  Bar Codes. In foodservice, bar codes are used just like the ones found in grocery and many other retail stores. Bar codes allow electronic equipment to record the fact that an item has been sold and/or that it is still in inventory. These data are then transferred to a computer that quickly calculates the amount and dollar value of inventory on hand.

  POS Systems. Point-of-Sale systems closely resemble and mimic cash registers, except that POS systems are really small computers or are, on occasion, linked to a computer as part of a total information network. If used properly, these units will not only record sales dollars and the number of customers purchasing items during any meal period, but will also provide foodservice management with a complete breakout of every item sold by product category, the time it was sold, and average checks.

If linked to a computer running appropriate software, management can also use POS systems to factor in labor costs, productivity ratios (such as sales per labor hour worked), actual food cost, actual labor cost, and other controllable expenses.

Debit Cards. With the introduction of POS systems and electronic card readers, the debit card has become, for some organizations, the only or primary way of making foodservice transactions. In fact, many schools and college/university foodservices that have regular meal plans handle most of their sales through debit cards. Many companies also offer debit cards that patrons can fund via purchases in set dollar increments or through authorized payroll deductions. The fact that cashiers do not have to handle cash for debit card transactions is a tremendous way to speed up what is normally one of the slowest customer service processes in foodservice.

CONCLUSION

Almost without exception, today there is a machine or process that will considerably speed up foodservice's preparation, cooking, portioning, and customer service time. As pointed out earlier in this chapter, administrators should perform a cost/benefit analysis prior to making any large-scale food equipment purchases. While a high-speed bread-making machine costing in the neighborhood of $250,000 would be a nice feature, a foodservice operation only using about 150 to 175 loaves per day would find that even the smallest bread-making equipment (which can produce that many loaves in an hour) is of dubious utility.

All in all, it is simply a good practice from both an operational and financial results perspective for administrators to purchase equipment and research new foodservice technologies with a clear head and a defined purpose firmly in mind.

Exhibit 10-2
AN INTRODUCTION TO CENTRAL COOK-CHILL KITCHENS

Before embarking on a central kitchen project, it is important to understand what a central kitchen is and what it can accomplish in terms of providing foodservice to multiple sites/facilities. Simply stated, a central kitchen permits the production/preparation of all or a major portion of the hot and cold foods to be served in different facilities located either on a single campus or over a large geographical area. Generally, these kitchens employ a food preparation technology called cook-chill-rethermalize.

There are several viable alternatives for implementing a cook-chill-retherm process. Obviously, each alternative has some strengths and weaknesses to consider. It is important to understand the needs of each given department/facility. What is a pro argument for a system at one facility may be a con argument at another. The best central kitchen cook-chill retherm system is one that is designed to meet the defined short and long term needs of the facilities served by that system.

What is cook-chill?

Cook-chill is defined simply as a mass feeding system based on conventional preparation and cooking of food followed by rapid chilling, storage in a temperature-controlled environment near 32 degrees F. and then rethermalizing the food immediately before consumption.

What is the purpose?

The primary purpose is to prolong product shelf-life while maintaining quality. Rapid chilling inhibits the multiplication of bacteria and other microorganisms to slow down the deterioration of food that occurs at normal temperatures. The danger zone for food handling is between 40°F and 140°F. It is best to complete the chilling process in 120 minutes or less and to limit rethermalized food handling and portioning to 30 minutes or less.

How can foods be rapidly chilled?

There are two basic methods of chilling food rapidly. One is to transfer the food from the cooking kettles into polyethylene bags, which are sealed and either manually transferred or moved by conveyor belt to a tumbling ice water bath. The chiller is a perforated drum that rotates in a tank of circulating cold water. The bags are designed to withstand gentle tumbling in the ice water while they reach the desired temperature.

The other method is to place the food no more than two inches deep in pans on carts and roll them into a blast chilling unit. These blast chillers resemble roll-in refrigerator units. They can rapidly circulate cold air around the pans until the food has reached the desired temperature. In some situations it is appropriate to chill polyeurethene bags of food in a blast chiller.

Do I need a whole new kitchen to convert to cook-chill?

Blast chillers can essentially be added to a smaller (under 500 meals per meal period) standard kitchen and production converted to partial cook-chill

Figure 10-2 continued

with relative ease. The other necessary ingredient is sufficient walk-in refrigeration space in which to store the chilled food until use.

Tumble chill systems are highly automated and are, therefore, designed from the start to operate as a total system. The system includes steam-jacketed agitator kettles, pump-filler stations, conveyors, and tumbler chillers/cook tanks. The system is extremely labor-efficient because there is little direct handling of the food during the process. Due to the fact that greater quantities of chilled food are stored for longer periods of time, this system requires even more refrigeration space than the blast chill system.

How long will cook-chill foods keep?

Blast chilled food has a shelf life of up to a week or more; however, it is recommended that it be served within the first four days. Due to the limited handling and its air-tight packaging, tumble chilled food has a shelf life of approximately 30-42 days.

Can I prepare/serve any food I want by the cook-chill method?

Food such as soups, casseroles, roasted meats, stews, and similar items that will fit into a hotel pan can be blast chilled. Tumble chill systems work best with liquid or viscous products such as sauces, soups, stews, or pureed or creamed vegetables. However, the tumble chiller can double as a cook tank when hot water is used. For example, packaged meats slow cook in their own juices followed by automatically circulated cold water that arrests cooking and rapidly chills the food.

Can we use the same recipes that we use now in our facilities?

The same types of food can be prepared from the same recipes. Experience has shown that some ingredients such as flour used as a thickening agent in sauces, do not "hold up" in the cook-chill product. There are substitute starch thickeners that will work. With some testing, most recipes can be adapted to cook-chill.

Do you have to cook-chill every item once you are on the program?

No. In fact, some foods never get cooked until the point of service. For example, frozen vegetables are already blanched before they are frozen; that is to say, they were "cooked" for a minute or two, then "quick-frozen" so there is no need to do anything with them until service time, when they are rethermalized with the rest of the cook-chill food. Frozen deep-fried foods also do not need to be processed prior to use.

What about food quality?

One of the things that comes to mind when people first hear about cook-chill is "TV dinners," which conjure up different images for everyone. As with any system, when good food is properly prepared according to detailed recipes/directions and stored appropriately, food quality is maintained. When the staff fails to follow procedure, the system breaks down and the food quality may suffer.

Figure 10-2 continued

Given proper management and supervision, there is no reason for food prepared by cook-chill to be inferior in quality. A well-managed cook-chill program should improve the overall quality of the food served.

What are the major advantages of cook-chill?

Labor Savings:

- Management and production staff can concentrate on specific tasks all day with little or no peak mealtime production tension.
- In most systems, seven days worth of food can be prepared in a four- or five-day work week in the kitchen.
- Key cooking staff can be kept to a minimum, since relatively unskilled labor can be used for the rethermalization and service of food.

Food Cost Savings:

- There should be less wasted product due to spoilage and overproduction. If there is overproduction of an item, it can be frozen and used at a later date.

Energy Savings:

- More efficient use of production equipment results in reduced energy costs.
- If food is prepared on a five-day work week to be served over seven days, the kitchen can be shut down two days, resulting in energy savings.

Consistency:

- There is more control and uniformity of production techniques to assure that a product will be the same each time it is made.

Service Flexibility:

- With product in inventory, special diets, and off-peak feeding are simplified.

Space Savings:

- Since bulk production equipment is usually used, total kitchen space is reduced, despite the need for increased refrigeration.

The foregoing is a very short explanation of a highly complex process of preparing and serving food. Essentially there are two potential methods for implementing a cook-chill program. These chilling methods are described below.

Alternative #1

Standard cooking equipment is used for batch cooking. Chilling is done in blast chillers, which are essentially refrigerator-like cabinets with the capability to rapidly lower the temperature of food that has been rolled into the unit in 2 1/2 inch deep pans on a rolling cart.

Figure 10-2 continued

Results: Food has a shelf life of from two to five days.

Alternative #2

Large capacity cook tanks are used to prepare large quantities of solid meat contained in sealed polyeurethene bags simultaneously. When the cooking process is complete, the water drains and the tank fills with cold water in which the bags of cooked meat are tumbled in an ice water bath until chilled (below 38°F).

Results: Food has a shelf life of up to 30-42 days.

Are there alternatives to cook-chill?

Basically, there are two alternatives to a cook-chill program.

- Central kitchen preparation of hot food to be shipped in bulk directly prior to service time.
- Maintenance of individual cook-and-serve kitchens at each facility.

What are the positive and negative aspects of central kitchen preparation with hot bulk shipment of food prior to mealtimes?

+ The central kitchen gives you control over the consistent production of food.

+ Savings result from not having to fully equip the unit kitchens.

– The food is shipped hot right before a meal. This means that if there is a truck breakdown or other delay, the meals may not arrive on time and/or at the proper serving temperatures.

– Hot food is difficult to transport as it is prone to spillage.

– Serving times may not be flexible on the receiving end. The food must be served within a reasonable amount of time after arrival. If there are late patrons or other factors that preclude immediate service, quality control is lost.

– The kitchen must be fully staffed seven days a week.

Then why not just keep the cook and serve system?

The maintenance of individual cook and serve kitchens at each facility is the most costly alternative and the most difficult to control/manage. Costwise, there is the need to fully equip every kitchen to prepare and serve meals. It is also necessary to have trained cooking staff at each site seven days a week. There is still no assurance of consistency in quality of food.

What happens to the food once it is cooked and chilled?

It must be placed immediately into refrigeration as "cooked food inventory." Essentially the kitchen builds a food bank of prepared foods ready to be sent to where ever it is needed.

When is the food shipped?

Figure 10-2 continued

That depends upon the type of service required at each facility. Some cook-chill programs ship all the food for a full day's meals one or two days in advance. Others ship it a few hours ahead of service. It depends on several factors including the proximity of the service sites, the amount of refrigerated storage at each site, and the manner in which the food is to be served (cafeteria style, preportioned trays, or other).

How *is* the food served?

The answer to this question is strictly dependent on each individual facility. One of the beauties of cook-chill is the flexibility it offers in the serving scenario. One facility might serve preportioned trays, another might serve from a cafeteria line. One facility might serve everyone at one time, another might prefer to stagger meal serving times throughout the facility. The options are restricted only by the serving site's equipment and space, the desires of the administration, and the ability of the central kitchen to deliver the product.

How is the food transported?

Depending on the distance to be traveled, the food is either placed in refrigerated or nonrefrigerated carts. Just prior to meal service, the food carts are loaded onto a truck, strapped in to prevent tipping/spilling, and delivered. Depending on the climate and the distance traveled, the truck should be refrigerated. Sometimes trucks are fitted with battery packs that enable the carts to be plugged in during transport.

At the point of transport, are the meals in bulk or portioned onto trays?

They can be available either way, depending on the needs of the facility. Some facility managers choose to receive hot packs and cold packs of portioned meals. Designated personnel simply reheat the hot food, place it on a tray with the cold food, and serve. This is an especially valuable option in units such as medical wards where not everyone may be fed at the same time and in psychiatric units, where patients sometimes need to be fed individually.

Others receive the food in bulk, retherm it, and then portion it onto insulated trays for delivery to the housing units. Some juvenile and rehabilitation units choose to rethermalize food in bulk, place it in serving bowls/platters, and serve tables of eight to ten family style as a part of the "normalization" process.

Still another scenario provides for the food to be sent in bulk, rethermalized, and served on a cafeteria line or from portable serving lines setup in housing units. This individual on-site rethermalization results in a hot meal for everyone, not just the first person served. Again, the flexibility permitted by the cook-chill system is one of its real assets.

How do you reheat the food?

There are a variety of ways to reheat food. It depends on many factors, including how it will be served.

- If the people to be fed all come to a central area and are served from a tray line, the food can be rethermalized in bulk in convection ovens and

Figure 10-2 continued

placed on a steam table for service. This rethermalization can take place in the central kitchen and food sent to the units in electric hot and cold carts. This is the least efficient method. It is much more effective to ship the bulk food cold and rethermalize it at the point of service.

This type of system works well when there are a number of existing kitchens/dining rooms to be served by a central kitchen. The ovens, steam table, and existing refrigeration can all be used. The remainder of the kitchen preparation area need not be maintained/replaced. Depending on the situation, some space may be recovered for other facility uses.

- If the people to be fed are served within individual units but there are no serveries in those units, the food can be rethermalized in bulk in the kitchen, portioned onto thermal trays, and distributed.

  Food might be brought to a facility cold, rethermalized in a central rethermalization pantry, and portioned hot for delivery. This system works well when there is no need to move the food outside from one building to another. Thermal trays lose temperature much faster when exposed to cooler outdoor temperature.

- If people are to be fed in units that contain serveries with ovens, the food can be portioned in the kitchen, sent cold to the units, and rethermalized as needed for service. One or two conventionally sized convection ovens can rethermalize up to 75 meals at one time. When only a few meals are served at a time over a period of one to two hours, microwave ovens might be used for rethermalization.

  When a facility has a number of buildings in a compound without connecting tunnels or walkways, rethermalization can also provide assurance that the food will be hot when served. This system, however, also requires the space and equipment for a servery at or near the point of service.

Is cook-chill good for every situation?

Full cook-chill production is not the solution to every foodservice problem at every facility. It is simply an alternate program that was developed from increased knowledge of food storage and advanced equipment technology.

Where is cook-chill most effective?

Generally, it is most effective when large quantities of a single menu are required for service at multiple sites or at flexible time schedules. The airlines were the first to use the cook-chill system. Schools and corrections facilities are the fastest-growing segments of the marketplace for cook-chill systems. Both these types of facilities meet the criteria for successful implementation of cook-chill. When an institution/agency meets the criteria, it should carefully consider the concept(s) in its long-range master plan.

What does the term "food factory" mean?

Figure 10-2 continued

A food factory is a cook-chill kitchen that processes foods into "convenience" foods for resale or serving at multiple locations. This may mean that some of the food is "cook-chill" while some is not. For example, a food factory may produce bean burritos. The bean filling may be cooked and chilled then rolled into the burritos, Or the bean filling may be purchased ready to use in cans and the burritos filled. The goal of the food factory is to produce a ready-to-heat and serve burrito. A food factory may make sandwiches that are wrapped and sold in a deli case or vending machine.

Pizza may be prepared and partially cooked, ready-to-heat and serve at the point of sale. A good point of reference is the convenience store, which sells many ready to eat items. Many of those items come from food factories or commissary kitchens.

Some food factories make bulk and/or individual servings of foods that are ready to serve in much the same way that some of the commercial products like Le Menu, Stouffer's, Swanson's, and other companies sell products in the grocery store. The food factory allows a school district, for example, to utilize commodity products to make items that can be easily served in the individual schools. For example, commodity tomatoes or tomato sauce, cheese, and flour are all used to make pizzas.

What are the key elements that make a cook-chill program successful?

- A well-thought-out program document that defines the goals of the program prior to the design and construction of a facility. This should include not only kitchen operation, but the delivery and service program specifications as well.
- Adequate provision for staff training prior to opening the facility.
- A foodservice management software program to control raw product inventory and prepared food inventory as well as all production management. This system would receive and consolidate the daily requirements of each facility and develop exact delivery requirements to control the delivery of product from the central kitchen to the service points.
- A progressive transition plan for converting facilities from standard cook-and-serve to cook-chill units. This transition may take from one month to several months, depending on the number of satellite units.
- Adequate supervisory staff to assure quality control.
- Specific cook-chill recipes to assure that the food holds up during the initial cooking and rethermalization process.

CHAPTER ELEVEN

Quality Assurance

"Today's the day," Jones thought, driving to work while fortifying himself with a fast-food restaurant breakfast sandwich and coffee. "Harry's agreed to come back for a visit to share a formal inspection of our main cafeteria and to walk me through Quality Assurance criteria. Now I just have to make sure he explains the audit process in detail and shows me how to interpret finished audit forms so I'll know how we're doing in the future. Looks like I'll be a few minutes late," Jones noted, finishing his sandwich, "but at least I won't be hungry when we inspect the kitchen."

"Glad you could make it, Dana," Harry Daulton said, offering a cup of black coffee to Jones as he entered the cafeteria's empty servery. "Your secretary reminded me you have that benefits office meeting at 11:00, so I'd like to take you right into my old office and show you what a Quality Assurance audit is all about. We'll go over audit scoring and what to look for when doing an inspection tour. Okay?"

"Sounds good, Harry," Jones agreed. "Only thing is, I already have a coffee, see? Put a lid on that one, though, and I'll drink it later."

"I'd better pour it out," Daulton smiled, moving toward the servery's beverage island. "I kept meaning to tell my replacement to order those lids, but you know how it is. We'll draw you a fresh cup later."

Seated in Daulton's small office, crowded with menu blanks, product samples, promotional materials, and professional mementos, Jones listened as the recently retired foodservice director described the purpose of a Quality Assurance audit. Daulton explained that such inspections are intended to measure the efficiency and effectiveness of a foodservice program. During an audit, special attention should be focused on the quality of offered foods and services, as well as the care being extended in and general cleanliness of the cafeteria and catering facilities.

Regardless of the sort of organization a foodservice is operating in, the program and its facilities should be formally audited every three months. Periodic informal, walk-through inspections should be conducted by the foodservice administrator. (Administrators with foodservice oversight responsibilities should prepare timely reports of all formal audit and walk-through inspection results.) The purpose of walk-through assessment is not to reinspect entire facilities, but, rather, to ensure that deficiencies turned up during the quarterly formal audits have been corrected and that no new ones have developed.

Hearing this, Jones logically wanted to know the sorts of deficiencies formal Quality Assurance audits are supposed to turn up.

The universally applicable answer he received included problems with food quality and operational inefficiencies, unsanitary equipment and facility conditions, and patron survey scores. As an example, the sample Quality Assurance Form presented at the end of this chapter is designed so that when evaluated, all foodservice resources and facilities must record total scores of 90 percent or better in order to pass inspection. Should an audit reveal a score of less than 90 percent in any area, then the entire facility in which the problems have been identified should be considered to have failed. A failing facility's manager must respond to the audit's results by immediately writing a report addressing each deficiency noted during the audit and citing corrective steps that will be undertaken to prevent reoccurrences of the deficiencies.

Seeing Jones jotting down his prescriptions, Daulton added the advice that formal audits should always be held without prior announcement to foodservice personnel, to eliminate the possibility that existing problems will be covered up. "Besides, the health inspector never gives *us* any warning when *he* comes to visit," Daulton confided to Jones. It is a good idea, however, to schedule and conduct the first audit with the foodservice manager or management team along. In this way, everyone can gain a clear understanding as to what the audit will cover as well as the methodology for determining point deductions.

Jones quickly flashed back to his military experience, remembering how those Saturday morning inspections appeared to focus solely on what was wrong with the outfit. He vowed right then that his Quality Assurance audit process was not going to be adversarial. He would focus on the good things being done along with those items that required improvement.

Scoring a formal Quality Assurance audit is a matter of apportioning fractions of the total available score to different program aspects in each facility. One successful scoring method is to allot 25 percent of available points to judging the quality of food items made for or at different serving stations. Another 25 percent should be reserved for evaluating the operational effectiveness of management and staff, as well as the quality of customer service. The final 50 percent of audit scoring should be applied to evaluating whether facilities and equipment are in proper repair and meet all applicable sanitation codes and standards. Obviously, a regular and thorough evaluation of a foodservice's sanitation practices (*and* their results) is critical to the healthy functioning of any facility, so it is especially important that deficiencies in this audit area be identified and rectified. Since the Quality Assurance Form is just a model, the actual weighting of scores may need to be adjusted to fit the specific circumstances of a particular organization.

Trying to assimilate all these new criteria and beginning to realize the magnitude of auditors' responsibilities, Jones next asked how audit scores are recorded.

Daulton replied by pulling a blank Quality Assurance Audit Form out of a desk drawer. (See Exhibit 11-1 at the end ot this chapter and on the accompanying disk.) He explained to Jones that the first step to completing any audit is to have the auditor(s) fill out each facility's location, the name of its manager, the date and time of the audit before signing their names. Completed audit forms should always be stored in chronological order in secure files.

Daulton then took a blank Food Matrix Quality Attribute Guide from a different drawer, displaying this, too, to Jones. (See Exhibit 11-2 at the end of this chapter and on the accompanying disk.) This form, Daulton noted, is used to help auditors evaluate food items' quality, appearance, taste, portion size, and similar values. Again, it is important to note that this model will need to be adapted to the circumstances of each individual foodservice situation. In many cases, the standards already in place are used. If well operated, there should be ample back-up of written procedures, approved recipes and preparation procedures, as well as diagrams and/or pictures to provide a specific frame of reference as to how food is to be prepared and served. Brandishing both forms in a meaty fist, Daulton asked Jones if he was ready to conduct a formal Quality Assurance audit.

"Frankly, not yet," Jones admitted.

"Don't worry. By the time we finish this one, you will be," Daulton said reassuringly. You're new to foodservice and I've retired after 30 years in this business, so the best way for *you* to learn is to follow me through our facilities and to see them through *my* eyes. There are four key steps to keep in mind as we go through the process. They are:

- Food Preparation and Presentation
- Operational/Management/Customer Service Assessment
- Facilities and Equipment
- Front of the House

The former foodservice director and Support Services administrator began the second step of their unannounced, formal Quality Assurance audit by conducting a quick walk-through of the entire foodservice facility. Harry noted that the quick walk-through is the best way to spot problems that might require immediate attention (such as a dirty dining room, missing cashier, or other customer service related issue). The balance of the audit would help ascertain the problem(s) cause(s). The formal audit commenced by entering the servery or customer service area to evaluate the quality of foods and beverages—both those stored and those being prepared for that day's lunch. For audit purposes, all menu items are divided into seven categories: hot foods, grill items, salad bar selections, sandwiches, plated salads, desserts, and beverages. On occasion, as when plated salads are deleted in favor of extensive salad bar selections, an auditor will have to adjust the "points allowed" column correspondingly on the audit form.

When auditors perform their estimation of food quality, it is vital that they identify any deviances from the standards set forth in the Food Matrix Quality Attributes Reference Guide. If any items are determined to be not up to identified food quality standards in the areas of appearance, temperature, portion-control, preparation, and variety (as specified by the day's menu), auditors must deduct rating points according to the severity of the observed discrepancies.

For example, if one of four grill items inspected fails to meet minimum temperature requirements (is too cold), a quarter of the available points in this category should be subtracted and a brief factual description of the failure added to the audit record.

While mastering the scoring mechanisms is not difficult, administrators (and others new to foodservice) may find subjective factors such as appearance and preparation quality harder to evaluate consistently. Besides familiarizing themselves with quality standards for different products (available from those items' manufacturers and/or distributors or the foodservice departments' own recipe and product specification files), the best way to judge if a food product is up to quality standards is to "eye-ball" it.

FOOD PRODUCTS

Garnish and Appeal

Garnishing food is a process whereby it is made to look as attractive as possible to the patron. Appeal relates to an assessment of how the food itself looks.

In the kitchen, for instance, Jones learned that his foodservice director always checked the baked fish entrée (being prepared for that day's lunch) to see that chefs had garnished it with parsley and lemon slices, as per his instructions. He was somewhat perturbed to find that the chefs had allowed the fish to stay in the oven too long so that it had dried edges. Daulton further advised Jones to gain experience by studying department recipes and photos of sample plates, in order to learn what different finished dishes must contain and look like when served. (Recipes and photos were currently kept loosely in boxes in the director's office.)

Continuing their inspection of entrées being prepared for that day's lunch, the auditors looked for other factors that can add or detract from foods' appeal. In addition to the presence of specified garnishes, auditors should check for under/overcooked items, whether any products have "unnatural" colors or aromas, and how attractively foods have been positioned in serving pans. In short, appearance quality is achieved by ensuring that no aspect of foods presented to customers can be considered a "turn-off."

Temperature

Food temperature was the next quality factor the auditors inspected. Since assessments in this area must be both objective and stringently accurate (mismeasurement of food temperatures can allow the growth of infectious pathogens), all foodservice auditors should possess food thermometers. These instruments come in two types: pocket-size dial probe thermometers (which currently sell for approximately $6.00 to $12.00) and battery-powered thermometers featuring digital readouts (these are now sold for about $35.00 to $125.00). Food thermometers can be purchased from restaurant equipment and supplies companies.

The reason auditors must have and know how to use food thermometers is that all fresh and processed menu items must be prepared and served within rigid and consistent temperature ranges in order to ensure their healthfulness and nutritional values. For example, auditors must ensure that all cold foods such as salad dressings and potato salad are stored below 40°F. Any such items stored at higher temperatures should receive a failing score in this section of the audit (points deducted should be proportionate to the number of items reviewed and found to be at proper temperatures) and, if there is any reasonable doubt, they should be thrown away *immediately*.

Hot foods, too, have their temperature requirements. All solid-form meats (such as roasts, steaks, and chops) must be cooked to an interior (or core) temperature of *at least* 145°F before the local Department of Health will consider them acceptable for service. Hamburgers and ground meat products such as meatloaf must be cooked to an internal temperature of 155°F. Pork and poultry products require an even higher internal temperature of 165°F. The above temperatures, along with recommended cooking and holding times, reflect the model standards suggested for all kitchens wishing or mandated to adopt a Hazardous Analysis Critical Control Point Program (HACCP), see Chapter 6. Actual minimum acceptable temperatures will be different depending on where the organization is located and whether it is subject to federal, state, or local rules. These extra degrees of doneness will not only ensure that pathogen contamination has been eliminated, but will also help keep hot food *hot* as customers spend time selecting other food in the servery and queuing to pay a cashier.

During Jones' tour, Daulton took pains to emphasize that accurate, daily food temperature inspections of dairy, pork, beef, poultry, egg-based, and mayonnaise-based products are especially important. Equally important is for management and staff to constantly monitor the temperatures of the refrigerators and display units where these products are held. "This is because these items are most susceptible to spoilage and infestation from pathogens that can cause food-borne illnesses," Daulton explained as he and Jones stood in foodservice's chilly walk-in refrigerator. "The most frequent cause of food-borne illnesses is improper temperature holding of the items you see here," Daulton added, "so *whomever* is operating this foodservice program, make sure that director is a stickler on temperature control!"

Due to a number of highly publicized food contamination and poisoning incidents, it is anticipated that food temperature cooking and holding standards will be extensively reviewed and possibly revised. All temperature standards should be verified with state and/or local health authorities. Where there is a conflict or ambiguity, it is recommended that foodservice staff adopt the optimum food safety standard.

Portion Control

The auditors next moved to a central makeup table where salad bar selections and other items were being prepared to evaluate staff's portion control practices. A cardinal principal of Quality Assurance, portion control should be regulated by standards expressed in writing and illustrated in a price and portion guidebook maintained by the foodservice management team. This practice should be adhered to by self-operators and contractors alike.

The purpose of auditing portion control procedures is to ensure strict compliance with established standards. The benefits of applying portion control standards include effective control of food costs; support for customer satisfaction, assuring all patrons receive equally sized menu items; and reduction in "wasted" labor, since equal-sized portions are easier for cafeteria staff to serve. From a visual and price/value perspective, the portions should be appropriately sized for the service plate or dish selected (i.e., it is not so large that it overflows the plate and it is not so small as to leave the impression that it is too small of a portion). Equally important, proper portioning will speed up self-service options, since customers find it easier to select standard-sized food. There have been times when patrons will reach to the very back row of product to take the largest piece. Usually, they manage to drag their shirt or blouse sleeve through one or more of the items to reach it. Portions may be unequal because the foodservice employee is not using/has not been trained to use the appropriately sized or type utensil. There are occasions when serving line personnel increase portion sizes for special friends or tend to discriminate by giving men larger portions than women. While cost is certainly an important issue, bad public/customer relations can extract a stiff penalty if unequal portioning practices are permitted to continue.

Typically, foodservice staffs find that customers are most concerned about portion control of entrée items as they are generally the most expensive. Products stocked in salad bars, soup (especially where there are meat, vegetables, or pasta products included) and bread stations, beverage areas, and dessert cases are of equal concern because in self-service areas patrons do not want to feel that someone else got a "better deal." Not only do diners expect such items to be uniform and consistent in size and appearance; they also expect them to be easy to pick out and presented in a sanitary and efficient manner. Most salad bar choices, for instance, should be precut into bite-sized pieces, so that customers can take as many or few of the items as desired. Finally, to facilitate the convenient service of all items, regardless of portion size, auditors should be sure that staff have put out appropriate type and size serving utensils (such as spoons, ladles, and tongs) at every serving station. The staff will need to check periodically throughout the meal period to make sure that the utensils, serviceware, and surrounding area are maintained in a clean, sanitary condition.

Preparation Quality

Next, the audit trail led Daulton and Jones to the kitchen's ranks of burner-topped stoves to review the preparation quality of items to be served that day. Calling on his decades of foodservice management experience, Daulton explained to the Support Services administrator that the key evaluative principle in this phase of their audit was to look at foods as customers would.

"What you want to ask yourself," Daulton said, "is whether I, as a customer, can look at these foods and feel confident that they were properly prepared with clean, wholesome ingredients according to generally accepted cooking methods. If so, I'll order these items again. If the ingredients were wilted or aged or if they were over- or undercooked, I and my fellow customers will stay away until this foodservice closes."

One of the cooks handed Harry a small cup of navy bean soup with a spoon. Daulton spooned up a taste. "I let our cooks do their own thing a little bit. I just tell them that as long as *I* like the way foods taste, our customers will, too." The retired foodservice director laughed, patting his ample paunch. Jones immediately thought of what was wrong with that philosophy. It was perhaps a coincidence, but Dana had stopped purchasing soup in the cafeteria for the very reason that Harry had just endorsed. It never tasted the same from one time to the next. A quick note was made to insist that the cooks follow established recipes to the letter.

In evaluating as subjective a factor as preparation quality, auditors may wish to check for "off" flavors or aromas, mushy textures, or other conditions that would indicate that foods were misprepared. Auditors should base their scoring for this area (as with food appearance) on adherence to established recipes and cooking practices. Most often, cooks decide to "free lance" a recipe by adding or subtracting ingredients they believe will make the product better. In addition, they may decide to skip steps or speed up the cooking process if they have fallen behind. Either or both situations will result in a less than satisfactory product and/or negatively impact food cost. If its appearance (the item is "swimming in grease") or smell (a rancid or fishy odor) is offensive, patrons will refuse to order it, resulting in an expensive trip to the garbage can.

In most noncommercial situations, cooking needs to be an exact science. Even if the product looks good, it is both appropriate and within an administrator's scope of responsibility to sample selected items throughout the audit process. While the food item may not appeal to one's personal taste, it is important to determine if it has been correctly and consistently prepared.

Preparation quality is intended to address convenience and ready-to-serve items, as well. Fresh fruit that is too ripe or has scars/discoloration will be just as unattractive as a poorly prepared salad. Food items such as carton milk, yogurt, and packaged snacks that have expiration dates should be checked. Food items beyond their pull dates should not be presented/sold as fresh.

Variety and Specifications

This is a two-part evaluative process. Variety relates to the balance of available choices. With respect to specifications, most foodservice managers, whether self- or contractor-operated, are expected to prepare or have ready to sell a certain minimum number of items in each sales category (such as entrées, salads, grill items, desserts, and beverages). This is done to avoid having patrons feel or perceive that there are not a sufficient number of choices.

To determine if food variety and specifications are "as advertised" (i.e., as promoted on the day's menu), auditors should next refer to menu descriptives (such as "fresh" peas and "vegetarian" lasagna), as well as additional specifications promised or agreed to by foodservice's self-operator or contracted provider. In particular, variety should be evaluated on the basis of type, number, and quality of offered menu items. The purpose of this phase of auditors' reviews is to ascertain whether foodservice is daily offering acceptably balanced menus of promoted food. That is, a sufficient diversity of food types, nutritional qualities, colors, textures, and compositions should be regularly provided. An example of a well-balanced lunch entrée selection might include a solid meat item such as roast turkey with dressing and gravy, poached fresh Petrale sole, and linguine with pesto sauce. Note that balance relates to more than just color, texture, and taste. It is expected that one of the three choices will appeal to those wanting meat and potatoes, healthful/nutritious items, or foods with a little spice/flavor.

It is also important for the foodservice provider to use proper nomenclature or terminology on its menu. For example, patrons may become upset when they find that their beef Stroganoff is not solid pieces of beef but hamburger. They may also get upset if they thought they purchased a crab Louis salad and the crab is really an imitation product. If it is a "classic" dish, the best advice is not to permit foodservice personnel to make creative changes without first changing its name or making sure that patrons know that it is prepared differently.

It is important to keep in mind that menu making is an art. Those with experience in foodservice management know that menu development is a process of learning and keeping up with what customers want, how often they want it, when they wish to purchase different items, and what makes them feel good about their food choices. In other words, daily foodservice menus should contain not only an agreed-to variety of prespecified foods, but also the particular balance of items preferred by each organization's customers.

OPERATIONAL ASPECTS—MANAGEMENT

By this point, Daulton and Jones had reached the third step in the Quality Assurance audit of foodservice: the evaluation of operational aspects. Three areas of activity fall under scrutiny during this audit phase: management practices; customer service; and personnel performance.

The best way to learn how to appreciate these factors is to look at the auditors' expectations and standards for each (the Defined Expectations are in Exhibit 11-3 at the end of the chapter and on the accompanying disk). It is vital that those with oversight responsibilities for foodservice fully familiarize themselves with these terms and their standards. While administrators may wish to alter or amend these definitions in accord with the specific foodservice programs being offered in their organizations, a common evaluative *purpose* should be maintained. Overall, auditors should assess the level of attention cafeteria managers and/or assistants are maintaining toward both the front (dining areas, serveries, and catering sites) *and* back of their operations (kitchens and storage areas). This review should be combined with an evaluation of how well staff are being managed and how responsive department members are to customer needs.

Most administrators will recognize that this auditing activity is similar to assessing the aptitudes and attitudes displayed by *any* managers and staff on an individual and team basis. The conclusions auditors draw from their assessment, periodic walk-throughs, reviews of customer comments, and their own experiences as foodservice customers will, in sum, reflect the quality level of foodservice's hiring, training, and management practices.

Therefore, if auditors believe that an operational aspect only partly fulfills their (or predefined) expectations, the appropriate point value should be deducted. There are two essential issues here. The first relates to the problem itself (i.e., someone has failed to periodically clean and restock the salad bar throughout the meal). In that case, there should be zero points given for appearance in that category. The second relates to whether management was doing its job by actively supervising the service area and should have caught the problem. In this case, there should be corresponding point deductions under the "Management" category.

Food and supply item outages can be terribly frustrating for patrons. Dana's personal frustration with the lack of lids for the carry-out coffee cups is a perfect example. Patrons do not need to be told that "someone" forgot to order such and such items more than once, as a number of competitive foodservice choices are usually located nearby. Patrons who choose to eat at the end of the meal period deserve the same opportunities to select from a wide variety of foods attractively presented in a clean, neat environment.

When there are consistent problems from one audit to the next, management must be held responsible for its inability to fix them.

OPERATIONAL ASPECTS—CUSTOMER SERVICE AND PERSONNEL

There is an ongoing debate as to which is more important, food quality or customer service. The easiest and best answer is that they are mutually important. If one is lacking, the other is bound to suffer. Customer service is simply more difficult to quantify in terms of satisfaction. This is the point in the process when the auditor must use his or her powers of observation to get a "feel" for the foodservice operation's "personality"—the attitude and aptitude that should be displayed in the foodservice organization every day.

Dining out, which encompasses any food and beverage consumption outside the home, is really a form of entertainment. It offers a break from work or classes, which engender a wide range of physical and psychological needs. Taking care of a hunger pang or thirst takes care of physical needs. Psychological needs are far more complex. Suffice it to say, we all have basic needs for nice surroundings, pleasant human contact, and an overall safe comfort level.

With that understanding as a foundation, Dana Jones carefully observed the foodservice staff as they greeted patrons, took orders, prepared/portioned the food, and provided other customer services as necessary. The amount of time it took to get the food and pay for it was just as important as the food quality, price, and the fact that the cashier smiled and said thank-you to each patron.

Daulton pointed out to Jones that he should be especially watchful of the way foodservice employees look, dress, handle food, and observe all essential sanitation and safety procedures. Jones reminded himself to look in the National Restaurant Association's "Servsafe" Program (see Chapter 14). With all of the recent publicity on food poisoning and contamination incidents, patrons are very concerned that their food servers and cooks look and act professionally.

FACILITIES AND EQUIPMENT

The fourth step in the foodservice Quality Assurance audit process is a detailed and extensive one: the evaluation of facilities and equipment. During this phase, auditors inspect and score the general conditions, order, cleanliness, and sanitation levels of 10 specific foodservice areas. (See Quality Audit form entitled Facilities and Equipment for area list.) Please note that a full 50 percent of the total audit score is to be recorded during this inspection phase, so auditors must be consistent and exacting in finding and identifying substandard conditions. In addition, if sanitation and maintenance programs are managed separately in your organization, then special care should be given to identifying problems in these areas distinctly, and making sure the responsible managers respond with corrective actions. With respect to equipment, please refer to Chapter 10 before conducting this portion of the audit.

As the voice of experience, Daulton at this point shared with Jones a series of insights designed to help the administrator better assess sanitation issues. He stressed that cleaning and sanitation is really about whether the foodservice staff has developed good work habits. In this regard, foodservice staff are trained to adopt a "clean as you go" philosophy, so that all of the cleaning work is not held until the end of the day. Daulton proceeded to take Jones through the kitchen on a work-area-by-work-area basis.

Cooking Equipment—General

Cooking equipment (especially) must be kept clean *at all times*, whether in use or not. Daulton reminded Jones that auditors should find ovens, griddles, and broilers free of burned-on food spills. Otherwise, the taste of foods and the equipment's cooking efficiency will be adversely affected. In addition, neglected spilled foods or grease can start fires in cooking areas. Equipment doors and lids, as well as splash/splatter areas should also be inspected for evidence of food or grease. Finally, auditors must ascertain that all kitchen equipment is in good working order; if not, repairs should be underway and documented.

Hoods

Daulton explained that the ventilation units (known as hoods) built in above some cooking equipment need to have both their external and internal surfaces cleaned regularly. Auditors must ensure that these surfaces are being cleaned even if the hoods are manufactured to be "self-cleaning." This is because most self-cleaning systems sanitize only those hood surfaces hidden from view; all other surfaces must be manually cleaned. In addition, most ventilation units contain removable filters that should be taken out and washed and/or replaced. Frequency depends on the volume and type of cooking being done. A large, high-volume foodservice operation that does a lot of cooking on grills (also known as griddles) and deep-fat fryers may require cleaning on a weekly or semiweekly basis. A low-volume foodservice where most of the food is prepared in steam equipment may have to wash the hood only once a month.

It is vital to remember that hood systems that have been improperly cleaned pose *critical* grease and electrical fire hazards for foodservice departments. To prevent potential hazards from becoming accidents, hood systems, including their enclosed fire extinguishing systems, should be professionally cleaned and repaired *at least* twice a year by a qualified, properly licensed outside hood-cleaning contractor. This contractor will be a good source for advice as to how often the removable filters should be cleaned as well.

Steam and Water Reliant Equipment

Having looked into the ventilation system maintenance situation, Daulton then explained to Jones how auditors should conduct Quality Assurance inspections of kitchen equipment that use piped water or live steam for cooking foods. Daulton noted that such equipment, including steamers, steam-jacketed kettles, ice machines, coffee brewers, and dishwashers, is susceptible to buildups of minerals (like lime) that originate in water sources or pipes.

In areas of the country where hard water is a known problem, auditors will want to ensure that foodservice staff and building/equipment maintenance personnel are carefully monitoring equipment that uses significant amounts of water or steam, such as coffee makers, dishwashers, steam-jacketed kettles, steam tables, and bain maries. Hard water contains a number of naturally occurring minerals. In large concentrations, these minerals can build up a scaly crust that clogs water lines and drains and significantly reduces cooking/use efficiency. If left untreated, the mineral deposits will eventually cause corrosion, which results in expensive repairs or replacement long before that equipment has reached its useful life expectancy. Hard water has a distinct "taste" and, as a result, can materially impact the taste of coffee, hot/iced tea, and fountain-style soft drinks. Regular use of a chemical "deliming" agent (approved for use by the equipment manufacturer, local sewer/waste water authority or, perhaps, your safety or hazardous materials use committee) is the only known way to eliminate mineral deposits before they begin to cause damage. The installation or use of water filters or softeners is a very appropriate preventative measure that can generally be cost-justified in lower maintenance costs.

Deep-Fat Fryers

Another type of kitchen equipment that should be given auditors' special attention is the deep-fat fryer. Daulton emphasized to Jones that the fat from these machines must be strained regularly. How regularly depends on how much use the units get and, most important, how many different products are cooked during a normal meal service or production day. The frying medium (vegetable or animal fats) must remain clean at all times through constant filtration if foodservice is to produce fresh-tasting and wholesome fried foods. Newer deep-fat fryers (see Chapter 10) have an automatic filtering system, which reduces the number of times the unit needs to be cleaned. Older deep-fat fryers may have to be emptied/strained and washed once a day. In all cases, the auditor should verify that the units are being cleaned and maintained in accordance with the manufacturer's specifications.

Foodservice staff should filter frying media (such as oils) *at least* once a day to remove foreign elements like breading. Unfiltered and/or overused frying liquids will give off excessive smoke and/or rancid odors during cooking, thus further indicating a food quality/equipment sanitation problem. In essence, the fat is breaking down (chemically) due to excessive use and high, constant heat. And, since frying oils are relatively expensive, the more often foodservice staff clean and filter, the longer these liquids will last.

In sum, Quality Assurance auditors should be on the lookout for greasy or dirty frying equipment, uncleaned filters, and unfiltered frying liquids. Grease fires and careless handling of hot frying oils are two major causes of accidents in kitchens and on cooking lines today.

Coffee Brewers and Dispensers

Since many foodservices sell more coffee than any other item, and often brew throughout the day, coffee brewers and holding/dispensing units must be cleaned, at a minimum, once a day. Heavier use may require cleaning after each meal service. Daulton pointed out that all coffee-brewing equipment should be washed out with special stain-removing chemical(s) available from coffee suppliers. "The secret to making a *really* good cup of coffee," Daulton said, "is to use equipment, including pots and dispensers, which are completely clean." As noted previously, the quality of the water (hard versus soft) can make a difference, especially to the discriminating coffee drinker.

Other Beverage-Making/ Dispensing Units

After evaluating the kitchen's coffee-brewing and serving equipment (and taking points off for problems like using a filter basket that had not been cleaned in days), the auditors moved next to inspect beverage units dispensing milk, soft drinks, fruit juices, powder-mix fruit-flavored drinks, iced tea, and ice water for overall cleanliness. It is especially important to check milk-dispensing units to ensure they are operating and holding product at the proper temperature (below 40°F). If dispensing units are *not* operating within this temperature range, the held milk will soon turn sour and unservable. It is also important to inspect all cold beverage units' dispensing heads and surrounding splash areas, as spills and syrupy residues are most likely to occur here, reducing units' efficiency and creating poor food quality and unsanitary conditions.

Floors and Walls

Other surfaces where dirt and/or grease are likely to build up is a foodservice department's floors and walls. Keep in mind that in a busy operation, floors and walls are certain to become soiled during the course of daily activities. The distinction that Quality Assurance auditors must draw is between those areas dirtied by recent spills and splatters and other surfaces (such as work tables, shelves, and racks) on which dirt has accumulated over an extended period of time. The best way to determine if floors and walls are being properly and consistently cleaned is to check beneath and behind equipment, storage racks, and tables located against walls and in corners, as it is in these locations that truly unsanitary conditions are most often found.

Daulton further told Jones that special attention should be paid during this audit phase to unattended food spills. There are both sanitation and safety reasons why such spills should not be left uncleaned. First, water, grease, or food spills can obviously cause a potentially injurious accident. In addition, an uncleaned kitchen will inevitably attract bugs and other pests.

Pest Control

Should either a formal Quality Assurance audit or an informal walk-through reveal a pest problem, the following actions should be taken immediately.

- If your company/organization has a pest control company under contract that visits on a regularly scheduled basis, it should be contacted and asked to fix the problem.
- The pest problem may be "new" in that it arrived in a recent delivery of food. It may be necessary to inspect produce boxes/cases, flour, sugar or rice sacks and other case goods to see if the problem was brought in from the packing house or food supplier warehouse. In the case of produce, the problem might be sourced to the fields where products are harvested and packed. If this is the case, products need to be removed from their shipping containers and placed in clean storage units. Shipping containers need to be disposed of immediately and the surrounding area thoroughly cleaned and treated with appropriate, authorized chemicals.
- Pest problems may be a sign that the foodservice staff is not cleaning the kitchen and storage areas properly.

To prevent pest infestations, foods must not be stored on floors. In most states, local Health Department codes mandate that foods be stored anywhere from three to six inches above floor surfaces. Entering a dry storage area, Daulton reminded Jones that "All rooms, racks, drawers, and shelves should be free of dust, grease, and food spills or you take off audit points. You've also got to be real sure that these areas are inspected for bugs and vermin, because this is where you are likely to find them."

Refrigerators and Freezers

The other food storage areas where special care must be given to maintaining cleanliness and temperature controls are refrigeration and freezer units found in most kitchens and service areas (such as walk-ins and upright and undercounter reach-in units). Besides applying the same Quality Assurance standards for sanitation in these areas, auditors must also check that all required precautions have been taken to ensure that freezers and refrigerators are operating in mandated temperature ranges. Most states' Health Departments, for instance, require that all refrigerated storage units be equipped with operator-installed thermometers to back up the unit thermometers installed by manufacturers. Auditors also need to know that freezer units should be able to maintain an internal temperature of -10°F to 0°F. Refrigerated units should maintain temperatures between 34°F and 38°F.

Leading Jones into one of foodservice's large walk-in refrigerators, Daulton introduced the administrator to some of the points auditors must cover. Daulton explained that all foods should be completely covered or wrapped, dated, and identified on labels. Drip pans should be positioned beneath all defrosting products. Special care must be taken to make sure that hot, leftover foods have been placed in shallow pans to allow rapid cooling and prevent harmful pathogen growth. Hot food in a large container such as a 10 gallon pot can take up to 16 hours to reach 40°F or less. Daulton also pointed out that refrigerators and freezers should be organized in a logical, neat, orderly fashion. Too often, food items get "buried" and have to be thrown out because they are too old. A disorganized refrigerator or freezer also causes a terrible waste of productive time as it takes longer to find things, Daulton noted.

All refrigerators' internal and external cooling fans, as well as cooling equipment, should be free of dust and grease. In addition, nothing should obstruct the free flow of air throughout these units. All door seals must be inspected for wear and replaced if gouged, ripped, or abraded. Finally, all freezer and refrigerator external and internal surfaces, especially door handles and shelving, should be checked for cleanliness. In the case of freezers, an excessive buildup of ice and/or frost means that there is probably a mechanical or structural problem that needs immediate attention. The unit should be defrosted as soon as possible to avoid any potential temperature maintenance violations.

Food Preparation Equipment

From the chilled regions of the walk-in refrigerator spaces, Jones and Daulton next proceeded to the kitchen's bright, open food preparation area. Here, Daulton explained, is where auditors should make random inspections of pots, pans, utensils, and cutting boards to ensure that all have been properly washed, dried, and stored in sanitary areas.

Dana picked up four pans and found dried food in one and a heavy grease smear in another. An embarrassed Harry quickly took them to the pot washer for a thorough cleaning.

The former foodservice director noted that if an inspected piece of food preparation equipment (such as a slicer, chopper, processor, or mixer) is ready to use (fully assembled) *and* found to be improperly cleaned, then a point(s) deduction should be recorded. The reason for the deduction is that an employee will almost always use a fully assembled piece of equipment as he or she finds it, and will not reinspect or reclean it before use. This represents an ideal opportunity for cross-contamination to occur.

"You've got to pay extra close attention to can openers, cooks' knives, meat thermometers, scoops and 'dishers,' and any utensils stored in drawers, because these are tools used to handle foods with the greatest potential for point-of-service cross-contamination," Daulton emphasized. "Also, cutting boards should not only be clean, they must also be free of deep grooves that can trap food particles. Many operators have elected to use color-coded cutting boards that are matched to specific food product groups."

While on the subject of contamination, Daulton steered Jones into the dish and pot/pan washing area. He noted that there are rigorous temperature and procedural standards for washing dishes and serviceware. Essentially, hot water units (as opposed to those that use chemical cleaners and resulting lower temperatures) should maintain a wash temperature of 150°F and a final rinse of no less than 180°F. Special care must be taken to assure that the proper amount of soap and rinse solution is being used. In most operations, this entails checking to see if the automatic dispensing units are working properly. As with all other pieces of equipment, the dish and pot/pan washers needs to be drained and cleaned out as often as necessary, but no less than after each meal period. Larger-volume operations may need to stop once or twice so that the machines can be drained and the traps (to catch food particles) emptied and cleaned prior to restarting them.

Having walked his Support Services administrator through a thorough inspection of cooking equipment, Daulton then went over the sanitation requirements for foodservice's most important resources—its employees. In order to satisfy auditors, all hand sinks should be easily accessible and stocked with liquid hand soap and disposable paper towels. During an audit, foodservice employees should be seen "sanitizing" their hands after using toilets, taking breaks, *and* before starting new work assignments. "And, of course, no audit is complete until you've given a thorough review to both employees' rest rooms and locker rooms," Daulton advised Jones. The employees' locker room and rest area should represent the standards of cleanliness and sanitation expected throughout the balance of the facility. For food-handling/preparation and service personnel, it is essential that the bathrooms be clean and properly supplied with soap, paper towels, toilet tissue, and ample hot water for handwashing.

Front-of-the-House

Last, but certainly not least, the "front-of-the-house"—the entry way, servery, and dining room—needs to be clean and inviting. All light fixtures should be working properly and at the specified levels. Music, if any, should be appropriate for dining (i.e., not fast-paced or frantic). The dining room should be neat and orderly, with clean tables and chairs/benches. If specified, each table should have napkins, salt and pepper, and ashtrays. Patrons who are asked/expected to return their trays to a drop-off point (usually a conveyor belt into the kitchen) should expect to find this area equally neat, clean, and free of offensive odors.

SCORING THE AUDIT

Overall, if Quality Assurance auditors find foodservice's equipment and work/changing spaces to be in good operating condition, clean, and maintained according to applicable sanitation standards, the full number of audit points should be awarded. On the other hand, should equipment or areas be found not to be in expected order, clean, and properly maintained, all or a percentage of available points should be deducted.

Keep in mind that auditors must determine and record fractional scores in a consistent manner. Fractional scores, therefore, should be based on the observed degree a piece of equipment or work area is in compliance with all audit standards.

"Now, before we go back to my old office and finish up by reviewing overall audit scoring, let me give you one more audit hint," Daulton said to Jones. "It is real important for administrators to study the local Health Department's inspection forms and processes, and make sure that no changes are made by foodservice in the future to bring *our* forms or processes into conflict with the Board of Health. Okay? Let's go grab a cup of coffee and talk about audit scoring."

Seated across Daulton's bare desk, Jones sipped a cup of foodservice coffee ("Not as good as that first cup from the convenience store; we need better beans," he thought) and took notes as the retired director recited the foodservice audit scoring process.

First, points awarded for food quality, operations, and facilities and equipment should be divided by the total of possible points. Remember that product categories and items or equipment not available to be scored should be eliminated and the total number of possible points reduced. For example, if your foodservice does not operate steam kettles, the points available in this section should be eliminated from the total. In addition, weighted percentage scores in each category should be carried over into the final audit score.

"The bottom line," Daulton said, "if this department receives 90 percent or more of the possible points, it passes the audit. If the score is under 90 percent, foodservice fails."

It is strongly suggested that administrators discuss audit results with cafeteria or department managers as soon as possible after scores have been tallied. It is better yet if auditors take managers on brief post-audit facility tours and point out the actual deficiencies mentioned in their reports. These walk-throughs also provide advantageous times for auditors to point out some of the many things that foodservice is doing *right*, especially in the areas of food quality, customer service, and facility/equipment sanitation. Finally, a copy of completed audit forms should be forwarded to the person responsible for administering foodservice if it is self-operated or to the contractor's district or corporate headquarters for immediate review and follow-up.

Another benefit of personal communications between administrators and foodservice managers is that it will help prevent Quality Assurance audits from becoming adversarial. It is important for all involved to consider that an audit provides a honest "snapshot" of a foodservice operation on a "typical" day. This is why both negative *and* positive findings should be shared with foodservice managers.

In order to preserve the "chain of command," under *no* circumstances should audit results be discussed with foodservice staff. The reason is obvious: To do so would risk undermining one or more department managers' authority. There also may be instances in which managers may attempt to justify or rationalize deficiencies found during an audit, in order to avoid a failing score. In such cases, administrators will have to consider the merits of individual arguments to determine if audit results should be altered.

In the event one or more foodservice facilities fail their audits, administrators should receive a written report within 10 days (from either self-operated or contracted department management). These reports should describe applied solutions to identified problems, when the problems were or will be corrected, and what has or will be done to prevent the problems from reoccurring. Then a reaudit should be conducted of just the failing facilities within 10 days of receipt of the manager(s) reports.

Lastly, audit scores of 90 percent or above do not require any follow-up correspondence. However, as Daulton concluded to Jones, "Just because a facility passed, you still have to make sure the manager corrects whatever deficiencies *were* found within a specified time frame. Got it?" "Got it," Jones affirmed, draining the last of his now-cold coffee. "Now I'm ready for the audits to come. Thanks."

Exhibit 11-1

QUALITY ASSURANCE AUDIT
ACME UNITED FOOD SERVICES

UNIT NUMBER ____________ AUDITOR ____________

UNIT MANAGER ____________ TOTAL SCORE ____________

DATE OF AUDIT: ________ TIME: ________

SUMMARY FOOD QUALITY			*SUMMARY FACILITIES & EQUIPMENT*		
	POSSIBLE	*ACTUAL*		*POSSIBLE*	*ACTUAL*
Hot Food	8		Front of House	15	
Grill Items	6		Short-Order Stations	9	
Soup/Chili	4		Hot/Cold Stations	10	
Salad Bar	6		Beverage Equipment	8	
Sandwiches	6		Back of House	10	
Plated Salads	4		Cooking Equipment	6	
Desserts	4		Storage Equipment	6	
Beverage	2		Preparation Equipment	7	
			General/Sani/Safety	13	
			Refrigerator/ Freezer	6	
TOTAL	40		TOTAL	90	
OPERATIONS	*POSSIBLE*	*ACTUAL*	*SUMMARY*	*POSSIBLE*	*ACTUAL*
Management	18		Food Quality	40	
Customer Service	16		Operations	50	
Personnel	16		Facilities/ Equipment	90	
TOTAL	50		TOTAL	180	

PASSED _____ FAILED _____ SCORE _____ %

GENERAL COMMENTS

UNIT # ______ PAGE TWO

FOOD QUALITY		
HOT FOODS	*POSSIBLE*	*ACTUAL*
1. Garnish/Appeal 2. Temperature 3. Portion Control 4. Preparation Quality 5. Variety/Specifications	1 2 1 2 2	
TOTAL	8	
GRILL ITEMS	*POSSIBLE*	*ACTUAL*
1. Garnish/Appeal 2. Temperature 3. Portion Control 4. Preparation Quality 5. Variety/Specifications	1 1 1 2 1	
TOTAL	6	
SOUP/CHILI	*POSSIBLE*	*ACTUAL*
1. Garnish/Appeal 2. Temperature 3. Preparation Quality 4. Variety/Specifications	1 1 1 1	
TOTAL	4	
SALAD BAR	*POSSIBLE*	*ACTUAL*
1. Garnish/Appeal 2. Temperature 3. Preparation Quality 4. Variety/Specifications	1 1 2 2	
TOTAL	6	
SANDWICHES	*POSSIBLE*	*ACTUAL*
1. Garnish/Appeal 2. Temperature 3. Portion Control 4. Preparation Quality 5. Variety/Specifications	1 1 1 2 1	
TOTAL	6	
LARGE AND SMALL PLATE SALADS	*POSSIBLE*	*ACTUAL*
1. Garnish/Appeal 2. Temperature 3. Portion Control 4. Preparation Quality 5. Variety/Specifications	0.5 0.5 1 1 1	
TOTAL	4	
DESSERTS	*POSSIBLE*	*ACTUAL*
1. Garnish/Appeal 2. Temperature 3. Portion Control 4. Preparation Quality 5. Variety/Specifications	0.5 0.5 1 1 1	
TOTAL	4	

UNIT # ______ PAGE THREE

BEVERAGES	*POSSIBLE*	*ACTUAL*
1. Temperature	1	
2. Preparation Quality	1	
TOTAL	2	

OPERATIONS

MANAGEMENT	*POSSIBLE*	*ACTUAL*
1. Availability/Attitude	2	
2. Production Needs	2	
3. Operational Problems	2	
4. Line Control	1	
5. Attention Front of House	2	
6. Attention Back of House	2	
7. Attention Employees' Work Habits	2	
8. Attention Employees' Appearance	2	
9. Attention to Walkouts and Security	2	
10. Cashier Price Accuracy	1	
TOTAL	18	

CUSTOMER SERVICE	*POSSIBLE*	*ACTUAL*
1. Serving Line Flow	2	
2. Cashier Line Flow	2	
3. Attentiveness to Customers	3	
4. Suggestive Selling	2	
5. Knowledge of Items Served	2	
6. Attitude/Personality	2	
7. Menu Board Appearance/Complete	1	
8. Menu Board Price/Accuracy	1	
9. Tray Availability/Cleanliness	1	
TOTAL	16	

PERSONNEL	*POSSIBLE*	*ACTUAL*
1. Infections & Sores Restricted	2	
2. Hands Washed, Hygienic Work Procedures, No Smoking	2	
3. Clean Clothes, Hair	2	
4. Handling of Food/Use of Gloves	2	
5. Food (Ice) Dispenser Utensils Used	2	
6. Name Tags/Security Badges	2	
7. Approved Uniforms	2	
8. Personnel Safety/Sanitation Habits	2	
TOTAL	16	

FACILITIES & EQUIPMENT

FRONT OF THE HOUSE	*POSSIBLE*	*ACTUAL*
1. Tables, Chairs (Arrangement/Clean)	1	
2. Tables (Salt/Pepper/AshTrays)	1	
3. Condiment Stations	1	
4. Entry to Serving Area	1	
5. Tray Cart Return Area	1	
6. Sanitation During Meal	1	
7. Appearance/Cleanliness of Cashier Station(s)	1	
8. Cleanliness of Floors	2	
9. Walls	2	
10. Decor Treatments	1	
11. Menu Board Cleanliness	1	

UNIT # ______ PAGE FOUR

12. Service Counters/Sneeze Guards Clean 13. Microwave Oven	1 1	
TOTAL	15	
SHORT-ORDER STATION	*POSSIBLE*	*ACTUAL*
1. Toaster 2. Deep Fat Fryers 3. Griddle and Broiler 4. Heat Lamps 5. Exhaust Hood and Filter 6. Fire Protection System (HD/EX) 7. Sneeze Guards/Service Centers 8. Special Equipment (Hot Dog Grill, Etc.)	1 1 2 1 1 1 1 1	
TOTAL	9	
HOT/COLD FOOD STATIONS	*POSSIBLE*	*ACTUAL*
1. Hot/Cold Pass Throughs 2. Soup Wells 3. Steam Tables 4. Hot/Cold Carts Pass Throughs 5. Display Units/Cold Pans 6. Salad Bar 7. Sandwich Bar 8. Popcorn Machine 9. Displays (Cookie, Etc.) 10. Dessert Cases	1 1 1 1 1 1 1 1 1 1	
TOTAL	10	
BEVERAGE EQUIPMENT	*POSSIBLE*	*ACTUAL*
1. Coffee Urns 2. Iced Tea Dispenser 3. Milk Dispenser 4. Juice Dispenser 5. Ice Dispenser 6. Water Dispenser 7. Soft Drink Dispenser 8. Milk Shake Unit/Soft Serve	1 1 1 1 1 1 1 1	
TOTAL	8	
BACK OF HOUSE	*POSSIBLE*	*ACTUAL*
1. Exhaust Hoods and Filters 2. Fire Protection (Hood/Exhaust) 3. Fire Extinguishers (Other) 4. First Aid Kit 5. Refrigerator Compressors 6. Walls 7. Floors 8. Floor Drains 9. Electric Conservation 10. Water Conservation	1 1 1 1 1 1 1 1 1 1	
TOTAL	10	
COOKING EQUIPMENT	*POSSIBLE*	*ACTUAL*
1. Ranges and/or Hot Plates 2. Convection Ovens 3. Steamers 4. Steam Kettles	1 2 1 1	

UNIT # ______		PAGE FIVE
5. Tilting Skillets	1	
TOTAL	6	
STORAGE EQUIPMENT	*POSSIBLE*	*ACTUAL*
1. Storage Cabinets/Areas	1	
2. Work Tables	1	
3. Pots/Pans	1	
4. Smallwares/Drawers	1	
5. Shelving/Carts/Racks	1	
6. Ingredient Storage Bins	1	
TOTAL	6	
PREPARATION EQUIPMENT	*POSSIBLE*	*ACTUAL*
1. Can Openers	1	
2. Sandwich Makeup	1	
3. Slicer	2	
4. Mixers	1	
5. Carving Boards	2	
TOTAL	7	
GENERAL SANITATION & SAFETY	*POSSIBLE*	*ACTUAL*
1. Trash Cans and Lids	1	
2. Trash Compactors	1	
3. Garbage Disposal	1	
4. Dishwasher	1	
5. Sinks, Sanitizing Solution	1	
6. Wash Hands Signs, Soap, Towels	1	
7. No Smoking Signs	1	
8. Pest Control	1	
9. Food Storage Wrap/Temperature/Label	1	
10. Thermometer, Use/Accuracy/Location	1	
11. Food Properly Thawed Before Cooking	1	
12. Self-Service Foods Properly Protected	1	
13. Wiping Clothes Clean and Sorted	1	
TOTAL	13	
REFRIGERATOR/FREEZER EQUIPMENT	*POSSIBLE*	*ACTUAL*
1. Refrigerators (Walk-in/Roll/Reach)	2	
2. Freezers (Walk-in/Roll/Reach)	2	
3. Ice Cream Freezer	1	
4. Ice Maker	1	
TOTAL	6	

Exhibit 11-2

FOOD MATRIX QUALITY ATTRIBUTE REFERENCE GUIDE

	GARNISH AND APPEAL	*TEMPERATURE*	*PORTION CONTROL*	*PREPARATION QUALITY*	*VARIETY/ SPECIFICATION*
HOT FOODS	Garnish of same type at all times. Appears fresh, no burn-on.	Minimum of 145°F temperature. Desired temperature 160°F.	As specified in price and portion book.	*Not* overcooked, seasoned or excessively dry, raw or tough in texture.	Per facility addendum. No run outs. Items offered are not similar in ingredients.
GRILL/FRYER ITEMS	Garnish of same type at all times. No sign of shrinkage or discoloring.	Raw items held under refrigeration. Room temperature avoided at all times.	As specified in price and portion book.	Free of excess grease and liquid, free of crusty burn on, tender, not overgrilled. Fryer oil free of particles and discoloration.	Per facility addendum. No run outs of posted items through duration of meal.
SOUP/CHILI	Garnish not required. Free from pan burn on.	Minimum of 145°F temperature. Desired temperature 160°F.	Self-serve	Ingredients cooked and tender. Free of floating grease and overseasoning. Ample ratio of ingredients to liquid.	Per facility addendum. Minimum variety of one soup and/or chili daily. No run outs of variety posted.

Exhibit 11-2 continued

	GARNISH AND APPEAL	*TEMPERATURE*	*PORTION CONTROL*	*PREPARATION QUALITY*	*VARIETY/ SPECIFICATION*
SALAD BAR	Salad bar area decorated with fresh vegetables, fruit.	Desired temperature 38°F-40°F. Any temperature above 40°F unacceptable.	Not applicable	Ingredients fresh, crisp, free of discoloring, blemishes. All pieces ''bite-size.'' Dairy/ starch items free of mildew, starch firm.	Per facility addendum. At least one large bowl of salad greens and 10 accompaniments. No run outs of any item through duration of service.
SANDWICHES	Garnished with pickle and chips. All ingredients fresh. No sign of drying out.	Cold sandwiches maintained at 40°F.	As specified in price and portion book.	Fresh, free of fat. Meat cut against grain, sliced thin or wafered.	Per facility addendum. Minimum variety of at least six selections through services. No run outs of posted sandwiches.
PLATED SALADS	All salads garnished in same manner. Lined. Free of liquids. Wrapped to prevent drying.	Desired temperature 38°F-40°F. Any temperature above 40°F unacceptable.	As per price and portion book. Same salads must be uniform in size.	Fresh, free of fat. Meat cut against grain, sliced thin or wafered.	Per facility addendum. Variety posted is available throughout service.

Exhibit 11-2 continued

	GARNISH AND APPEAL	*TEMPERATURE*	*PORTION CONTROL*	*PREPARATION QUALITY*	*VARIETY/ SPECIFICATION*
DESSERTS	Garnish not required. Product must be fresh, no sign of drying.	No requirements other than dairy-based or cream products must be refrigerated.	As per price and portion book. Portions must be uniform and consistent in size.	Fresh, no film buildup or sign of aging. Crusts tender, items not stale or frozen.	Per facility addendum. At least one variety of cake, pudding, and three or four varieties of cookies.
BEVERAGES	Not applicable.	Desired temperature 38°F-40°F for cold beverages. 160°F-180°F for hot beverages.	Not applicable	Proper carbonation in soft drinks, milk free of off-taste (sourness). Fruit drinks not artificially flavored. Coffee proper strength.	Per facility addendum.

Exhibit 11-3
DEFINED EXPECTATIONS

I. CUSTOMER SERVICE

Area	*Defined Expectations*
Serving Line Flow	Points of service free of bottlenecks. Lines moving smoothly in all areas. Minimal cross-traffic in lines.
Cashier Line Flow	Cashier line free of bottlenecks. Cashier should be efficient. Number of cashiers should be adequate for customer flow.
Attentiveness to Customers	Customers/employees being assisted at all points of service, no waiting. Foodservice management and personnel looking for problems, anticipating needs.
Suggestive Selling	Foodservice employees assisting customers in making selection(s). Recommending additional items to complement initial order by customer.
Knowledge of Items Served	All foodservice employees knowledgeable of what they are serving, (i.e., type of meat, ingredients in product, price, etc.). Foodservice employees able to adequately respond to customer questions regarding what they are serving.
Attitude/Personality	Positive attitude maintained by foodservice employees. Foodservice employees are pleasant, courteous, and helpful. No grumbling and/or negative comments exchanged with customers.
Menu Board/ Pricing Accuracy	Menu boards are clean and depict what is being served. Items are priced correctly.
Menu Board Accuracy	Menu boards accurately depict what is being sold. Items posted are available, and menu strips are removed when product is sold out.
Tray Availability/Cleanliness	Trays are available. All trays are free of any food particles, clean, and dry.

II. MANAGEMENT/AWARENESS ATTENTION

Area	*Defined Expectations*
Availability/Attitude	Manager on-site in cafeteria, readily available to customers and their employees.
Production Needs	Manager knowledgeable of and addressing any/all production needs, (i.e., run outs, restocking). Production problems being resolved immediately.

Operational Problems	Manager actively looking for and resolving situations that could result in potential problems, (i.e., health/safety hazards, fire marshal codes, equipment breakdowns, attitude problems, long lines, etc.).
Line Control	Manager aware of and actively addressing lines at all points of service for problems that potentially could impede service and security of sales. Manager takes immediate steps to resolve line confusion, cross-traffic.
Front of House	Manager addressing and correcting situations that detract from appearance of cafeteria, (i.e., dirty tables, full ashtrays, spills on floor, cleanliness of dining and serving area).
Back of House	Management aware of and correcting problems related to back of house, (i.e., security of inventory and office, cleanliness of kitchen, productivity of staff in kitchen). Assures back of house in good order.
Employee Work Habits	Management aware of, addressing, and correcting poor and unacceptable employee work habits, (i.e., touching hair while preparing food, overhandling food, handling cash and utensils, unacceptable sanitation practices, etc.).
Employee Appearance	Manager aware of and actively addressing employee appearance, (i.e., employees in clean uniforms, wearing name tags, hair neat and trim).
Attention to Walkouts	Manager/staff alert to potential problems that could result in customer walkouts, (i.e., unavailability of cashier, failure to put register chains up, lack of management and staff in service area at peak periods).
Cashier Price Accuracy	Manager assures posted prices are accurate and prices charged at register coincide with prices posted. Management takes immediate action to correct any errors.

III. PERSONNEL

Area	*Defined Expectations*
Infections & Sores Restricted	Personnel appear healthy, no visible sores, sneezing, coughing.
Hygienic Work Habits/ Smoking	Employees exhibit hygienic work habits, wash hands, no touching of nose, hair, or face. No smoking.

Clean Clothes, Hair	Uniforms are clean and neat, no stains, Hair is trimmed and restricted from movement.
Handling of Food/ Use of Gloves	Hand gloves are used (if policy). Food/ice and hand contact is confined.
Food (Ice) Dispenser Utensils Used	Food dispensers and utensils used for ice and all foods. No direct hand/food contact.
Name Tags/Security Badges	All personnel wearing name tags and/or security badges.
Approved Uniforms	All employees in approved uniforms.
Personnel Safety/ Sanitation Habits	Step stool used, all safety guards in place and used, proper safety and sanitation habits.

CHAPTER TWELVE

Accountability and Management Reports

After several months of "running the show," Jones had become confident of his ability to understand and evaluate "his" foodservice department's basic operational performance. An area of administrative responsibility he had been avoiding, however, and one that definitely needed his attention, was foodservice's financial management. Sitting in his quiet office late one afternoon, Jones realized that he had to acquire sufficient foodservice management understanding in order to ensure that sales were being completely and accurately recorded, cash and charges had been properly processed and accounted for, and all expenses were appropriate and approved. Based on his previous experiences administering contracted services, Jones knew that the key to building a successful relationship would be gaining enough knowledge about foodservice financial management to ensure that he would not find himself at the mercy of his services provider.

One of any administrator's primary communication tools is the financial reports that will be generated by either the self or contractor operated foodservice management team. Most administrators are not threatened by the prospect of reviewing and analyzing financial statements, they do it all the time. Foodservice statements, however, are different to a sufficient degree to cause even the best of administrators to have second thoughts about trying to interpret the meaning of the data provided.

Understanding the purpose of the various reports and how to effectively use them as management tools is critical. A brief discussion of the typical reports is presented on the following pages.

WEEKLY OPERATING REPORTS

The weekly operating report generated in a well run foodservice operation contains a great deal of information that can be useful to the administrator. These reports are typically generated for each operating unit with a summary report for the entire foodservice department or, in the case of the contracted operation, for the account. Valuable information relative to daily sales activity (including customer counts and average checks) by service period, productivity data (total number of labor hours worked, average sales per labor hour worked and overtime hours) and a breakout of food costs by category should be included in each report.

The data in the weekly operating report will be useful should the administrator have to approve a change in the service levels or an increase in staffing. One key requirement for this report is to insist that sales as well as food and labor costs be broken out by source. Catering sales should not be "lumped in" with retail and vending sales. If there is a national or regional branded outlet within the operation, it would be helpful to see separate sales for that unit. Is it doing significantly better than the non-branded units? Would it beneficial to the organization to install more branded concepts? If food cost is significantly higher and franchise or license fees are high, the branded unit may generate more gross revenue but contribute less to the bottom-line. These and other questions are answered in part by reviewing the financial statements.

MONTHLY/PERIOD OPERATING STATEMENT COMPARED TO BUDGET AND PAST ACCOUNTING PERIODS

Ideally, sales and expenses are compared to budget; the prior month; last fiscal year; and year-to-date data (see Exhibit 12-1). Unfortunately, some contractors generate this information on two separate statements. This

Exhibit 12-1
PERIOD FINANCIAL REPORT

CURRENT PERIOD							YEAR TO DATE (YTD)					SAME PERIOD PREVIOUS YEAR				
Actual	*%*	*Budget*	*%*	*Variance*	*%*		*Actual*	*%*	*Budget*	*%*	*Variance*	*Actual*	*%*	*Budget*	*%*	*Variance*
						SALES Cafeteria Coffee Cart Catering Snack Bar Cold Vended Food										
						TOTAL SALES										
						COST OF GOODS SOLD Bakery Beverages Dairy Grocery Meats Produce Miscellaneous										
						TOTAL COST OF GOODS										
						LABOR COSTS Management Hourly Premium Pay Vacation & Holiday Group Insurance										

Exhibit 12-1 continued

CURRENT PERIOD							YEAR TO DATE (YTD)					SAME PERIOD PREVIOUS YEAR				
Actual	*%*	*Budget*	*%*	*Variance*	*%*		*Actual*	*%*	*Budget*	*%*	*Variance*	*Actual*	*%*	*Budget*	*%*	*Variance*
						Payroll Taxes										
						Workers' Comp										
						TOTAL LABOR COSTS										
						CONTROLLABLE EXPENSES										
						Direct Operating Expenses										
						Paper Supplies										
						Cleaning Supplies										
						Laundry										
						Flowers										
						Uniforms										
						Replacements										
						Advertising										
						Donations										
						Advertisements										
						Promotions										
						Utilities										
						Administrative and General										
						Payroll Processing										
						Bank Charges										
						Bad Debts										
						Office Supplies										
						Telephone										

Exhibit 12-1 continued

CURRENT PERIOD							*YEAR TO DATE (YTD)*					*SAME PERIOD PREVIOUS YEAR*				
Actual	*%*	*Budget*	*%*	*Variance*	*%*		*Actual*	*%*	*Budget*	*%*	*Variance*	*Actual*	*%*	*Budget*	*%*	*Variance*
						Travel Expenses Over/Shorts Printing Miscellaneous Maintenance and Repair Painting/Decorating Equipment Repairs Maint. Contracts										
						TOTAL CONTROLLABLE EXPENSES										
						NONCONTROL-LABLE EXPENSES Depreciation Insurance Taxes, Licenses & Fees Management Fee Commissions										
						TOTAL NONCON-TROLLABLE EXPENSE										
						NET PROFIT										

report is important in sales and costs analysis, planning and forecasting, capital equipment replacement and operating budget forecasts.

Timeliness is of the utmost importance. An administrator should expect to have the monthly/period operating statement in hand within 15 days of the period end. Another feature is to have the sales and expense figures stated in dollars and as percentages of the total. The percentages will be critical in comparing the operation with other organizations food-service performance.

As the administrator becomes more familiar with the operating statements, it will become apparent when there are unexplained shifts in the information. For example, food cost jumps 4 percentage points over one or two months. Such an increase should serve as a "red flag" to the administrator. The first action taken may be a discussion with the food-service manager to determine whether or not there is an obvious explanation for the increase. If, after identifying the problem and a possible solution, the increases continue, it may be time to conduct an informal audit of that portion of the program. Later in this chapter there is a discussion of how to conduct such an audit of various aspects of the food-service department.

SALES INFORMATION

Sales should be broken down into various revenue categories such as cafeteria, catering, vending, carts, concessions and branded concepts. Sales volume in any given period can be positively or negatively impacted by any of the following:

- The number of days in the period.
- The number, if any, of holidays in the period.
- Weather
- Pay dates

  In a college environment, sales will be impacted as the term and year ends. Students may have less to spend than they did at the beginning of the year.
- The number, type and attendance of catering events.
- The season of the year. November through December represents the peak catering demand in most organizations.
- Special events and promotions in the foodservice units
- A change for the better or worse in food quality or service levels.
- Improper sales recording.

- Failure to properly ring up sales and account for all cash received.
- External factors such as rapid inflation or a dramatic downturn in the economy.
- Internal factors such as major management changes or down sizing.
- Changes in the level of competition.

When there are significant changes from one period to the next or over several periods, it is important to take action. Working with the foodservice management may resolve the problem.

If the situation is not resolved, then the administrator is wise to refer to the audit section of this chapter.

COST INFORMATION

Operating expenses will generally fall into one of four categories:

- Product costs
- Labor costs
- Controllable operating costs
- Non-controllable operating costs

The following is a discussion of each of the four categories.

Product/Food Costs

This category will include all of the food items purchased and may or may not include paper products such as cups, plates and take-out containers directly associated with the sale of food. In operations which use very little disposable serviceware, paper product may be shown in the product or food cost section. If a program is dependent to a large extent on disposable serviceware, that cost should be shown as a part of controllable operating costs. To the purist, the latter is the preferred treatment for paper products. The product cost categories are normally:

- Bakery Goods
- Beverages
- Dairy Products
- Groceries
- Meat, Poultry, Seafood

- Produce
- Miscellaneous

If purchased frequently, liquor may be a separate category. As mentioned above, disposable supplies may also be one of the product cost categories. The total food cost would be tracked as a percentage of revenues and each of the subcategories as a percentage of total food cost. This later calculation will provide a basis to identify abnormal trends. Food cost is generally calculated as follows:

Food Cost = Beginning Inventory + Purchases – Ending Inventory

All things being equal, there should be a proportional relationship established that will be consistent on month to month basis. If the pattern is disrupted, it may be for the following reasons:

- Mathematical error
- Inaccurate inventory count
- Purchases applied to the wrong product category
- Excessive food waste
- Food theft

Labor Costs

Labor costs include:

- Wages
- Casual labor costs
- Benefits & payroll taxes
- Wage accruals (such as vacation and sick pay)
- Foodservice employee meals

Labor is a volatile, expensive commodity which can dramatically alter the financial budget for any operation. Staffing at optimum levels for the efficient operation and best possible service without over staffing requires skilled management. Changes in staffing levels need to be approved by the administrator, whether the facilities are self-operated or contracted. It is important that the administrator take time to understand the service level requirements and resultant staffing needs at a facility. Failure to adjust staffing to meet demand is one of the most common reasons for a foodservice operation to not meet its budget.

The administrator should carefully evaluate monthly labor expenses in terms of total cost, percentage of sales and their relationship to previous months. Your labor cost, as a percentage of sales, should remain somewhat constant from period to period. Some of the factors that can affect labor cost are:

- Changes in service levels
- Changes in operating hours
- Dramatic increases/decreases in sales volume
- High rate of employee turnover
- Transition to new management or a contracted operation
- Fluctuations in the number and type of catering events
- Wage increases not accompanied by corresponding price increases
- Management not monitoring employee check-in-check-out times
- Lack of management supervision to maintain productivity
- Management is not monitoring and approving overtime

Many of the above are directly related to management's performance. Every effort should be made to communicate and resolve the issues with the inhouse or contract management. Failure to respond within specified time-lines may require personnel action regarding the manager or meetings with District or Regional contractor staff.

Controllable Operating Costs

The most common controllable operating costs which can be actively managed include:

- Cleaning Supplies

  Brooms, mops, and cleansers are included in this category and should remain relatively constant.
- Paper Supplies

  If not included as part of the food costs, this will include the balance of the paper and disposable products used in the operation.
- Advertising and Promotion

  From an operational point of view, it is wise to run periodic promotions and special events. This is especially important for noncommercial foodservice when the market is the same from day to day as people get tired of the same food and surroundings. Any advertising and promotion plan should be preapproved by the administrator.

- Equipment Repairs and Maintenance

  Preventive maintenance is critical in any foodservice operation (see Chapter 7). Adequate time and materials should be budgeted to provide for that preventive maintenance. Records should be maintained, as described in Chapter 7. When repair costs begin to increase, it may be the red flag that you have some equipment which should be replaced or is being mishandled.
- Laundry

  This category includes all expenses related to the purchase and maintenance of linens and uniforms. Some organizations chose to rent these items rather than own and replace them. Linen and uniform rental contracts vary and care should be taken not to enter into an agreement that is based upon minimum costs rather than on an as used basis.
- Equipment Rental

  This category usually relates to the periodic need to rent furniture and equipment for catered events.
- Flowers

  Flowers are often purchased for a cafeteria and for catered events. Fresh flowers are nice but they are expensive and an administrator will want to make sure that there are purchasing policies and guidelines to control this expense.
- Small Equipment Replacement

  Pots, pans, utensils are all reported in this category. There should be a dollar amount which differentiates small equipment from capital equipment.
- China, Glass and Flatware

  This grouping may be included in the small equipment budget, especially if very little china and glass is purchased/used. However, if permanentware is used in the cafeteria, it should be kept as a separate line item.
- Vehicles

  The foodservice department may need to own or lease a vehicle(s) to transport food and supplies to other foodservice units from a central warehouse and/or commissary kitchen. Employees may also be asked to use their personal vehicles to accomplish certain business tasks. The costs for these should be reflected in this category.

- Administrative and General Expenses

  The expenses included in this account are those necessary to operate the business but which are not directly related to the service of the customer. Office supplies, postage, telephone, data processing, dues and subscriptions, traveling expenses, general insurance, commissions on charged cards, cash shortages, professional fees, protective services, are just a few of the administrative expenses that would be applied to this category. In a contractor operation these expenses might be under the non-controllable expenses group and would simply be a percentage of revenues negotiated into the contract.
- Miscellaneous Expenses

  All expenses assigned to miscellaneous should be clearly identified when the monthly/period statement is presented. It should not be used as a "diversion account" for the purpose of bringing other categories in at or under budget.

Some of the expenses to look for and question on a foodservice operating statement for contracted operations in particular are:

- Air express charges. For a contracted operation this is a potential problem. If the contractor's management is late in getting reports into its district, regional or corporate offices, it may chose to use air express. These charges, generally speaking, should not be charged to the organization.
- Excessive long distance phone calls.
- Travel and training expenses.
- Unapproved promotion and/or contractor signature/branded items.

Non-Controllable Operating Costs

Expenses included in this group are associated with fixed overhead costs. A listing and short explanation of each is presented as follows:

- Amortization & Depreciation.

  These costs reflect the period costs for any equipment. There should be a policy for the length of time to be used for amortizing or depreciating these items. In a contracted operation, the rate of interest should also be agreed to in advance.

- Insurance

  In a self-operated program the cost of insurance may be blended into the other insurance for the organization and not easily identifiable. In a contractor operated facility there will be insurance costs passed through to the foodservice. Wherever possible it is best to identify these costs as an actual cost of doing business.
- Taxes, Licenses & Fees

  Income, business or use taxes, licenses and fees required to operate a foodservices program should be reflected here.
- Management Fee (Contractor operations only)

  If there is a management fee contract in place that management fee would be accounted for in this category. This is usually a fixed, negotiated amount.

MEASUREMENT TOOLS

Jones sat back and thought about the situation. Once he had completed all the audit processes he had defined, how would he begin to understand the overall financial statement and, especially, how would he measure productivity? His SFM seminar had addressed the topic, and he pulled out that file to determine how he might use the information. The seminar leader had called these measurement tools "red flags," saying that all they did was point out that a problem might exist. The administrator would still have to analyze the situation to determine the cause. In Jones' notes were the following productivity measurement tools or potential "red flag" warnings.

Participation

A simple yet effective measurement of a foodservice program's success is to track participation. In most noncommercial situations, it is relatively easy to estimate the actual or projected number of persons located in a particular building or on a site/campus. Assuming that each foodervice outlet is tracking the number of cash register rings or transactions, participation can be calculated by dividing the number of transactions by potential patrons. Therefore, if there are 1,000 persons assigned to a site and the cafeteria and espresso cart averages 750 transactions per day, participation will be 75 percent.

Initially, a 75 percent participation level would appear to indicate that the foodservice is being used by three fourths of the population on an average day. There is a need, however, to factor in multiple transactions such as the person who may purchase breakfast in the morning, coffee during the A.M. break and lunch. In actuality, participation may be much less. In order to get a better sense of participation, the calculations should be done by meal or service period. In this way, the foodservice administrator can track what percentage of the population is utilizing the foodservice at peak periods such as lunch or dinner.

Revenue Measurement Tools

How do you know if your facility is generating the revenue it should? Is it meeting the customers' needs in a way that maximizes revenue? These are not easy questions to answer. There is no formula or industry standard that fits all situations. What must be done is to trend certain data over a period of time and determine which idiosyncracies drive your operation. An admistrator needs to select the measurement tools that fit his or her specific units.

Per Capita Sales

When a market potential can be narrowly quantified, per capita sales becomes a viable measurement tool. For example, a zoo can use the number of paid visitors per period to determine its per capita sales. A company cafeteria with a fixed number of employees to serve can do the same. A visitors' cafeteria in a hospital, however, may find this measurement tool less important because foodservice cannot accurately measure the number of visitors who come in and out of the hospital per period.

One transportation system with retail foodservice on each route found per capita sales, rather than per transaction sales to be an effective tool in determining potential sales increases that might be achieved with more modern equipment and menus. Since there was more than one foodservice unit in the system, management compared potential customer bases. They found that one unit had 100,000 annual passengers and another one had 80,000 annual passengers. The 100,000-passenger unit had higher total sales but, when calculated on the per capita basis, was underperforming the unit with fewer passengers. Observation in the units showed that both units were busy for the entire 30-minute duration of the ride. In fact, not all customers on the 100,000-passenger unit were served before it was time to disembark. It was determined that placing an additional cashier station in the unit with the higher number of passengers would increase the sales to the per capita level attained by the other unit. The additional revenue more than paid the salary of the additional cashier and increased passenger satisfaction dramatically.

Jones thought about his own situation. One of his units was generating more sales per employee market base than another. He would ask his foodservice manager to help him try to determine a course of action to correct this situation.

Average Sale per Cash Register Transaction

Tracking the number of cash register transactions recorded in a day or time period sometimes provides a misconception that all of a potential market is pleased with and uses the cafeteria frequently. It is important to view the number of transactions in relationship to other data.

For example, one foodservice administrator was very proud of the fact that, with 1,200 employees in a given office building, there were 1,025 daily transactions in the cafeteria. The mistaken assumption was that 85.4 percent of the building population was eating in the cafeteria. What was not taken into account was that only 230 transactions occurred in the cafeteria at the peak (lunch) period. This figure provides a measurement tool that can be compared to other cafeteria and foodservice operations.

Jones recalled that transactions were high in his cafeteria, but the customer surveys and comment cards suggested that satisfaction levels were not as high as the transactions would indicate. Fewer people were actually using the cafeteria than his manager thought.

Check Averages

Average check is often misunderstood by those unfamiliar with the foodservice industry. The label "average check" is actually a misnomer for this important piece of data. Many people interpret it to be the average sale for each check rung into the cash register; that is, average sale per transaction, such as described above.

In restaurants, executive dining rooms, and other operations where one person frequently pays the bill for multiple patrons, the sales per transaction figure is not sufficient to measure productivity and financial control. The other important element is the number of customers included in each check. The average check, then, is average revenue per person served. Just as the number of cash register rings in a cafeteria can inflate participation figures, single transactions in a restaurant often deflate the number of customers served. The average sale per customer served is the figure that can be compared to other operations and which, when tracked over a period of months, will indicate whether the operation is improving, remaining stagnant, or declining.

Costs as a Percentage of Revenue

Tracking costs as a percentage of revenue is a critical measurement tool in the foodservice industry. Every administrator should insist that financial statements be presented in a format that not only includes the difference between budgeted and actual figures for a given period, but also the expenses by percentage of revenue. This is true whether that revenue is a fixed amount such as for a college board plan or a variable amount based on a la carte sales in a cafeteria.

Tracking costs as a percentage of income/revenue will provide the necessary data to compare with other similar operations. It will also allow you to identify valuable trends over a period of time. One of the most valuable handbooks that any foodservice administrator should at least be familiar with is the *Uniform System of Accounts for Restaurants*, which is available from the National Restaurant Association (see Chapter 14). While the entire system is not always adaptable for every organization, the basic principles do have application. For example, one operation had food costs that ranged from 35 percent to 45 percent of revenue for a basic fast-food concept over a 12 month period. There should not be such a wide discrepancy in food cost percentage from month to month. Since pricing was in line with the commercial foodservice industry, there had to be an explanation for the fluctuating food costs. Further analysis showed that every product delivered from a major vendor was assigned to food costs because it was on that invoice. Since that vendor supplied all of the paper and janitorial products and often delivered extra cases of glassware, flatware, and other nonfood supplies, the operation was not tracking a true food cost. Assigning certain items and products to accounting categories will differ from operation to operation. Using the *Uniform System of Accounts for Restaurants* as a guideline for assigning those costs will result in data that can be compared to information published by a variety of public and private sources, such as those described in Chapters 13 and 14.

Productivity Measurement Tools

Measuring tools to monitor labor productivity and personnel management were important to Jones. He knew that people were an expensive resource and that it was his job to learn whether AU was getting the most for its dollars in that category.

- Meals served per labor hour worked

  This measurement tool is best applied when patrons are consuming full meals. Examples include hospital patients, college students in "all-you-care-to-eat" dining programs, and inmates in corrections facilities. Managers in these and other institutions find this a valid tool for measuring productivity.

  One operation served 20 meals per labor hour worked and another similar operation served only 16. Following close review of the two operations, it was easy to see that in one operation the cooking was done on the serving line so that staff could be brought from the kitchen to work the line during the meal periods. The other operation required that all the food be prepared in the kitchen and then portioned on the line. This resulted in the need to have staff in the kitchen and on the line during the meal periods, creating a lower per meal served factor.
- Revenue per labor hour worked

  This measurement is more valid for retail foodservice operations such as employee cafeterias, concessions operations, retail food courts, and others that primarily sell a la carte rather than full meals.

  One company had two cafeterias for its employees. One of them was generating $10.00 more sales per labor hour worked over a week period. The administrator was, of course, concerned that one unit was overstaffed. Further analysis showed that both cafeterias were full during every lunch period. At the recommendation of the foodservice manager, the adminstrator began to track half hourly sales in both cafeterias. It appeared that one of the two cafeteria building populations had the option of coming to work early and leaving early. The result was that in that cafeteria very few people took an afternoon break since they were leaving as early as 3:30 P.M. The old policy had been that both cafeterias were to operate until 4:30 P.M. A decision was made to close the second cafeteria at 2:00 P.M. each day. The labor savings were dramatic and sales did not decline noticeably. In fact, vending sales went up slightly, compensating for the lost cafeteria revenue.
- Labor cost per meal served

  Dividing the total payroll including benefits by the total meals served in the same period will provide a dollar labor cost per meal served. This measurement is especially useful, when combined with product cost, in determining prices for full meal service in college residence halls, hospitals, corrections units, and other institutions.

- Seat utilization

  Dividing the total number of customers dining during a specified period by the total seats in the operation will provide what is referred to as the "seat turns." If 200 lunches are served in a 115-seat cafeteria during a 90-minute period, the seat turns would be 1.72. This is a high seat utilization number for the time period.

  Seat turns can provide useful information, though one is never certain where the results will lead. In one instance, a manager was perplexed because the seat utilization in a 200-seat cafeteria was only one during a two-hour period. The facility had a market potential of 600 customers, there was no nearby competition, and food and service ratings were high. In fact, the customers' biggest complaint was that the cafeteria was always full. The manager finally asked an outside foodservice acquaintance to come and take a look at the operation. One look and the objective visitor saw the problem. All of the 25 round tables seated eight persons. What was happening was a single diner or a group of two or three would come to the cafeteria, get their meals and then could not find a "table" for their lunch. Some either quit coming to the cafeteria or bought items to take back to their desks. The manager replaced all but four of the round tables with two- and four-person tables, still netting a total seating capacity of 200. Within the month the seat utilization had gone from 1 to 1.5, with sales rising accordingly.

Other Measurement Tools

Special Function Records

Keeping a periodic summary of the number of special events, number of attenders, and average check will enable a foodservice manager to monitor trends and spot variances that might indicate either operational or financial problems. An administrator should request that the foodservice manager, if not already doing so, prepare such a summary, ideally on a monthly basis.

Employee Turnover

Hiring and training new employees is costly and interrupts the operation. Turnover in the foodservice industry is usually higher than overall employee turnover; however, organizations that include employees in the benefit program and operate their foodservice on a five-day-a-week basis tend to have lower turnover than the fast-food or general restaurant industry. An administrator can develop a good long-term measuring tool by tracking employee turnover in the foodservice department. First, it is important to determine if there are times during the year when turnover is higher. Could that turnover be lower or is it a part of the organization's business pattern? For example, college and universities that use not just casual student labor, but also hire and train select students for supervisory positions will generally have increased turnover at graduation and/or the end of a given term.

If turnover levels increase and remain at a higher level over several months, it may signal a need to look at the supervisory situation. Has a new, ineffective supervisor created increased turnover? Has management changed some policies that are resulting in increased turnover? It is not necessary to assume that increased turnover is always bad. It may be that a large number of individuals were ready for and took retirement or the company's early retirement offer was taken by more foodservice staff than anticipated. A fluctuation in and of itself is not a problem. It is simply a "red flag," indicating the need to ascertain the reasons.

Inventory Turnover

Many institutional and corporate dining programs once operated on the philosophy that they needed anywhere from three to five weeks' inventory on hand at any given time. Institutions, especially, purchased in bulk for a quarter year or even longer and stored the products. Today, suppliers are able to deliver product more readily; the cost of storing and handling products has increased; and the cost of tying up working capital is high. As a result, most operations maintain inventory levels of from one to three weeks, depending as much on location or potentially bad weather conditions as any other factor. Turning inventory over in a two-week period is common for many operations.

A quick measurement tool for determining the inventory turnover is to divide total annual purchases by the average weekly/period inventory.

THE AUDIT

Jones knew he did not need to acquire the skills to conduct a complete financial audit, but he did need to learn an informal means of verifying critical aspects of foodservice's bookkeeping and accounting system.

According to a fellow foodservice administrator Jones had met, what he needed was a process that would enable him to look for "red flags" or "holes in the system." The process referred to must provide administrators with the means to verify that foodservice staff are doing everything possible to collect, accurately record, and manage/control the department's cash. Because many organizations have subsidized cafeterias, these organization have an important financial interest in assuring that foodservice staff accurately report all sales and expenses. In addition, it is important to keep accurate operations data such as customer counts, average sales per customer, and sales by time period.

The Society for Foodservice Management's annual meeting Jones had attended in New York City in early October had been very informative, he recalled. One of the workshops had been on the topic of financial management. The speaker had stated that it is important for administrators to have a quasi-audit system that allows them to follow an "audit trail" (i.e., permit the easy tracking/validation of all critical financial transactions over a set period of time). If a foodservice is contracted, prior to commencing an audit the auditing administrator needs to ascertain the accounting time frame the contractor utilizes. Most contractors prefer to operate according to accounting periods (blocks of four weeks followed by a five-week block or only blocks of four weeks resulting in 13—not 12—accounting periods per year) as opposed to calendar months. Therefore, in some cases, administrators will be reviewing multiple tracking periods. For example, cafeteria sales will have to be reconciled on a weekly basis, payroll biweekly (if employees are paid every two weeks), and food cost whenever fully priced inventories are taken.

When preparing to do an initial audit, administrators need to ask their organization's foodservice managers or, if applicable, their contractor's managers, to "talk and show" them through the sales and expenses reporting process currently being used. Administrators will want to get copies of and explanations for each of the accounting forms used. If a foodservice is contracted, administrators will find that most contractors follow the same general process, though each one has developed its own nomenclature and forms. When foodservice is self-operated, on the other hand, accounting systems may be less standardized. Thus, it is advisable for administrators to consult all individuals who might participate in the financial cycle, including purchasing and bookkeeping employees.

With these thoughts in mind, Jones first decided to gain a good understanding of how the foodservice accounting process actually functioned. He would then use these data and the information from the SFM seminar to guide him toward adopting an audit program that would work for him, his department, and AU. To this end, he decided that it would be helpful initially to develop a "preliminary" audit program and use it for the first evaluation. Based on the results of the preliminary audit, appropriate adjustments could be made and a final program adopted.

Before auditing the contracted operations, an administrator must read and clearly understand the contract. As the contract administrator, Jones spent time refamiliarizing himself with the relevant details of those documents.

Critical audit categories include:

1. Sales and Cash/Charge Accountability: cafeteria sales, catering sales, retail store sales, cart sales
2. Total Income: vending sales and commissions
3. Product Costs
4. Labor Costs
5. Operating Costs: controllable and noncontrollable

Jones sat back, pleased with the draft outline of his audit process. He felt sure now that his general background in financial management would be useful in managing foodservice's finances, as well. His subsequent work is presented on the following pages. The recommended process and procedures for conducting an audit of each category are presented. Because each of the nine audit categories will generally be conducted at different times, each section is written to "stand alone," resulting in some unavoidable redundancy. The goal is to permit an administrator to review an entire section without having to refer to the other sections.

Sales and Cash/Charge Accountability Audit

Before starting a sales audit, administrators should give some thought to the foodservice sales process. A department's primary role is to provide an exchange of food or service for payment. Payment can be received in the form of cash, charged meals, meal vouchers, catering charges, or income from products supplied to vending machines. The challenge for auditors is to ascertain that the exchanges were proper, and properly recorded, in each instance. Foodservice managers must have a keen interest in maintaining strict controls over sales. Any audit of sales should be easily accomplished by utilizing the control procedures foodservice managers or contractors' managers have established for properly and accurately recording sales. Therefore, a substantial part of each audit will be spent ascertaining that the established control procedures and paper trail are being utilized.

I. Determine the period of time that sales are to be verified (such as by meal period, day, week, one accounting period, multiple accounting periods, or year).
   A. Notify the foodservice manager or contractor's representative and request their assistance in conducting an audit.
   B. Request that foodservice manager(s) provide necessary supporting documentation.

      Weekly sales reports with cash register tapes, over-ring slips, cashiers' diaries, meal vouchers, meal charge slips, and catering orders with supporting documentation should be inspected. (If the audit is for a period of time in excess of a week, additional information should include monthly or period sales reports and monthly or period financial statements for all foodservice operations.)
   C. Set an appointment with foodservice manager(s) to conduct the audit. It is important that an appropriate amount of time be set aside. A first audit may take several hours, but subsequent evaluations should take less time.

Conducting the actual audit was comparable to solving a puzzle for Jones. He first wanted to verify that foodservice's recorded sales were accurate. To accomplish this, he proceeded thusly.

Step 1: First, Jones matched cash register tapes with cashiers' work sheets and daily/weekly sales reports. Jones was amazed at the amount of paper foodservice managers had to process on a regular basis; he had always thought they just had to know how to cook for, serve, and manage people. For his audit, Jones elected to review one week of tapes and daily sales reports at random. If all was in order, he would spot check a couple of days in other weeks. If he found regular discrepancies, he would review documents covering the entire period.

Step 2: Jones' next step was to verify that all charges and meal vouchers had been registered as sales. An attender at the SFM seminar had pointed out that employee meals needed to be run through the system both for tax purposes and to ascertain the validity of submitted food and labor costs.

Jones remembered questioning Harry Daulton a few months back about why foodservice employees received free meals. "Wouldn't it lower our subsidy if they at least paid a portion of their meal costs?" Jones had wanted to know. Daulton explained his theory. "If we didn't give them free food, they would probably find a way to eat 'free' anyway. I think it's better to give them meals that we record on our registers. That way, I keep better control of the system." Daulton had noted, though, that the employees were prohibited from including certain expensive items (such as steak and shrimp) in their free meals. He then recounted the story of a colleague who had found foodservice staff ordering twice as many lobsters as were usually served in that company's executive dining room, so that each staff member could have lobster themselves. The colleague, Daulton recalled, had quickly put a halt to *that* practice.

During this conversation, Daulton also made another germane point. In most cases, foodservice employees will take greater care during preparation of foods that they themselves will be eating. In addition, employees learn about foodservice's various menu items by eating them and are, therefore, better able to answer questions from the customers. Jones was convinced; free foodservice staff meals offered from a restricted menu would remain. He did resolve, however, to keep a watchful eye on the recording of those meals on cashier register tapes.

Step 3: This involved verifying that all customer payments for AU owned vending machine items had been registered as sales. In some cases, a cafeteria may be supplying foods to such machines, while their revenue is being recorded on the vending area's statement. When this is the case, a corresponding credit/payment should be recorded from vending to the cafeteria for the dollar value of the food and labor supplied. This amount should reflect the *actual value* of the food items supplied. This way, a cafeteria will not be subsidizing vending.

Jones realized that he had a new problem to deal with, since he was still in the process of determining what to do with AU's vending when the contract to operate its 36 machines came up for renewal. Right now, some of his machines were contracted, while others belonged to AU and were only serviced by the foodservice department. Where the vending machines were contracted to an outside operator, Jones would have to conduct a separate audit process.

Step 4: Jones next matched individual catering invoices to the weekly catering sales reports. He was careful to verify that each had been recorded as sales. He also confirmed that each catering invoice had been properly priced and that all price extensions and totals were correct. Daulton had once told Jones about a time several years ago when he had found that the catering manager was giving a "better" price to certain departments. It turned out that the staff in those departments were good personal friends of the catering manager and had the power to make sure that the catering manager had occasional use of the company condo in the mountains in return for his favors.

Jones found himself wishing silently that employees would use some of their creative energies to benefit their organization, rather than finding ways to defraud it. While he did not like to think of people as basically dishonest, he had to admit that it would be naive not to recognize the need to monitor all aspects of foodservice's program.

Jones then verified that each catering order had been properly approved and charged to the correct customer/account code. Because of AU's new in-house policy on interdepartmental services, he also had to verify that a purchase order number had been established for each order. AU had made that move during its first-of-the-year reorganization to ensure that all costs were properly charged and that departments did not go over budget without realizing it. At AU, purchase orders could not be authorized by anyone but a vice president if a department or division had met or exceeded its budget in an allotted category.

The next step in the audit process was for Jones to verify that the prices for all "special orders" (i.e., not listed in the price and portion book, such as equipment rentals and extra/overtime labor) had been approved and paid for by the department or person responsible for each order.

Daulton advised Jones to verify during audits that "X"

> readings from cash registers had been carried forward to the next shift/day. On most cash register systems, the "X" reading represents the cumulative or running total. When an "X" reading is taken, the closing reading from the prior shift or day must be brought forward and subtracted from the new reading to calculate the total sales for that shift/day. Daulton had also pointed out the importance of inspecting actual cash register tapes to be sure that the correct readings had been recorded.

If a foodservice manager is taking "Z" readings (i.e., instead of maintaining a cumulative or running total, machine totals are returned to zero at the end of every shift/day), he or she would then want to verify that cash register transaction counts were being properly monitored. (The transaction count is an allegedly tamper-proof cash register mechanism that records each time the register is used. An unexplained break in the transaction count record should be investigated, as it may represent evidence of theft or fraud.)

By conducting a sales review, an administrator will be able to verify that all over-rings have been recorded in cashiers' reports with a cash register tape attached and approved by a foodservice manager for verification. Administrators should look for a pattern of frequent or large dollar-amount over-rings. Such activity may well indicate a theft problem. Cashiers should not have the authority to use their cash registers' "Manager's Key" to correct their own over-rings. In addition, all other "noncustomer transaction" entries (such as "No Sale" rings, etc.) should be monitored for frequency and timing.

This phase of the audit process provides administrators with an excellent opportunity to determine that their foodservice's price and portion book is current. Additionally, now is the time to verify that all catering orders are being priced uniformly.

Jones understood that once he had verified, via the sales audit, that all receipts had been recorded, his concern became making certain that all monies, in whatever form, were deposited in the bank. Because most cafeteria sales are in cash, this is the area of financial management that has the greatest potential for dishonesty. Remember, should anyone be manipulating cash, he or she is stealing from the organization. Therefore, it is very important to look for ways that cash is being inappropriately handled. Income, as we are using the term for the purposes of this audit, is another way of saying money. The audit of income (money) should be seen as an extension of the sales audit.

Total Income Audit

Jones referred to his notes to review how to audit a foodservice's money-handling procedures.

Preparation

Step 1: Determine the period of time during which total income is to be verified (such as meal period, day, week, one accounting period, multiple accounting periods, or the year).

Step 2: Notify the foodservice manager or, if applicable, contractor's representative of the intent to audit.

Step 3: Request the following information from the foodservice manager or contractor:

- Weekly sales reports, cashiers' work sheets/reports, paid out items such as petty cash slips, vouchers, and the employee meals log
- Individual vending machine sales records, weekly vending sales reports, commission calculation reports
- Bank deposit receipts

Conducting the audit

Step 1: Cash should be reconciled for/by each cashier at the completion of each shift. The cash reconciliation process starts with the verification of sales figures on cash register tapes. All deductions from sales must be verified as valid. Match the paid-outs to the weekly sales report and the cashiers' work sheets.

- All paid-outs must be supported with valid receipts and approved by a foodservice manager.
- Vouchers must be fully filled out and authorized by a foodservice manager. The reason(s) for the payout should be clearly stated.
- Verify that cashiers' change banks are audited regularly.

Step 2: Look for a pattern of cash shortages or overages on a cashier-by-cashier basis. Such activity may indicate a possible theft problem.

Step 3: Look for an unusual number of "No Sales." Each no sale represents the cash drawer being opened without a sale.

Step 4: Match the bank deposit receipts to the weekly sales report.

In units where cash receipts are picked up by an armored car company, the bank receipts may be included in the following week's paperwork. In some cases, catering payments will be recorded separately. Verifications over a sample period of time (such as a week or an accounting period) and an attempt to match up all catering invoices with payment checks should be made.

If catering payments are made directly by departments or divisions to a foodservice department or on-site contractor, it should be fairly simple to match up payments. If catering payments are made to a remote location, however, administrators will have to have their contractors supply a payment record and/or copies of the checks. The last part of this process will be to verify that the current invoices outstanding equal the amount shown on foodservice's accounts receivable ledger or balance sheet.

Step 5: Verify that each weekly sales report is mathematically correct (i.e., that it balances).

Step 6: If an audit is to extend beyond a week, administrators must verify that the total of all weekly sales reports equals the amount of total income listed on period or monthly financial statements.

Step 7: Review the employee meals log to make sure that all transactions are properly recorded and that employees are not taking more than permitted by the employee meals policy.

Step 8: If self-operated, match individual vending machine records with the weekly vending report. Proof the combined vending machine sales total. Match the combined individual vending machine total with the vending commission calculation report. Where cafeteria food is being supplied for vending, administrators will also want to audit the food production records and "discard reports" to ascertain that all products and revenues have been accounted for. It is also advisable to proof the commission calculations.

In some cases, a vending contractor tracks its inventory and sales by price categories. Where this is so, administrators will have to audit the process by tracking the product and/or price groups for each machine. Another way of verifying vending machine sales is to audit the transaction counter readings from one period to another. The ultimate goal is for administrators to assure themselves that sales are being accurately recorded and that the organization is receiving all of its due commissions. Since AU received a commission on some vending machine sales, Jones knew it was important to verify vending sales to ascertain that correct commissions were being paid by its vending supplier.

Step 9: Catering invoices are controlled documents and should be consecutively numbered. Administrators will want to account for all invoices. Once used, they should be listed on the period-ending catering sales reports and billing invoices sent to all departments from which catering orders have emanated. An administrator will want to make sure that transfers were all credited to foodservice or, if the department is contracted, that the organization's payment was credited to the proper bank account and shown as "paid" on its contractor's books.

Step 10: The vast majority of catering events are charged to in-house accounts or outside organizations. That's why it is important that the accounts receivable ledger be audited. Foodservice's records should have a complete listing of all accounts outstanding on an "aged" basis (those unpaid over a 30-, 60-, and 90+-day period). Bills not paid after 90 days may require investigation and follow-up collection action.

Since past-due catering bills may be charged to foodservices' operating subsidies, administrators will want to make sure that a corresponding credit is received once each bill has been paid.

Product Cost Audit

Conducting a complete audit of a foodservice's product cost during one accounting period, multiple accounting periods, or for a year would be an intensely laborious task. Administrators' needs will be well served if they simply focus on reviewing one or two categories of significant product invoices. The audit process in this area includes:

Step 1: Determine which purveyor(s) should be audited.

Step 2: Notify foodservice managers and/or contractor representatives, as applicable, of the intent to audit these expenditures and request their assistance.

Step 3: Request that foodservice managers and/or contractor representatives provide the following information:

- Inventory records/book, invoices from selected purveyor(s), petty cash slips used to purchase food or supplies, applicable transfer journal entries (for food and supplies transferred from one unit to another or, if contracted, from another contractor's unit to an organization's), ordering/receiving records, and purveyor price book. When applicable, administrators should ask for copies of all merchandise return memoranda and purveyor credit slips.
- Should administrators decide to expand the scope of the audit to encompass an entire week or accounting period, they will need copies of the applicable starting and ending product inventories in correctly priced and extended forms.

Step 4: Verify that all purveyors are authorized suppliers.

Step 5: Verify that all items purchased are appropriate for the organization's cafeteria and/or conform with specifications agreed to in the contract.

Step 6: Match prices as they appear on invoices with purveyor's price books or quote sheets.

Step 7: Proof all price extensions and total the invoices.

Step 8: Verify that invoiced amounts for individual items have been applied to appropriate cost accounts (such as meats and groceries). This check should include verifying the proper distribution of petty cash slips.

Again, administrators will want to track all special purchases for catering to make sure that the expenses were anticipated or included as part of the customer charge.

Since food costs are tracked by product category, it will be necessary to set up a work sheet as a means of validating that the food cost totals are correct.

Step 9: Verify that individual invoice items were properly recorded in receiving records.

If an audit is to be restricted to verifying several invoices, it may be well worth an administrator's time to ask foodservice managers or contractors' representatives to supply invoices for an entire accounting period. Rather than proof each one's mathematical accuracy, administrators may wish to review them in a random manner to make certain they are from authorized suppliers and that no "unusual" products are being purchased. Special attention should be paid to those invoices filled out and calculated by hand. Oftentimes, these are from smaller vendors like bakeries, produce companies, or flower shops. As administrators look over these invoices, they should take the time to check the quality and quantity of items being ordered. This way, they will be able to make certain that one foodservice facility is not buying products for another cafeteria or for someone's personal use, and that corners aren't being cut on food quality in order to save a few dollars.

Step 10: Verify that items being purchased with petty cash are appropriate. Look for patterns. Is the same item being purchased consistently with petty cash? Are there a number of petty cash purchases from the same supplier?

It is always helpful to ascertain which items a foodservice department or contractor is buying with petty cash funds. If there is a pattern of buying regularly purchased food and supply items, administrators should remind managers or contractors' representatives to buy these items via normal wholesale methods, rather than paying retail prices at local stores. Administrators will want to make sure that this practice is curtailed, as it certainly will have a negative impact on food and/or supply costs. Look for the same person's initials as handling or authorizing payments. Unless there is only one person designated, a single individual's initials may indicate that one person is manipulating the payouts to his or her own personal gain.

Labor Cost Audit

To conduct an audit of an entire week's or accounting period's labor costs would require a prohibitive amount of time. Administrators' goal of verifying record-keeping accuracy will be equally well served if a representative number of employees' records are reviewed and their related labor costs verified. In smaller cafeterias, it will be just as easy to audit time and payroll records for all employees. The following steps should be followed to conduct this phase of the audit:

Step 1: Determine which employees you intend to audit.

Step 2: Notify foodservice managers of the intent to audit and request their assistance.

Step 3: Request the following information:

- Time cards or computer summary sheets for selected employees

- Weekly staff schedules
- Employee meal logs

Note: If an audit covers a period of time in excess of one week, it will be necessary to request additional information to cover the time period.

Step 4: Review the amount of hours worked by staff against their posted schedules. Ascertain the reason for significant differences, if any appear. This is necessary to verify that the wages paid were equal to the hours worked. Another reason for verifying the scheduled hours is to assure compliance with bargaining unit and/or state/federal employment laws regarding time records.

Step 5: Verify the calculation of hours worked. Match the hours on time cards to the weekly time sheets. Verify that the wage rate is accurate. Administrators will want to question any unusual or unexplained overtime charges. Verify that employee meal charges are accurate.

Step 6: For contract-managed foodservice programs, administrators will need to verify that all employees listed on weekly time sheets are actually contractor's employees assigned to specified foodservice facilities. The easiest way to do this is by matching names on the payroll register to faces.

Step 7: At contracted foodservice programs, it is also important to match the contractor's transfer journal entries for insurance, vacation accrual, and other claims against weekly time sheets. Unused accruals should be credited back to the applicable site.

Jones wanted to determine if the correct amount of compensation and related benefits were being paid. A verification of accruals for wages, vacations, insurance, and other benefits can answer this concern and is an excellent use of an administrator's time. Dishonest contractors may transfer labor and benefit accruals from a P&L account to a fee account, to hide their real costs and transfer expenses to unwitting clients.

Carrying "ghost labor" on a payroll is a favorite way for a dishonest person to make a few extra dollars. For instance, Jones recalled hearing at the recent SFM meeting how one administrator had uncovered a situation where phony overtime was charged by a contractor manager to certain employees, who then shared their ill-gotten gains with that manager. While he had no reason to suspect that type of abuse was occurring at AU,

Jones was not going to leave any stone unturned. "Better to prevent than cure" had always been his workplace motto.

Another horror story that one person had shared was the issue of casual laborers. Management was hiring a day laborer from an agency. Company policy allowed that time of temporary service to be a maximum of five consecutive days, with the laborers paid cash at the end of each day. Management hired the employee to work on Monday and paid cash. Each of the next four days the manager put in a cash payout for labor but the individual did not actually work. The money wound up in the manager's pocket.

Jones began looking for patterns in labor scheduling. Were the same individuals consistently receiving overtime? Was the amount of overtime always the same? If supervisors have solicited the aid of employees in padding time worked, they often will repeat the time each week, under the assumption that if the total does not change, no one will suspect. An employee may agree to "mark up" hours for a share of the return.

Jones chuckled as he recalled another attender at the SFM meeting saying that such "time theft" was the reason he did not want to contract his organization's foodservice. To that fellow's dismay, however, two people in the group had spoken up to describe similar incidents at their own *self-operated* programs. The contractor-wary fellow had had to admit that fraud was possible everywhere, not just in contracted foodservice units. Jones swore he'd do all in his power to see to it that fraud did not occur in any of his foodservice program components. After all, he reasoned, "The buck stops at my desk."

Controllable and Noncontrollable Operating Costs Audit

An audit of controllable and noncontrollable operating costs should be conducted in the same manner as the process used to determine product costs. Controllable costs are purchases of such items as cleaning materials, paper supplies, small equipment, laundry service and uniforms, rentals, and maintenance. In contract foodservice situations, noncontrollable costs are generally charged to each client-organization facility's account by intercompany transfers originated by the contractor's regional accounting office. Noncontrollable charges are usually fees and licenses, insurance costs, and contractors' fees. Is a foodservice getting what it is paying for? Is it paying the correct price for what it gets? To find out:

Step 1: Select a purveyor(s) to be audited. Advise foodservice managers or contractors' representatives of the intent to audit, ask their assistance, and request the necessary supporting documentation.

Step 2: Use the same procedures as outlined previously in validating the process of posting and assigning these expenses.

Step 3: Validate any nonrecurring expenses. In the case of contracted programs, the contract may require that any nonrecurring expenses (i.e., special purchases) must receive administrators' prior approval.

This subject area represents the greatest opportunity for contractor-client "misunderstandings" as to what is an appropriate expense to be charged to foodservice. As noted in the introduction, it will be very important that administrators carefully review their contracts to determine which "normal operating expenses" their foodservice contractors are responsible for. Special attention should be paid to charges for proprietary materials such as manager's manuals or software. For example, one contractor was passing a charge through to a hospital for the development and maintenance of diet manuals. These hospital-specific, customized manuals were prepared by on-site dietitians already being charged as a labor expense to the hospital. At the end of the contract period, when a new contractor had been selected, the contract management company was claiming the manuals as proprietary. There was no language in the prior contract to clarify this issue.

A good rule of thumb to use when writing contract language is that any materials that the account/client paid for in connection with that account should be the property of the account/client. Materials purchased and/or provided as part of the contractor's management fee that are generic to that contractor should remain the property of the contractor. In the case of the previously mentioned hospital, the manuals would have remained as its property. On the other hand, that same contractor used a computer software program developed by its corporate offices. The ending data remained at the hospital, but the software was taken back by the contractor. (Note: It is important in setting the specifications for a contract that you consider the type of software program that a contractor proposes to use. To assure continuity, it is preferable that an operator uses a generic brand of software that can be purchased from the vendor by the organization or its succeeding contractor. If a contractor uses a program it has developed internally, the transition to self-operation or another contract is that much more difficult.)

Jones was both exhilarated and exhausted by having finally developed a clear picture of the foodservice's financial operations. With a sense of the measurement tools at his disposal and a defined audit process he was confident that he had what he needed to succeed in his new role.

CHAPTER THIRTEEN

Research Data/ Customer Knowledge

It was hard for Jones to believe that almost a year had passed since AU had began restructuring and dropped the "hot potato" of foodservice administration into his lap. He felt he had learned a great deal, even though just "learning the ropes," from solving the problems he had faced. In short, Jones at last felt he had become a competent foodservice administrator, but true to his career values, he was not content just to "do the job." Returning to his office one cold Monday afternoon following the Thanksgiving holiday, Jones let his mind wander to the possibilities of improving AU's foodservice programs, along with the planned facilities remodeling and eventual construction of the new foodservice facility across the freeway. "Ultimately," Jones thought, "we will have to increase foodservice's revenue and eliminate its subsidy."

But before reaching that point Jones knew that foodservice would have to continue upgrading its operational performance. Throughout the past year, his office had received letters of complaint, some anonymous, about different aspects of foodservice's program. He had either responded to each letter or had different foodservice managers respond, depending on the nature of the complaint. Foodservice managers, Jones had discovered, would often pass on the verbal compliments customers offered about the program, but they rarely mentioned any customer complaints. "Of course," he thought, "that's natural. Would I tell my new boss when customers criticized my services? Probably not!"

To further complicate Jones' assessment of his foodservice customers' degree of satisfaction, he had begun to receive several foodservice trade publications that regularly printed sales and demographic data for various types of foodservices. Jones' problem was that he did not know enough about customers' opinions of his operations to be sure he was accurately comparing AU's programs against these industry standards. The time had come, Jones decided, to rectify this situation. After a few conversations with several foodservice administrators at other local organizations, he learned that many of them had developed multiple means of keeping track of customer data.

TYPES OF CUSTOMER RESEARCH

Jones recognized the need to conduct two distinct types of internal research in order to compile data for different analytical purposes. The two types of research include:

- Assessment of the overall foodservice program.
  These data will tell operators what their customers think of the food and service. The results provide an assessment of what *is*, not what *should be.*
- Analysis of dining habits and preferences.
  This type of internal research can help define customers' overall dining habits and preferences, spending patterns, and other data. This research is aimed at helping operators and administrators define what their foodservice program *should be*, not to provide an assessment of what it *is*.

FREQUENCY OF RESEARCH

There must be some reasonable way for customers to express their opinions about foodservice on a regular basis. But that process alone will not generate customer preference data and is certainly unlikely to elicit information as to why some organization members never participate in the program. Jones could see that he would need to do both ongoing research, as well as periodic surveys of organization members' opinions of foodservice.

- Ongoing process
  This is a system for receiving and responding to customer

comments on a day-to-day basis. Such opinion sampling can be carried out either by distributing comment cards or by posting a suggestion box in each dining facility.

- Periodic surveys

  These surveys provide administrators and operators with a repeatable process of obtaining in-depth customer perceptions and needs/preferences relative to foodservice. The process might include using one or more survey forms (verbal/written/electronic) and/or focus groups (formal/informal) to produce desired information.

ONGOING COMMUNICATIONS WITH CUSTOMERS

To ensure program satisfaction, customers should be given a means of communicating their likes and dislikes regarding the foodservice program. Most commonly, this process involves distributing comment cards and/or putting out a suggestion box. In the noncommercial foodservice market, these cards are used primarily to monitor customer satisfaction by eliciting data on their attitudes toward the food, service, and general ambience. In other words, cards allow customers who use an organization's foodservice to forward comments regarding operational issues that most directly affect their dining satisfaction. (A sample comment card is shown in Exhibit 13-1 and on the accompanying disk.)

To be effective, comment cards need to be brief. Few if any customers will fill out a lengthy form just to make a point about foodservice preference. In addition, comment cards tend to be more effective if they are distributed on a scheduled basis (e.g., once a quarter each person who goes through a cashier line gets a comment card with his or her receipt). In between the scheduled distribution periods, comment cards should be displayed at cashiers' stands, where customers can pick them up if they feel compelled to voice a positive or negative comment. The randomly gathered feedback will lead to different findings during a "survey" period than would be the case if all or a percentage of customers had been specifically asked to fill out cards. Theoretically, customers fill out these cards only when they have a strong opinion.

A brightly decorated, locked deposit box positioned near egress points will assure customers that their responses will be kept confidential.

When designing comment card questions, it is important for a foodservice department's management first to stop and detail exactly what

Exhibit 13-1
COMMENT CARD

	Ex.	*Good*	*Fair*	*Poor*	*Comments*
Temperature of Food					
Taste of Food					
Size of Portions					
Value for Money					
Cleanliness					
Courtesy					
Speedy Service					
Other					

Date ______________ Time ___________ AM/PM

How often do you use the cafeteria?
1 x per week _____ 2–3 x per week _____ Every day _____

Your name and phone number would be appreciated; however, if you wish to remain anonymous, we will still value your comments.

____

____

information they wish to obtain from the survey process. Are cards just to be used by customers to rate the organization's food and service, or should they be designed to solicit open-ended comments?

With the advent of electronic mail (E-mail) in many organizations, comment cards are now being placed on the computer for customers to fill in and send via E-mail to the foodservice administrator. Other operations are installing a computer terminal in the cafeteria so customers can stop and input comments. Obviously, the easier it is for customers, the more input the department will receive. Jones thought about the old adage, "For every customer who complains to you, 10 others just go out and spread the bad word to their friends." He would much rather have the feedback, address the problem, and hopefully keep customers satisfied.

Filled out, returned comment cards, if monitored over time, can begin to show trends and, therefore, identify potential or emerging trouble spots within foodservice operations. This information should enable astute foodservice managers to correct identified problems before they impact sales dramatically. One foodservice manager recently noted an increase in complaints about hot food being cold. By checking the temperatures on the hot food lines it was determined that the food was at the top end of the temperature range at the point it was served. Looking around for other causes for the complaint, the manager observed that the lines were longer than they had been in the past. The hot food was cooling off by the time customers sat down in the dining room to eat it. By adding another cashier station during the busiest times, customers were served more quickly and the complaints about cold food went away.

Please note that one of customer comment cards' major limitations is that they reflect *only* the opinions of those members of an organization who use the foodservice facilities. Therefore, other types of customer surveys must be used if administrators intend to determine who is not using their foodservices and why.

Putting out a suggestion box offers another, less formal means of allowing customers to communicate their foodservice likes and dislikes. A locked box stocked with a stack of note paper or comment sheets will allow customers to pass along open-ended comments about the program. If comment forms are printed, they should have spaces in which customers can enter names and telephone numbers or addresses, so that respondents can be contacted by foodservice's management with an explanation, apology, or other appropriate response.

Jones had heard of another idea that appealed to him. An administrator at one organization had the foodservice manager or assistant manager stationed at the cafeteria exit two or three times a month to ask customers about the food and service. That same administrator also insisted that the manager or assistant manager be in the serving and dining areas during every meal period. No sitting in the office for that management team, especially during meal periods.

Jones decided that making printed forms and locked suggestion boxes available would be a good addition to AU's foodservice operations. He needed, however, to direct his foodservice managers to check boxes daily and to respond to all comments within 48 hours, even if their response was only to thank a customer and indicate any steps being taken to address his or her concern. He liked the idea of posting the comment and the response on the cafeteria bulletin board to show customers that AU's foodservice was responding to customers. *Communication* would have to become the department's watch-word. "We must not make our customers wonder what is going on with foodservice; we have to communicate with them," Jones reminded himself. He knew from administering other customer-relations programs AU had implemented that ongoing communications would eliminate many complaints.

PERIODIC IN-DEPTH ANALYSES

Jones then turned his attention to the need to conduct periodic in-depth customer analyses. This process would not only augment the comment cards and suggestion boxes, but would also provide data on those AU employees who did not currently use the organization's foodservice facilities, as well as define a profile of customer dining habits and preferences.

While it is important to conduct this market-wide research every two to three years, the frequency will ultimately depend on the size of each organization, its level of market participation, and related factors. However, even at organizations where customer turnover is relatively low, it is important for foodservice to test its market regularly as data soon become old due to changes in customers' expectations.

Colleges and universities use comment cards on an ongoing basis, usually conducting campus-wide surveys every four years, due to the near complete turnover in their student populations during that period. A two-year community college most likely will want to look at surveying biannually. In both cases, the faculty and staff which represents the "permanent customer" base should be surveyed as well. Hospitals, on the other hand, first need to establish what their staff turnover rate is before they can determine how frequently they should survey customers in employee/public cafeterias. Jones recalled one foodservice administrator from a local hospital telling him over the phone that by the time most patients could eat solid meals they were usually sent home! Auditoriums, sports arenas, zoos, and other public facilities also have to determine which surveying schedule meets their own particular needs. However, it is safe to assume that if no survey has been done by an organization's foodservice in the past three years, now is time to conduct one.

It is most critical that a survey be conducted just before a foodservice changes concepts, plans to remodel any facilities, or makes a determination to convert to contract foodservice. No master plan or strategic change in operations should be made without customer input.

A sample customer survey is included as Exhibit 13-2 at the end of this chapter and on the accompanying disk. A few reminders to guide survey developers include:

- Decide in advance the necessary level of statistical accuracy. Do you want to have a five percent sample of the total market, or are you planning to let everyone who wants to respond? One organization was of the opinion that only a handful would return the survey, so they sent it to all 2,000 employees. They were overwhelmed when they received over 1,300 completed surveys. Tallying the results became a far greater chore than they had anticipated. The biggest message they got from the process was an understanding of the high level of interest in the foodservice program.
- Plan how you will tabulate the results before you write the survey. If you do not, you may find that the results are not quantifiable or that the tabulation process takes far too long. It is recommended that, at least for the first survey, the organization consult its own management information systems people or use an outside research firm. Once the survey instrument and tabulation process are in place, many organizations can then assume responsibility for the periodic survey distribution, collection, and tabulation.
- Consider the use of the organization's E-mail to send and receive surveys. If this is possible, it will save untold hours in distributing, collecting, and tabulating results every time a survey is conducted.
- Keep the survey "clean"(easy to read).
- Whenever possible, develop a checklist of point measurements that makes it easy for respondents to position their answers along a continuum. For instance, if foodservice asks a question with which the department wants customers to agree or disagree, the continuum might look like this:

Agree	Agree Somewhat		Neutral		Disagree Somewhat		Disagree			
10	9	8	7	6	5	4	3	2	1	0

  To determine the potential impact of a program change on customer satisfaction levels, the survey continuum might appear thusly:

Increase Satisfaction Greatly		Increase Satisfaction Somewhat	Would Not Impact Satisfaction	Decrease Satisfaction Somewhat	Decrease Satisfaction Greatly	
10	9	8 7 6	5	4 3 2	1	0

Current satisfaction levels might be addressed as:

Completely Satisfactory	Somewhat Satisfactory	No Impact	Somewhat Unsatisfactory	Completely Unsatisfactory
10 9	8 7 6	5	4 3 2	1 0

The purpose of supplying such measurement scales is to allow customers to "vote" in a manner that results in relatable numerical scores.

In addition to assessing customer satisfaction with the food, service, ambience, and other factors, a survey should include questions designed to draw forth any or all of the following facts that apply to an organization's foodservice facilities:

Type of meal or snack purchased

Reason for coming to the foodservice operation (such as attending a meeting, visiting with friends, being hungry, too busy to go elsewhere, consider the cafeteria the best place around to eat, etc.)

Length of time available for the visit (i.e., length of break or meal period)

Number of visits to the facility per time period.

- Another critical component of a foodservice survey that administrators all too commonly overlook is a section designed to determine current "dining patterns." For example, foodservice's survey should ask customers: Where do you normally eat breakfast? Lunch? Dinner? (Typical answers might include at home, in a fast-food restaurant, at work, and so forth.) When customers eat meals out, what type of restaurant do they select (i.e., fast-food, coffee shop, family-style, buffet, or formal service)? How much do respondents spend for each type of meal or snack eaten away from home? Interestingly enough, many will report that they expect to pay $5.00 to $8.00 to eat lunch in a restaurant, but only $2.50 to $3.50 to dine in an on-site cafeteria serving comparable food. A properly designed survey will reveal such expectations. Sometimes revealed expectations can be changed through good marketing and educational efforts; in other instances, a department's major benefit is simply that it becomes aware of customers' likes and dislikes and gets a chance to respond to them through menu and service level changes.

  A survey should, at a minimum, attempt to elicit the following customer eating out habits/preferences:

* Amount usually spent for each meal/snack.
* Type of foods most often purchased for each meal/snack.
* Listing of favorite restaurants for various meals/snacks (i.e., for breakfast my favorite place is __________; for week night family dinner __________ for special occasion dinners __________) along with the price generally paid for each of these dining experiences. (Respondent to fill in blanks.)

- Sometimes administrators and foodservice managers can take advantage of an available source of data that profiles their potential market. Such profiles might include campus registration demographics, a company's human resources profile, or other profiles of a defined primary market. Even when such information is available, however, it is best to include a few basic questions that can be cross-tabulated to determine whether the survey profile attributes can be applied to everyone or if one segment of respondents has a particular bias and how much impact that group's opinion has on the evaluation of the total program. For example, one recent survey indicated that 30 percent of respondents wanted more healthful foods on the menu. Since the survey also asked demographic profile questions, a cross-tabulation showed that 48 percent of those who wanted more healthful food items were white-collar female employees. However, 55 percent of the women who responded to this survey indicated that they only ate in the cafeteria one to two times per month. That same group indicated that they ate at off-site restaurants about six to seven times a month, at an average expenditure of $5.00. The administrative team analyzing the survey was able to determine that if more healthful foods were served in the cafeteria and the white-collar female market segment could be attracted to the cafeteria even once a week, sales would increase dramatically *and* a segment of the market that was heretofore disgruntled would be satisfied.

If the survey is to be conducted by telephone, the format will be different. Exhibit 13-3 provides a sample telephone survey. The key to a telephone survey is to have trained survey personnel. This usually requires the use of an outside research firm and is often more costly than a written survey.

FOCUS GROUPS

Focus groups offer administrators another means of assessing their marketplace. The primary benefit of focus groups is the inherent opportunity they offer organizers to pursue and further clarify comments made by participants. For example, if a facilitator asks members of a group, in rotation, to give their primary reasons for not patronizing the cafeteria, one answer is likely to be, "It's too expensive." If offered in response to a written survey, the answer would lack detail. If presented in a focus group, however, a trained facilitator might follow up that response by asking, "Can you give me an example?" or "Which commercial establishment offers products within the price range you would expect at our cafeteria?" Foodservice focus groups are best conducted by outside consultants who are knowledgeable about the industry and not biased with respect to organizations' foodservice operations. It is important to keep objectivity at the forefront of the process.

Focus groups can be either formal or informal in nature. Formal focus groups are usually held in a special room with one-way mirrors so that interested parties can watch and hear without inserting themselves physically into the setting. These events are often videotaped. A rigid set of questions is adhered to throughout the process. The formal focus group is often directed at specific topics. For example, the topic may be the customer service aspects of the foodservice operation rather than food, service, and ambience. More informal focus groups work just as effectively in many settings. These groups are often held by forming participants into a circle, without the fancy facilities and video equipment. The planned questions often lead to other follow-up questions, and there is less rigidity to the overall process. The key to using either type successfully is to have a knowledgeable interviewer who is skilled at keeping the group "focused" on the topic.

COMPARABLE RESEARCH DATA

Once you know something about your own market, where do you go for comparable data? When he first began his surveying process, Jones had been uneasy about asking AU colleagues for demographic information, since people sometimes are reluctant to state their family income and other personal statistics on a survey form. He also had been unsure as to the relevance of demographic information until he spoke with one of the research specialists at the National Restaurant Association. (See Chapter 14 for more information on this and other professional foodservice trade associations.) Many associations and other organizations publish a wide variety of studies, most of them with demographic/economic profiles of the respondents. Jones could begin to understand why it was important to ask for demographic/economic data on his survey. In this way, he could match his results to those of other surveys.

Today, several sources of research data are available in the foodservice industry. Some of the sources offer studies that relate primarily to retail foodservice markets but have application to any foodservice program, whether in corporate, educational, medical, or other environments. The fact is that such a large number of people now travel, dine out, and, generally, have developed a sophisticated sense of quality food and service that the principles of retail foodservice have been adopted by operators in what has always been referred to as the "noncommercial" foodservice market. To be considered top-quality, corporate, health care, education, and other noncommercial foodservice programs must be operated according to these principles, which means providing customers with the same level, variety, and authenticity of food and service to which they have become accustomed from commercial sector dining experiences. The highest-quality noncommercial dining programs today, therefore, are being managed by professionals who stay up with the trends throughout the industry. Instead of touring only noncommercial programs to find new operating ideas, these progressive operators look to the shopping malls, fast-food industry, popular restaurants, and other contemporary foodservice entities. These entities have indeed become competition for most of what was once a captive noncommercial foodservice market.

Some of the sources of continuing research materials will be accessible through membership in the organizations described in Chapter 14. Some of the more useful sources/publications include the following:

- Professional organizations/associations

  The National Restaurant Association and many larger foodservice companies participate in the quarterly Chain Restaurant Eating-Out Share Trends (CREST) survey that tracks customer behavior patterns and expenditures in this segment of the foodservice industry. Some 10,000 families who model the economic/demographic profile of the average citizen, according to the United States Census, record all of their restaurant visits during a two-week period in each quarter of a year. Summaries of these data are published in *Restaurants USA*, the monthly publication of the NRA, and in other NRA publications. This process has been going on for many years and has provided the most consistent trending information. Other professional journals published by foodservice trade associations within their various market segments (see Chapter 14) also publish periodic surveys of customer behavior in their particular market segments. One should always be leery of survey write-ups that do not provide readers with the basis from which the sample was drawn or who sponsored and/or underwrote it.

Another service of the NRA is its monthly *Abstracts* publication. This bulletin publishes the titles and abstracts of various articles on segments of the foodservice industry. Subscribing to this publication is the fastest way for administrators to learn which resources are available on any given issue.

- Commercial publications

  Commercial publications offer another source of general market data. In addition to those listed in Chapter 14, *American Demographics*[1] offers timely and relevant information for the foodservice industry.

- University publications

  Tufts University's *Diet & Nutrition Letter* is the most up-to-date resource now available on diet and nutrition issues. Published monthly, this newsletter analyzes products, advises readers of new diet studies whose findings may affect customer health, and encapsulates legislative issues that will influence the ways foods are served. Other universities and colleges with foodservice programs or hotel and restaurant schools also publish data from time to time. Administrators can contact these institutions through the Council on Hotel Restaurant and Institutional Education (CHRIE) (see Chapter 14).

- Private research companies

  Roper, Gallup, and A. C. Nielsen are just a sampling of the firms that conduct market research and publish the results in bulletins available through subscription services. Through the NRA *Abstracts* it is possible to keep up with available information that might be useful to any given organization or its particular foodservice program. (For further information on sources relative to each industry segment, refer to the organizations listed in Chapter 14.)

[1] Published by Dow Jones & Company, Inc., 127 West State Street, Ithaca, NY 14850.

Reviewing his list of potential research resources, Jones fought back the now-familiar sensation of being overwhelmed by new information. All in all, he felt confident of his ability to direct and monitor an ongoing research process. He decided, however, to contact AU's Marketing department to find out whether anyone employed there could help him develop an in-house, organization-wide survey. Jones suspected, though, that if he wanted to bring true foodservice expertise to his surveying process, he would have to go to an outside resource. He knew he would want to retain a consultancy that had conducted similar foodservice studies and could demonstrate its experience. Reference checks would be vital in this process. With these conclusions carefully noted, Jones turned out the lights and left his office.

Exhibit 13-2
FOODSERVICE SURVEY

We are conducting a survey of your company cafeteria to understand your needs and the needs of others like you. Your participation will go a long way towards providing the kind of foodservice that will meet your needs. To complete the survey, simply circle the number that corresponds to your answer. Please return your completed questionnaire within 5 days through company mail.

Please indicate at which cafeteria you received this survey. CAFETERIA NAME

Answer all questions based on this location only. ______________

1. How frequently do you purchase food and/or beverages at this location for each of the following meals?

	5-7	3-4	2	1	Less than once/wk.	Never
Breakfast	5	4	3	2	1	0
Lunch	5	4	3	2	1	0
Dinner	5	4	3	2	1	0

2. Please indicate where you typically eat the foods and beverages you purchase at this location for each of the following meals.

	In the cafeteria	At my desk	Some other place	Never purchase/eat
Breakfast	4	3	2	1
Lunch	4	3	2	1
Dinner	4	3	2	1

3. How frequently during the work week do you . . .

	5-7	3-4	2	1	Less than once/wk.	Never
Bring lunch from home	5	4	3	2	1	0
Go to a restaurant for lunch	5	4	3	2	1	0
Skip lunch	5	4	3	2	1	0

4. Overall, how would you rate your satisfaction with this cafeteria, using a scale where 10 means extremely satisfied and 1 means not at all satisfied?

Extremely Satisfied	10	9	8	7	6	5	4	3	2	1	Not at all Satisfied

5. How would you rate this cafeteria on each of the following, using a scale where 10 means excellent and 1 means very poor?

	Excellent									Very Poor
Taste of food	10	9	8	7	6	5	4	3	2	1
Appearance of food	10	9	8	7	6	5	4	3	2	1
Variety of foods	10	9	8	7	6	5	4	3	2	1

Exhibit 13-2 continued

	Excellent									Very Poor
Food temperature	10	9	8	7	6	5	4	3	2	1
Offering contemporary foods	10	9	8	7	6	5	4	3	2	1
Friendliness of personnel	10	9	8	7	6	5	4	3	2	1
Appearance of service personnel	10	9	8	7	6	5	4	3	2	1
Speed of service	10	9	8	7	6	5	4	3	2	1
Consistency of service	10	9	8	7	6	5	4	3	2	1
Appearance of facility	10	9	8	7	6	5	4	3	2	1
Cleanliness	10	9	8	7	6	5	4	3	2	1
Price of meals	10	9	8	7	6	5	4	3	2	1
Convenience of hours	10	9	8	7	6	5	4	3	2	1

6. Overall, how would you rate the value of the meals you purchase in this cafeteria, using a scale where 10 means excellent value and 1 means very poor value?

Excellent 10 9 8 7 6 5 4 3 2 1 0 Very Poor

7. On average, how much do you spend each work day on meals and snacks purchased at on site foodservice locations?

1 Spend nothing	5 $3.00 to $5.99
2 Under $1.00	6 $6.00 to $7.99
3 $1.00 to $1.99	7 $8.00 to $10.00
4 $2.00 to $2.99	8 Over $10.00

8. Since this is a survey about food, tell us about what kinds of food you like by marking how often you eat each of the following kinds of food. (Circle one number indicating "how often" for each type of food.)

	Never	At Times	Often	Very Often
1 American; burgers, hot dogs	1	2	3	4
2 Italian/pizza	1	2	3	4
3 Chinese/Asian	1	2	3	4
4 Mexican	1	2	3	4
5 Chicken and ribs	1	2	3	4
6 Salads	1	2	3	4
7 Sandwiches	1	2	3	4
8 Soups	1	2	3	4
9 Fresh fruit	1	2	3	4

9. What is the name of your favorite chain restaurant when you dine out for lunch and dinner?

1 Lunch ______________________________

2 Dinner ______________________________

Exhibit 13-2 continued

THESE LAST FEW QUESTIONS ARE ABOUT YOU

10. Are you . . .

1 Male
2 Female

11. What is your primary reason for being at this location today?

1 Employee, regular work place
2 Employee, work in another building
3 Non-employee, regular work place
4 Visitor to the building

12. What is your age?

1 Under 25
2 25 to 34
3 35 to 44
4 45 to 54
5 55 to 64
6 65 and over

13. On average, how many days during the work week (Mon.-Fri.) are you in this building?

1 5 days
2 4 days
3 3 days
4 2 days
5 1 day
6 Less than 1 day per week

Any other comments or suggestions?

____

____

____

THANK YOU FOR YOUR COOPERATION

Please mail your completed survey in the attached postage paid return envelope.

Exhibit 13-3

ACME UNIVERSITY DINING SERVICES SURVEY

I.D. NO- ___ ___ ___ ___

INTERVIEWER- ______________ DATE- __________ SCHOOL ID- __________

Hello, my name is ________________ at Acme University. I am calling from our survey research center in ______________. We are conducting a survey of students of the University regarding campus foodservices.

Is this (NAME OF PERSON)- __________________

[IF WRONG NUMBER, TERMINATE INTERVIEW WITH: I'm sorry I have the wrong number. Do you have (person's name) new number?]

[NEW NUMBER]—(_____) _______-__________

[IF YES-START INTERVIEW]

[WHEN SELECTED PERSON ANSWERS, REPEAT INTRODUCTION]

[IF NOT]

May I speak with that person?

YES NO

When may I call back to reach him/her?

TIME ______________

DATE ______________

START INTERVIEW

Your name was randomly selected from a list of students attending your university. The questions will take 5-10 minutes. But before starting them, I want to mention that I would be happy to answer any questions about the study either now or later. Also, this interview is confidential and completely voluntary. If we should come to any question which you don't want to answer, just let me know, and we'll go on the next question.

-------------------------------- CALL RECORD --------------------------------

CALL NUMBER	01	02	03	04	05
DATE					
TIME					
RESULT					

IF INTERVIEW WAS REFUSED OR YOU PUT OTHER-WRITE OUT EXPLANATION HERE: ________________ NA = NO ANSWER B = BUSY SIGNAL NW = NOT WORKING BP = BUSINESS PHONE NE = NO ELIGIBLE RESPONDENT CB = CALLBACK R = REFUSAL OT = OTHER [EXPLAIN] CC = COMPLETED CALL. IF A NUMBER HAS BEEN CHANGED, RECORD THE NEW NUMBER. CHECK WITH SUPERVISOR BEFORE CALLING THIS NUMBER. IF YOU REACH A CALL FORWARDING/ANSWERING SERVICE OR MACHINE, RECORD THIS AS A NA – LEAVE MESSAGE ON MACHINE.

Campus I.D. _______

Exhibit 13-3 continued

ACME UNIVERSITY DINING SERVICE SURVEY

1. We'd like to begin by asking you some questions about where you eat your meals or purchase snack items as a substitution for a meal, when you are not on campus. When you eat off campus, do you *normally* eat (READ RESPONSES):
   1. something at home that you/someone else has prepared
   2. at a fast food restaurant
   3. at a sit-down restaurant
   4. at a cafeteria/buffet restaurant
   5. something from a take-out restaurant or delivery style restaurant
   8. DON'T KNOW
   9. REFUSED

2. When you eat in American style, fast food restaurants *usually*, what *one* type of food do you prefer the most? Would you prefer (READ CATEGORIES; PROBE FOR ONE RESPONSE)
   1. burgers or hot dogs
   2. subs
   3. chicken
   4. salads
   5. pastry or donuts
   6. OTHER (LIST) ________________
   8. DON'T KNOW
   9. REFUSED

3. When you eat at ethnic style, fast food restaurants *usually*, what *one* type of food do you prefer the most? Would you prefer (READ CATEGORIES: PROBE FOR ONE RESPONSE).
   1. Italian, including pizza
   2. Mexican
   3. Oriental
   4. Middle Eastern or Greek
   5. OTHER (LIST) ________________
   8. DON'T KNOW
   9. REFUSED

Here's another type of question. Using a scale from 1 to 10 with 10 being very important and 1 being not important at all, how important are the following factors in choosing a place to eat? (READ CATEGORIES):

	Very Important				Important			Not Important At All			
4. Convenient location	1	2	3	4	5	6	7	8	9	10	______
5. Hours of operation	1	2	3	4	5	6	7	8	9	10	______
6. Price	1	2	3	4	5	6	7	8	9	10	______
7. Menu	1	2	3	4	5	6	7	8	9	10	______
8. Quality of food	1	2	3	4	5	6	7	8	9	10	______
9. Pleasant atmosphere	1	2	3	4	5	6	7	8	9	10	______
10. Friendliness of staff	1	2	3	4	5	6	7	8	9	10	______
11. Cleanliness of facilities	1	2	3	4	5	6	7	8	9	10	______

Exhibit 13-3 continued

12. Thank you. Now I'd like to ask you some questions about where and what you eat when you're on campus. When you're attending classes, do you normally eat a meal, a snack or drink some beverage?

    1. Yes GO TO QUESTION 14
    2. NO GO TO QUESTION 13
    8. Don't Know
    9. Refused

    ______

13. Would you tell me why you don't eat or drink any food or beverages when you're on campus?

    ____

    ____

    NOW GO ON TO QUESTION 44.

14. When you're on campus how often do you buy food, snacks or beverages in a campus cash outlet each week? Would you say it's (READ CATEGORIES):

    1. several times a day
    2. daily
    3. several times a week
    4. once a week or less
    5. never

    ______

15. Where do you *usually* buy your food or snack items? Is it in (READ CATEGORIES):

    1. the residence hall dining room
    2. residence hall snack bar
    3. student union food outlets
    4. campus convenience or variety stores
    5. vending machines
    6. BRING OWN FOOD, SNACKS, ETC. (VOLUNTEERED)
    8. DON'T KNOW
    9. REFUSED

    ______

Would you tell me if you *always*, *sometimes*, *seldom*, or *never* eat the following items when you eat at a campus food outlet. (REPEAT CATEGORIES AS NECESSARY)

	Always	Sometimes	Seldom	Never	Don't Know	Refused	
16. Burgers and hot dogs	1	2	3	4	8	9	____
17. Salads	1	2	3	4	8	9	____
18. Deli items such as sandwiches	1	2	3	4	8	9	____
19. Hot entrees	1	2	3	4	8	9	____
20. Bakery items	1	2	3	4	8	9	____
21. Pizza	1	2	3	4	8	9	____
22. Beverages	1	2	3	4	8	9	____

Which of the following do you eat in a campus food outlet.

23. Breakfast	Yes	No	Don't Know	Refused	____
24. Lunch	Yes	No	Don't Know	Refused	____

Exhibit 13-3 continued

25. Dinner	Yes	No	Don't Know	Refused	_____
26. Snacks	Yes	No	Don't Know	Refused	_____

27. How much do you normally spend per visit to a campus food outlet? Is it (READ RESPONSES)

1. Less than $2 2. $2-3 3. $3-4 4. $4-5 5. $5 or more _______

28. Do you purchase snack items when you're on campus?

1. YES GO TO QUESTION 29 _______
5. NO 8. DON'T KNOW 9. REFUSED GO TO QUESTION *23*

29. Do you buy your snack items from the campus convenience store?

1. YES 5. NO 8. DON'T KNOW 9. REFUSED _______

30. From the AU Beagle's Bakery?

1. YES 5. NO 8. DON'T KNOW 9. REFUSED _______

31. From the Memorial Union Deli?

1. YES 5. NO 8. DON'T KNOW 9. REFUSED _______

32. From vending machines?

1. YES 5. NO 8. DON'T KNOW 9. REFUSED _______

33. Now I'd like you to rate the campus food outlets for various qualities on a scale of 1-10, with 10 being the highest.

	Poor			Average				Excellent			
34. Hours of operation	1	2	3	4	5	6	7	8	9	10	_____
35. Prices	1	2	3	4	5	6	7	8	9	10	_____
36. Menus	1	2	3	4	5	6	7	8	9	10	_____
37. Food quality	1	2	3	4	5	6	7	8	9	10	_____
38. Atmosphere	1	2	3	4	5	6	7	8	9	10	_____
39. Friendliness of staff	1	2	3	4	5	6	7	8	9	10	_____
40. The cleanliness of facilities	1	2	3	4	5	6	7	8	9	10	_____

41. Thank you! Now I'd like to ask you some questions about various ways to pay for meals and snacks on campus. Do you currently have a meal contract with campus foodservice?

1. YES 8. DON'T KNOW 9. REFUSED GO TO QUESTION *44* _______
5. NO GO TO QUESTION *42*

42. Have you ever had a meal plan contract?

1. YES GO TO QUESTION *43*
5. NO 8. DON'T KNOW 9. REFUSED GO TO QUESTION *44* _______

43. Why did you stop buying meal plan contracts? _______

____

____

8. DON'T KNOW 9. REFUSED

Exhibit 13-34 continued

44. Several methods for paying for meals and snacks are being considered for next year for all students on and off campus. These options may provide more purchasing power, convenience and flexibility. One method is a cash account in which a student deposits money and then uses a card to pay for anything bought in the cash food outlets on campus. This program could be either added to a regular meal contract or be offered by itself. If this type of program were offered which of the following options, if any, would you choose? Would you choose (READ ALL CATEGORIES):

    1. a meal plan without any cash or points.
    2. a meal plan with cash automatically added to it
    3. a meal plan with an option of add cash
    4. a cash plan only ________
    5. DON'T KNOW
    6. REFUSED

45. Would you choose to use a cash account bonus plan that offered a cash bonus for deposits of $50 and more?

    1. YES GO TO QUESTION *46*
    5. NO 8. DON'T KNOW 9. REFUSED GO TO QUESTION *44*

46. If you had a cash account, where would you most often use it? Would it be in (READ CATEGORIES):

    1. residence hall dining service
    2. residence hall snack bar
    3. student union food outlets
    4. campus convenience store ________
    8. DON'T KNOW
    9. REFUSED

47. Finally, I'd like to ask you some demographic questions that will help us with the statistical analysis of this survey. You don't have to answer all of the questions, but it will help us if you do.

47. What year in school are you? Are you a (READ):

    1. First year 2. Sophomore 3. Junior 4. Senior 5. Graduate Student ________
    6. SPECIAL 7. OTHER 8. DON'T KNOW 9. REFUSED

48. How many *credits* are you taking this quarter?

    8. DON'T KNOW 9. REFUSED ________

49. Are you taking any classes *after 5 PM?*

    1. YES GO TO QUESTION *50* ________
    5. NO 8. DON'T KNOW 9. REFUSED GO TO QUESTION *51*

50. Does the foodservice meet your needs during this time?

    1.YES 5. NO 8. DON'T KNOW 9. REFUSED ________

51. Do you live on campus in one of the residence halls?

    1. YES GO TO QUESTION *52*
    5. NO 8. DON'T KNOW 9. REFUSED GO TO QUESTION *53* ________

Exhibit 13-3 continued

52. How often do you leave the campus for the weekend? Is it (READ)
    1. 3-4 times a month
    2. 1-2 times per month
    3. less than once per month
    4. never
    8. DON'T KNOW
    9. REFUSED

    ______

53. Approximately how many miles do you live from campus?
    8. DON'T KNOW 9. REFUSED ______

54. What is your age?
    8. DON'T KNOW 9. REFUSED ______

55. What is your sex?
    1. MALE
    2. FEMALE
    8. DON'T KNOW
    9. REFUSED

    ______

Thank you for your time and cooperation. You've been very helpful!

INTERVIEWER – CHECK OVER INTERVIEW SCHEDULE FOR COMPLETENESS, ACCURACY, AND LEGIBILITY. PLEASE DESCRIBE ON THE BACK AND BRING TO A DIRECTOR'S ATTENTION ANY PROBLEMS WITH THE INTERVIEW, SUCH AS DIFFICULT QUESTIONS, CODING PROBLEMS, ETC. INSERT CONTACT SHEET FOR THIS SCHEDULE INSIDE THE SCHEDULE.

CHAPTER FOURTEEN

External Resources

Throughout his hectic but enlightening introduction to administering a multifaceted foodservice program, Jones had heard of many different foodservice trade organizations and the resources they made available to members of the industry. Because of his prior experience at AU, he already knew that professionals in each foodservice market sector (i.e., business and industry, health care, colleges/universities, schools, government institutions, not-for-profit organizations, and a myriad of others) appeared to have their own organizations, communications media, and formal or informal information-exchange networks. Over the past few weeks, Jones had started to keep a list of the professional groups and various trade publications that disseminated information about the world of foodservice.

On a crisp Saturday morning, Jones sat in his den, contentedly going over the paperwork he'd brought home from the office. As he started reviewing his rough "External Foodservice Resource" list, he was surprised to discover how many ways there were to access the various organizations' resources. Thanks to the help of several associates and his own trade publication research, Jones was able to put together a final resource listing, broken down into the following categories:

- Foodservice Industry—General
- Foodservice Industry—Specific Focus
- Other Organizations/Groups/Associations That Offer Foodservice Training/Education/Information
- Local Resources

Here is a summary of Jones' list and his notes on each organization's role in the foodservice industry.

FOODSERVICE INDUSTRY—GENERAL

National Restaurant Association

While no single organization represents every type of foodservice entity, almost everyone Jones asked identified the National Restaurant Association (NRA) as the only organization with the size, resources, and clout to be the recognized industry leader. Almost everyone Jones had talked to also suggested that AU's foodservice join the NRA, due to its vast network of services and distribution of timely, helpful information on pending legislation and government regulations. Jones' advisors were unanimous in their opinion that the NRA was also the best organization for assembling and distributing information on technical issues relating to food safety, market research, and operational topics.

Much of what the NRA has to offer can be accessed via its on-line computer network service, which is available on a subscription basis. In addition, the NRA holds an annual National Restaurant Show in Chicago, Illinois, around the third week of May. The show consists of literally thousands of food product, supply, and equipment exhibits and offers various industry-related seminars. Attendance at this exhibition is an excellent introduction to a complete cross-section of the foodservice industry for persons not yet familiar with it. NRA members receive free admission to the show, while a nominal registration fee is charged to nonmembers who wish to attend. The NRA show is not open to the public, so attendees may be asked to provide proof that they have a business purpose for attending. A word to the wise: The NRA Show is one of the biggest held annually in Chicago, so it is essential that travel plans and hotel reservations be made well in advance.

Information concerning membership, educational services, and show attendance can be secured by contacting the NRA at:

Executive Vice President
1200 Seventeenth Street NW
Washington, DC 20036-3097
202-331-5900

The NRA can also provide names and phone numbers of local or state restaurant associations that offer a variety of educational programs, food and equipment shows, and related services.

North American Food Equipment Manufacturers

When it comes to food preparation and processing equipment, the leading resource/organization is the North American Food Equipment Manufacturers (NAFEM). The main attraction of this organization is its biannual equipment show. Every other year and in different cities, NAFEM holds a convention and trade show that is solely dedicated to foodservice equipment. Any administrator who anticipates being significantly involved with opening or remodeling foodservice facilities and who wants to attain a greater familiarity with the range of foodservice equipment currently available will find this event well worth attending. Like NRA, NAFEM holds a series of informational seminars on industry trends and concerns in conjunction with its show.

Information concerning NAFEM in general, and the show in particular, can be obtained by contacting:

Executive Director
401 North Michigan Avenue
Chicago, IL 60611
312-644-6610
312-321-6869 (FAX)

FOODSERVICE INDUSTRY–SPECIFIC FOCUS

NRA and NAFEM and their respective shows have become magnets about which a number of industry groups have gathered. Almost without exception, every major foodservice industry group tries to hold a meeting just before or after a NRA or NAFEM event, to offer specific programming to their many members who attend. For the same reason, many equipment manufacturers and food processors hold special meetings or demonstrations for existing or potential customers in conjunction with NRA and NAFEM events. Here is Jones' list of the various specific-interest organizations and the roles they play in the foodservice industry.

The American Dietetic Association

Once thought of as just being active in hospitals, the American Dietetic Association (ADA) today is a nationally recognized certification organization whose members are all registered dietitians working for a variety of employers. Due to the increased interest in and, sometimes, legally mandated need for dietetic support in many foodservice environments, ADA members are involved in almost every industry segment. It is not unusual for dietitians currently to be managing or working in key support roles in foodservices at schools, colleges/universities, retirement communities or nursing care centers, jails/prisons, and corporate dining programs.

In order to retain their fully registered status, dietitians must take a minimum number of hours of continuing education courses throughout the year. Members also stay current in their field by subscribing to the ADA's monthly journal, which publishes highly technical papers on nutrition and dietary studies.

Information concerning the ADA and individual dietitians can be obtained by contacting:

Executive Director
216 West Jackson, Suite 800
Chicago, IL 60606-6995
312-899-0400
312-899-1979 (FAX)

The American Correctional Food Service Association

This association is affiliated with the American Correctional Association (ACA) and the American Jail Association (AJA), which, among other tasks, are charged with establishing minimum operating standards and certifying the operation of the nation's jails and prisons. The American Correctional Food Service Association (ACFSA) was established to provide both educational and networking opportunities for those professionals who directly operate or administer foodservice programs in adult correctional and juvenile detention facilities. This group holds an annual meeting in August or September in different cities that includes equipment and food product displays. In addition, its six regional groups hold smaller, local seminars and exhibits throughout the year.

Information concerning the ACFSA can be obtained by contacting:

Executive Director
2040 Chestnut Street
Harrisburg, PA 17104
717-233-2301
717-233-2790 (FAX)

The American Society for Hospital Food Service Administrators

As the name implies, this group is comprised of those professionals who manage and supervise foodservice operations in hospitals and associated medical/long-term treatment centers. The American Society for Hospital Food Service Administrators (ASHFSA) holds its annual meetings in different cities each June or July in coordination with the American Hospital Association. The organization has a number of state and regional chapters that meet throughout the year. Since many hospitals' and similar organizations' foodservice programs are operated by registered dietitians, ASHFSA maintains a close working relationship with ADA.

Information concerning ASHFSA can be obtained by contacting:

Executive Director
840 North Lake Shore Drive
Chicago, IL 60611
312-280-6416

The American School Food Service Association

This organization represents foodservice professionals who work at many of the nation's public and private elementary, middle/junior high, and high schools that operate breakfast and lunch programs. With its own monthly magazine and an annual meeting that is held in different cities each June or July, the American School Food Service Association (ASFSA) provides an excellent information and networking resource for administrators with an interest in school foodservices.

Information concerning ASFSA can be obtained by contacting:

Executive Director
1600 Duke Street, 7th Floor
Alexandria, VA 22314-3436
703-739-3900

The National Association of College and University Food Service

Whether members' programs are retail (cash) or board (residence hall) oriented, the National Association of College and University Food Service (NACUFS) serves the managers and supervisors responsible for providing foodservice on campuses in the United States, Canada, and around the world. NACUFS produces and distributes a variety of educational periodicals and pamphlets on topics of interest to members and holds its annual meeting every July in a different city. Regional and subregional member meetings are also held throughout the year. In addition to exhibits, a number of educational seminars are offered at each meeting.

Information concerning NACUFS can be obtained by contacting:

Executive Director
1405 South Harrison Road, #303
Michigan State University
East Lansing, MI 48824
517-332-2494

National Association of College Auxiliary Services and the National Association of College and University Business Officers

Two other college- and university-based organizations also address foodservice-related issues as part of their broader mandate to promote auxiliary enterprises and college business interests. Both the National Association of College Auxiliary Services (NACAS) and the National Association of College and University Business Officers (NACUBO) have an ongoing interest in foodservice, due to their members' operational and administrative oversight responsibilities.

Information concerning both NACAS and NACUBO can be obtained by contacting:

NACAS	NACUBO
Executive Director	Executive Director
P.O. Box 870	1 Dupont Circle, #500
Stanton, VA 24402	Washington, DC 20036

703-885-8826 202-861-2563
703-885-8355 (FAX) 202-861-2583 (FAX)

Society for Foodservice Management

The Society for Foodservice Management (SFM) was formed to represent the interests and meet the needs of professionals responsible for providing foodservices in corporate or business/industrial environments. There are four distinct member categories within SFM:

- Administrators of foodservice programs
- Corporate employees who operate foodservices for their particular organizations (known as "self-operators")
- Executives and managers from contract management companies (private firms that operate foodservice for organizations in return for a management fee or on a profit and loss basis)
- Representatives from companies that manufacture and sell equipment, food, and supply products or offer services to members/nonmembers in one or more of the first three categories

Because corporate dining, in many ways, parallels foodservice offered at many universities/colleges and hospitals (i.e., there has been a dramatic shift from traditional cafeteria and catering operations toward commercial-style retail marketing), SFM membership has broadened to include many foodservice professionals from these other industry segments.

SFM consists of six regions that hold meetings throughout the year. An annual meeting is held each year in September or October in various cities throughout the country.

Information concerning SFM can be obtained by contacting:

Executive Director
304 West Liberty Street, Suite 201
Louisville, KY 40202
502-583-3783
502-589-3602 (FAX)

There are numerous other organizations beside the above named that consider foodservice to be a critical support component for their primary missions. Whether foodservice is offered at a zoo, museum, auditorium, convention center, sports stadium, or airport (among many other potential locales), a membership group exists that addresses foodservice in general or has a specific subgroup or committee dedicated to that subject. Examples include the American Association of Zoological Parks and Aquariums, International Association of Auditorium Managers, International Association of Conference Centers, and International City/County Management Association.

FOODSERVICE RESOURCES–RELATED

Most key organizational managers and staff belong to one or more membership groups that support their involvement in a particular industry or career. Whether administrators' interests are directed toward personnel/human resources, office or site services, facility and equipment maintenance, accounting/auditing functions, or similar fields, their professional organizations periodically offer education and information on foodservice in their publications and at seminars. Some of the professional organizations and/or associations that specifically address foodservices include the following.

Hotel, Restaurant, Institutional Management, and Culinary Training Schools

The United States has a wide variety of publicly and privately operated, industry-oriented university, junior or community college, and vocational culinary training programs. Some, such as Cornell's School of Hotel Administration, Michigan State University's HRIM School, and the Culinary Institute of America in Hyde Park, New York, have earned excellent international reputations. Other university and community-level institutions are acquiring equally excellent reputations for teaching and graduating qualified young foodservice managers-to-be. Many foodservice training institutions maintain active contact with their alumni, often including job placement services.

The Council for Hotel and Restaurant and Institutional Education (CHRIE) is the organization that represents many of these schools. Information on the schools' various programs and opportunities to hire graduates is available from CHRIE, as well as the National Restaurant Association.

For information concerning CHRIE, please contact:

Executive Vice President
1200 17th Street NW, 7th Floor
Washington, DC 20036
202-332-5900
202-331-2429 (FAX)

As Dana Jones discovered, local university and community college hospitality industry education program directors can be excellent resources for adminstrators seeking information on foodservice operations and referrals to other industry resources.

Foodservice Consultants Society International

The Foodservice Consultants Society International (FCSI) consists of a group of consultants whose primary fields of knowledge include management advisory services and facility layout/design and equipment specifications. Some FCSI members' expertise is specific to an industry market sector (such as hospitals or schools). Others offer added service capabilities, such as interior design and laundry planning. The same diversity is true of many management advisory services members, who may offer a broad range of services or just specialize in computer applications or productivity enhancements.

When they qualify for membership, FCSI's professional members pledge that they will adhere to a strict set of ethical conduct standards, and will refrain from doing anything that will damage the integrity of their client-consultant relationships.

For information concerning or referrals to FCSI consultants, please contact:

FCSI Executive Vice President
304 West Liberty Street, Suite 201
Louisville, Kentucky 40202
502-583-3783
502-589-3602 (FAX)

Equipment, Food and Supplies Brokers, and Manufacturers' Representatives

No single organization represents all the brokers and equipment manufacturers' representatives working in the foodservice industry. NAFEM, introduced earlier in this chapter, represents many of these professionals, but other organization that can offer information and assistance on the manufacturing and distribution aspects of foodservice include the following.

International Foodservice Manufacturers Association
321 North Clark Street
Chicago, IL 60610
312-644-8989

The best way for administrators to get in touch with other foodservice organizations or individual professionals is to contact their city's or state's restaurant associations, check in local telephone business directories, or call selected manufacturers or food processors to receive a referral to their local representative.

As suggested in Chapter 8 (on vending), administrators are likely to want to gather information on this critical, mechanized sector of the foodservice industry. The vending market and its professionals are represented by the National Automatic Merchandisers Association (NAMA). Information concerning NAMA can be obtained by contacting:

Executive Director
20 North Wacker Drive, Suite 3500
Chicago, IL 60606
312-346-0370
312-704-4140 (FAX)

Most of the organizations listed by Jones have a variety of membership classifications. Purchasing an annual membership is generally not required if an administrator wishes to attend one or more of these groups' annual or regional shows/meetings. Most foodservice organizations, however, charge a higher fee for meeting attendance by nonmembers.

Trade Magazines and Books

There are a variety of foodservice industry publications that cover either the commercial or noncommercial foodservice markets, or both, and which are available on a free or qualified subscription basis. This section of Jones' list includes the various commercially published trade magazines (those not published by foodservice trade associations), along with a description of their editorial interests and information concerning subscriptions.

Food Management Magazine

Dedicated exclusively to covering the activities of operators in noncommercial foodservice, this monthly publication offers an abundance of informative news sections, one-page columns of expert advice, and at least three full-length features on a variety of operational, management, facility design, nutritional, and culinary topics in each issue. Information concerning subscriptions can be obtained by contacting:

Editor-in-Chief
Food Management Magazine
122 East 42nd Street, Suite 900
New York, NY 10168
212-309-7620
212-808-4189 (FAX)

or

Penton Publications
1100 Superior Avenue
Cleveland, OH 44197
216-696-7000
800-659-5251

FoodService Director

Also dedicated to covering events in noncommercial foodservice, this monthly, tabloid-format publication offers a large number of short reports on operators' program changes and menu successes. *FoodService Director* also conducts and publishes the results of frequent reader surveys and research projects. More information about *FoodService Director* can be obtained by contacting:

Editor
FoodService Director
Bill Publications
355 Park Avenue South
New York, NY 10010
212-592-6530

Nation's Restaurant News

This is a weekly, tabloid-format publication that, as its name implies, covers restaurant issues across the nation. It does, however, address subjects of concern to noncommercial foodservice operators and is an excellent source of timely government and general industry news. Information concerning *Nation's Restaurant News* can be obtained by contacting:

Editor
Nation's Restaurant News
Lebhar-Friedman, Inc.
425 Park Avenue
New York, NY 10022
800-447-7133

Restaurants & Institutions

This bimonthly publication bridges both the commercial and noncommercial segments by presenting a wide variety of articles on personnel management, design/decor, and food preparation. In addition, many issues contain research studies and survey pieces that analyze market trends, wage and benefit patterns, and customers' food preferences in different market segments. Information concerning this publication can be obtained by contacting:

Editor
Restaurants & Institutions
Cahners Publications Company
1350 E. Touhy Avenue
Des Plaines, IL 60017
708-635-8800
708-635-6856 (FAX)

Restaurant Business

This monthly magazine's editorial focus is on various facets of the restaurant industry, including fast-food, casual and fine dining, and independent and chain operations. In addition, the publication offers an annual "Restaurant Growth Index" that includes a comprehensive statistical profile on the restaurant business in every state, county, and major metropolitan area. Information concerning this publication can be obtained by contacting:

Editor
Restaurant Business
Bill Publications
355 Park Avenue South
New York, NY 10010
212-592-6505
212-592-6509 (FAX)

Restaurant Hospitality

This monthly periodical is a "sister" publication to *Food Management*, and its primary mission is to report on independent and chain restaurant operations, along with articles on food presentation and recipes. Information concerning this publication can be obtained by contacting:

Editor
Restaurant Hospitality
Penton Publications
1100 Superior Avenue
Cleveland, OH 44197
216-696-7000
800-659-5251

Cornell Hotel and Restaurant Administration Quarterly

Despite its name, the Cornell "*Quarterly*" has recently been expanded into a bimonthly publication. For the most part, this magazine offers a scholarly perspective on the hospitality industry with excellent, in-depth articles dealing with legal matters, human resources, and management organization. Information concerning this publication can be obtained by contacting:

Editor
Cornell Quarterly
Elsevier Science, Inc.
Madison Square Station
P.O. Box 882
New York, NY 10160
212-633-3950
212-633-3990 (FAX)

On-Campus Hospitality

As its name implies, this publication is dedicated to covering just college and university foodservice issues. Information concerning this publication can be obtained by contacting:

Editor
On-Campus Hospitality
Executive Business Media, Inc.
825 Old Country Road
Westbury, NY 11590
516-334-3030
516-334-3059 (FAX)

Correctional Foodservice

This is a quarterly publication that reports on adult corrections and juvenile detention issues involving foodservice. Information concerning this publication can be obtained by contacting:

Editor
Correctional Foodservice
International Publishing Company of America
665 La Villa Drive
Miami Springs, FL 33166
305-887-1700
305-885-1923 (FAX)
800-666-2565

Local Restaurants

A rewarding though indirect source of foodservice industry news can be accessed by administrators who keep up with what is happening on the local restaurant scene. Observing what is happening on the local commercial foodservice scene and holding conversations with knowledgeable people (such as restaurant operators, food brokers, and industry suppliers) about local trends and preferences can offer administrators an accurate reflection of the sorts of food items and service styles their foodservice customers (jail/prison inmates excepted) choose on their own time. The menus, service levels, and price points offered by local restaurateurs are often exactly what organizations' foodservice patrons wish to see in their programs. This is not to suggest, however, that an organization's foodservice program should mirror exactly that being offered in the commercial world. Due to the need to balance and meet a wide variety of food and service demands ranging from fast food to five-course dinners, it is the rare foodservice program that can operate as a commercial entity and still meet its organization's operational and financial goals and objectives.

Of all the resources herewith listed, perhaps the most important for administrators will be the people they meet. Forming a network of people who carry out the same professional responsibilities, share the same concerns, or have relevant specialized knowledge can be an invaluable asset to successful foodservice administration. A foodservice network should be seen as no different than any of the other network(s) that are found in various workplaces. The keys to maintaining a successful network are the same and include the following:

- Maintain regular contact with members of your network, either through one-on-one meetings or via membership in industry organizations.
- Be willing to share as much or more information as you take from others. Most networkers will have little patience with other professionals who only want information but will not share any in return.
- Be sensitive about asking for materials for which a colleague or organization has paid a substantial sum of money. As pointed out in an earlier chapter, the adoption of someone else's solutions can quickly become major problems for administrators who fail to see the benefits of cooperation.

Glossary

Administrative and general expenses Those expenses necessary to operate the business but not directly related to customer service.

A la carte Menu items are priced individually.

All-you-care-to-eat Customers are permitted access to a dining/serving area and can eat as much as they care to for the prepaid rate.

Back of the house Food storage, production, and preparation areas as opposed to front of the house which is the serving and dining or "public" area.

Bacterial infections A bacterial infection results when the victim swallows the actual bacteria that creates an infection in the gastrointestinal tract.

Blast chiller A refrigeration unit with circulating air capable of rapidly reducing the temperature of hot foods.

Board plan A contract between student, faculty, or staff and a college or university residence hall dining facilities.

Branded concepts Nationally or regionally trade-marked concepts that can be incorporated into a foodservice program for a franchise or licensing fee.

Branded product costs The cost of supplies that must be purchased from a specific vendor as part of a franchise or licensing agreement.

By-the-ounce A program whereby customers make their own salads or sandwiches and are charged by the ounce so that those who eat light pay less than those who have hearty appetites.

Catering To provide prearranged foodservice to the specific needs of any group.

Central kitchen Single production area where foods are prepared for and transported to multiple service areas.

Cleaning supplies Soaps and chemicals, disinfectants, brooms, mops, etc., required to maintain the facilities.

Client commissions The percentages paid to the contracting entities for the right to provide foodservice in a given nonsubsidized venue.

Combi-ovens An oven that cooks food by dry, convection, and/or steam heat.

Contract cleaning A service contractor for night cleaning, extermination, hood/ventilator cleaning.

Controllable expenses The total of all payroll costs, direct operating, advertising/promotion, utilities, administrative and general, repair and maintenance expenses.

Conveyor ovens The oven is set at one temperature and the conveyor line is timed so that the desired product is baked consistently each and every time.

Cook-chill The process of fully or partially cooking food then rapidly chilling it from the cooking temperature to below 40°F in two hours or less.

Cook-hold oven An oven for slow cooking, which reduces shrinkage (and loss of net weight) and improves flavor by removing less moisture. At the appropriate temperature the oven reverts a holding temperature.

C-stores Cash-and-carry convenience stores that vend a variety of sundries and groceries.

Convection oven An oven with a fan to circulate the heat, resulting in faster and more even cooking in a multiple shelved unit.

Cost of sales The $ total of all food and beverage used in a particular month or accounting period.

Cover A customer in a dining facility.

Direct operating expenses Those expenses directly attributable to food preparation and customer service such as uniforms, laundry, linen rentals, linen replacement, china, glassware, flatware and similar costs.

Direct subsidy Dollars paid to offset the difference between foodservice sales and expenses.

E. coli A bacteria found in raw meat and dairy products which, when transmitted to the human body, can result in serious illness or, in some cases, death.

Food cost The ratio of dollars of food purchased to revenue, expressed as a percentage. Unless certain paper products are directly related to the service of food (such as disposable plates, cartons, etc.), they should not be included in food cost.

Food poisoning The name for the gastrointestinal symptoms caused by a poison or a toxin released into the food, often by an offending bacteria.

Front of the house The serving and dining or "public" area of a foodservice facility.

FF&E Furniture, fixtures, and equipment including all of the furniture, fixtures (improvements to the space such as draperies, wall treatments, light fixtures) and equipment within foodservice areas.

General insurance All types of insurance not related to employee benefits or extended coverage on the premises or contents including, security, fraud/forgery, fidelity bonds, public liability, food poisoning, use and occupancy, lost or damaged articles, and partner's or officer's life insurance.

Griddle/grill A flat cooking surface.

Gross sales All revenue less applicable sales tax.

Indirect subsidy These are costs generally associated with the occupancy of a facility (such as rent, building/equipment maintenance, security, utilities, insurance and property taxes) and management/administrative overhead charges (such as those for human resources, purchasing and contract administration support).

Irradiation A method of preservation in which a radiation source is used to eliminate bacterial contamination and sterilize or pasteurize the food and/or spices.

K-minus Shorthand for a foodservice facility which has *no* kitchen. Usually food is brought in from a central kitchen.

Licenses & permits Federal, state, and municipal licenses including any special permits or inspection fees.

Management fee This is the fee that a contractor receives for managing an account. All non direct expenses (i.e., corporate overhead) and profit are normally included in this figure as a percentage of sales against a minimum return with a fixed dollar cap. Any monies above the fixed dollar cap can be proposed to be split between the contractor and the organization.

Manual foodservice A facility in which food and services are provided by human labor.

Marketing Includes all selling and promotion costs, direct mail, donations, souvenirs, favors, advertising, public relations and publicity, franchise fees and royalties or commissions, and market research (surveys).

MTO Areas where the food is made-to-order in a cafeteria or other foodservice outlet.

Menu cycle Repeating an established menu in a predetermined rotation. Generally, this is done every four or five weeks.

Menu explosion A process for determining the daily/weekly amount of each item on a menu that will usually be prepared in a specific kitchen. Done to determine the size of equipment necessary in a new or remodeled kitchen.

Paper products Disposable dish ware, flatware, drinking cups, napkins, table cloths.

Point-of-sale The point at which food and beverage is transferred to a customer. Cash registers are often referred to as point-of-sale units.

Printing and supplies All printed matter not devoted to advertising and promotion such as forms, account books, register tapes, letterhead, envelopes, and expendable office supplies.

Payroll tax & benefits Payroll taxes (FICA, FUTA, state unemployment, and state health insurance, social insurance, (i.e., worker's compensation insurance, welfare or pension plan payments) accident and health insurance premiums, and the cost of employee instruction and education, parties, and meals.

Productivity Measurable amount of work produced by the workforce.

Profit & loss contract A contractual arrangement whereby the contractor is responsible for the financial operation of the foodservice. The risk is placed upon the contractor to make money in the operation without a subsidy from the organization.

Rack oven An oven with one or more racks.

Replacements Replacement of all linen, china, glassware, flatware, and kitchen utensils.

RFB A Request For Bids sets all of the specifications and requirements and asked the proposing company to bid a price to perform the service or provide the products required.

RFP A Request For Proposals sets some of the requirements and asks the proposing company how it would operate a program and for what price.

RFQ A Request For Qualifications asks companies to submit their qualifications to perform a described level of foodservice. It is used to determine who is qualified to respond to an RFB or RFP.

Rotary oven An oven with one or more racks or shelves which rotate to assure even cooking.

Rotisserie A revolving spit which permits food to be cooked evenly.

Salad bar engineer An individual who has developed the skills necessary to stack and carry the equivalent of two fixed price, self service salads on one plate with out spillage.

Salaries & wages Include the salaries and wages, extra wages, overtime, vacation pay, and any commission or bonuses paid to employees.

Sales mix An item-by-item and/or sales group (such as entrees, beverages, desserts, etc.) listing showing the number and/or dollar amount sold for a specified period of time.

Servery In a cafeteria, the area where the food is actually served. In a catering operation, hospital or other facility it may also refer to the area where the staff will do the final dishing up in order to serve a meal.

Slicer Electric machine for slicing meats, cheese, vegetables, and other foods.

Smallwares All those items necessary to support the preparation and service of food with a per piece value of under a predetermined fixed amount. Smallwares include such items as pots, pans, serving utensils, china, glassware, serving platters/bowls, carving boards, etc.

Sous vide In French it literally means "cooked in a vacuum." Food is prepared and placed into a heavy duty plastic pouch (such as Cry-o-vac) and slow cooked at lower than normal temperatures in a vacuum chamber.

Subsidize To provide support other than that received from sales. May be actual dollar subsidy or may be indirect in the form of free rent, no utility charges or other waived costs.

Uniforms/laundry All uniform purchases, cleaning and repair to them, and badges as well as the cost of laundering table linens, napkins, and aprons.

Utilities Electricity, fuel, water, ice and refrigeration supplies, removal of waste, and engineering supplies.

Vegan A person who consumes only plant products, and who will not eat animal flesh or by-products such as dairy and eggs.

Vegetarian A person who consumes only plant products and animal by-products such as eggs and dairy.

Vendor Supplier.

Bibliography

Birchfield, John C., *Design & Layout of Foodservice Facilities.* New York: Van Nostrand Reinhold, 1988.

Borsenik, Frank D., and Stutts, Alan T., *The Management of Maintenance and Engineering Systems in the Hospitality Industry.* Third Edition New York: John Wiley & Sons, 1992.

Drummond, Karen E., R.D., *Nutrition for the Foodservice Professional.* Fourth Edition. New York: John Wiley & Sons, 1992.

Hansen, Bill, *Off-Premise Catering Management.* New York: John Wiley & Sons, 1994.

Hayes, David, and Miller, Jack E., *Basic Food and Beverage Cost Control.* New York: John Wiley & Sons, 1993.

Laventhol & Horwath. *Uniform System of Accounts for Restaurants.* Washington D.C.: National Restaurant Association, 1990.

Longree, Karla, and Armbruster, Gertrude, *Quantity Food Sanitation*, Fourth Edition. New York: John Wiley & Sons, 1987.

Warner, Mickey, *Noncommercial, Institutional and Contract Foodservice Management.* New York: John Wiley & Sons, 1994.

Appendix: Disk Documentation

I. About the Noncommercial Foodservice Diskette

This diskette product contains worksheets, requests for proposals, and contracts all of which are referenced in the text *Noncommercial Foodservice Management: An Administrator's Handbook*. These documents are designed to be easily modified and adapted. The files on the diskette have been formatted in Courier and Universe Scalable fonts. Some of the formatting might be lost if the diskette is formatted to a word processing program without the proper fonts. You will need to compare your printed disk copy with the copy included within the text.

II. Computer Requirments

This diskette requires an IBM-PC or compatible computer with DOS version 2.0 or later. It can be used in both DOS and Windows environments.

The files are formatted in Microsoft Word for Windows 2.0, WordPerfect 5.1, and ASCII, which is a universal text format for DOS computers. The files can be read into your word processing software program using the directions contained in this appendix. If your word processing program is not listed below, you can load the ASCII files by following the directions in your software manual. Using the index in your software manual, refer to the section on *Importing ASCII Files* or *Loading Documents from Other Word Processors.*

III. How to Make a Backup Diskette

Before you start to use the enclosed diskette, we strongly recommend that you make a backup copy of the original. Making a backup copy of your disk allows you to have a clean set of files saved in case you accidentally change or delete a file. Remember, however, that a backup disk is for your own personal use only. Any other use of the backup disk violates copyright law. Please take the time now to make the backup copy, using the instructions below:

(a) If your computer has two floppy disk drives:

1. Insert your DOS disk into drive A of your computer.
2. Insert a blank disk into drive B of your computer.
3. At the **A:>**, type **DISKCOPY A: B:** and press Enter. You will be prompted by DOS to place the source disk into drive A.
4. Place the *Noncommercial Foodservice* disk into drive A. Follow the directions on screen to complete the copy.
5. When you are through, remove the new backup disk from drive B and label it immediately. Remove the original *Noncommercial Foodservice* disk from drive A and store it in a safe place.

(b) If your computer has one floppy disk drive and a hard drive:

If you have an internal hard drive on your computer, you can copy the files from the enclosed disk directly onto your hard disk drive, in lieu of making a backup copy, by following the installation instructions on the following pages.

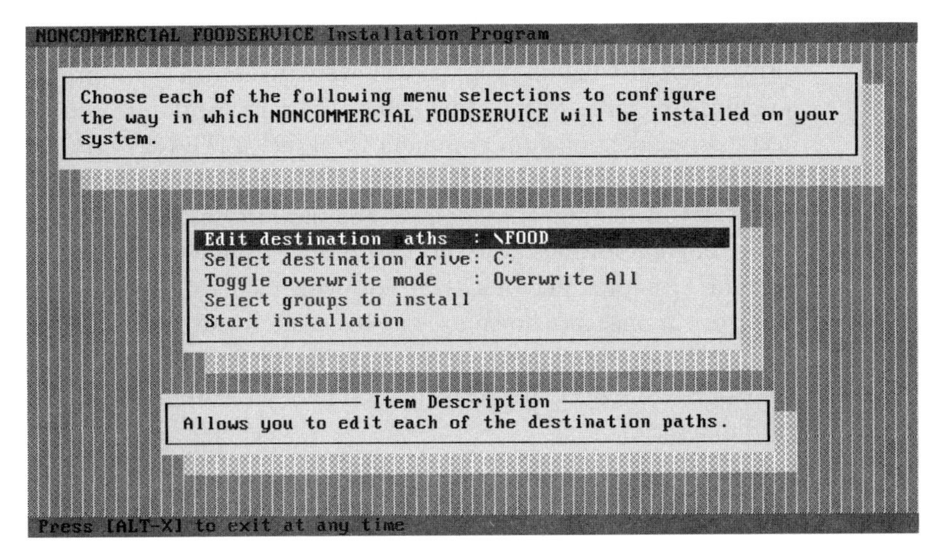

Figure 1

IV. Installing the Diskette

The enclosed diskette contains 18 individual files in a compressed format. In order to use the files, you must run the installation program for the disk.

You can install the diskette onto your computer by following these steps:

1. Insert the Noncommercial Foodservice disk into drive A of your computer. Type **A:\INSTALL** and press Enter.
2. The installation program will be loaded. After the title screen appears, you will be given the options shown in Figure 1.
3. The following Menu Selections will be listed: Edit Destination Paths, Select Destination Drive, Toggle Overwrite Mode, Select Groups to Install and Start Installation.
4. The **Destination Path** is the name of the default directory to store the data files. The default directory name is FOOD. To change this name, press Enter, hit the letter **P**, type in the name of the directory you wish to use and press Enter.
5. **Select Destination Drive** gives you the option of installing the disk onto a hard disk drive C:\ or, if you wish, onto a different drive.
6. The **Toggle Overwrite Mode** pertains to the directories and files you already have on your hard drive. Do *not* give the default

directory the same name as existing directories on your hard drive or the installation program will overwrite or delete any preexisting directories of the same name. The safest option to protect existing data on your computer is OVERWRITE NEVER.

7. The **Select Groups to Install** option allows you to install each directory on the disk one by one. The files on this disk are in three different formats: Microsoft Word for Windows, WordPerfect for Windows, and ASCII. If you wish to install the entire directory at once, tab down to Start Installation and press Enter. To install just one of these word processing formats, press Enter, hit the letter **G**, select the format you do not want to install, and hit Enter again.

The files are now successfully installed onto your hard drive.

V. Reading Files into Word Processing Programs

For your convenience, the files on the enclosed diskette are provided in three formats, ASCII, Microsoft Word for Windows, and WordPerfect for Windows. If you have Word Perfect 5.1 or Microsoft Word for Windows. The WordPerfect or MS Word files will be easiest for you to use because they are already formatted. Once the files are loaded into your word processor, you can customize them to suit your individual needs.

If you do not have Windows or you use other programs not compatible with MS Word or WordPerfect, the ASCII files are designed for you. Because ASCII format is standard format for all DOS computers, a number of different users with different word processing programs can read the disk. This means regardless of your particular word processing program (WordStar, MS Word for DOS, WordPerfect for DOS, etc.), you can still use this disk. Once the file is loaded into your word processor, you can customize them to suit your individual needs.

(a) Reading the files into Microsoft Word for Windows

To read a file into Microsoft Word for Windows, follow these steps: Load the Word for Windows program as normal.

1. When the Untitled document is displayed, select **OPEN** form the **FILE** menu.
2. The **OPEN FILE** dialog box will appear, as shown in Figure 2. At this box, make the appropriate selections for the drive and direc-

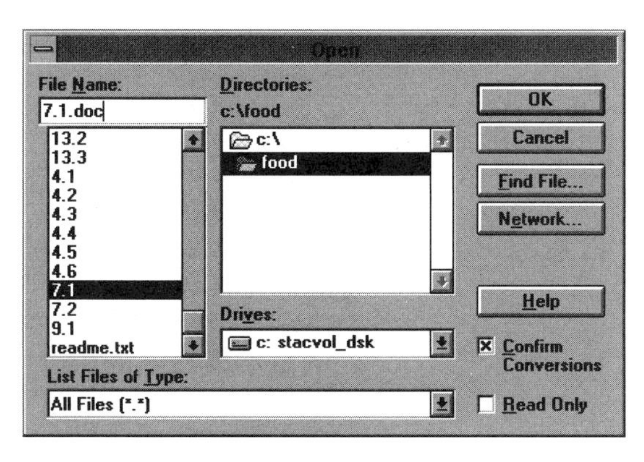

Figure 2

tory of the document you want to review. For instance, to open the file 7-1 in the FOOD directory, you must select drive C:\ and the directory FOOD and then type 7-1.DOC under the file name. Click OK to proceed. The file will immediately load into Microsoft Word for Windows.

3. Make your changes and revisions to the document.
4. To print the file, select **PRINT** from the **FILE** menu.
5. When you are through editing it, you should save it under a new name (to avoid overwriting the original file) before you quit.

(b) Reading Files Into WordPerfect 5.1 for DOS

To read a file into WordPerfect, follow these steps:
Load the WordPerfect program as normal.

1. When the blank document screen is displayed, press **SHIFT-F10** to retrieve the document.
2. To open the document **7-1**, from the directory FOOD, type **C: \FOOD\7-1.WP**. Press Enter when you have finished typing in the filename.
3. Make your changes and revisions to the document.
4. To print the document, press SHIFT-F7.
5. When you are through editing the document you should save it under a new file name (to avoid overwriting the original file) before you quit.

(c) Reading the WordPerfect files into WordPerfect for Windows

To read the files into WordPerfect for Windows, follow these steps:
Load the WordPerfect for Windows program as normal.

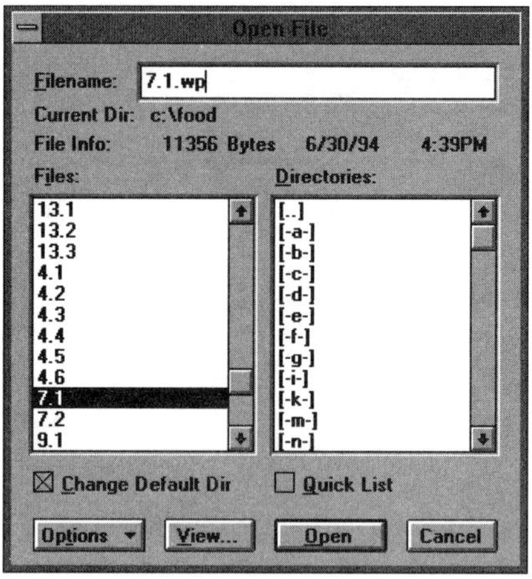

Figure 3

1. Select **OPEN** from the **FILE** menu.
2. The **OPEN** dialog will appear, as shown in Figure 3. At this box, make the appropriate selections for the drive and directory of the document you want to review. For instance, to open the file 7-1 located in the FOOD directory, you must select the directory.
3. Under the **FILES** option on the left side of the dialog box, enter 7-1.WP as the file name.
4. The file will immediately load into WordPerfect for Windows.
5. Make your changes and revisions to the document.
6. To print the file, select **PRINT** from the **FILE** menu.
7. When you are through editing it, you should save it under a new file name (to avoid overwriting the original file) before you quit.

Reading the ASCII Files into Other Word Processing Programs

To use these files with other word processing programs, refer to the documentation that accompanies your software. Often, the procedure is very similar to those already explained. The two primary steps involved in opening the ASCII files are:

1. Identify the file you want to load from the FOOD directory and indicate the filename to your word processor.
2. Identify the file as a DOS text file.

After these general steps, most word processing programs will immediately load the file.

VI. Summary Disk Contents

Exhibit Name	Description	Book Page Number
4-1	Tentative RFP Time Schedule	35
4-2	Sample Request for Qualifications (RFQ)	50–52
4-3	Model Request for Proposal (RFP)	53–59
4-4	Organization Manual Contract	60–76
4-5	Operating Proposal Evaluation	43–45
4-6	Telephone Reference Check Form	47
7-1	Food Facilities Consultant Request For Qualifications (RFQ) and Fee Proposals	119–121
7-2	Action Plan	105
9-1	Sample Vending Contract	142–149
10-1	Equipment Maintenance Record	167
10-2	Introduction to Central Cook-Chill Kitchens	175–181
11-1	Quality Assurance Audit	203–207
11-2	Food Matrix Quality Attribute Reference Guide	208–210
11-3	Defined Expectations	211–213
13-1	Comment Card	250
13-2	FoodService Survey	260–262
13-3	Telephone Survey	263–268

VII. User Assistance and Information

John Wiley & Sons, Inc. is pleased to provide assistance to users of this package. Should you have any questions regarding the use of this package, please call our technical support number (212) 850–6194 weekdays between 9 A.M. and 4 P.M. Eastern Standard Time.

To place additional orders or to request information about other Wiley products, please call (800) 879-4539.

Index